THE
DOUBLE
MIRROR

THE
DOUBLE
MIRROR

*A Skeptical Journey
into Buddhist Tantra*

Stephen T. Butterfield

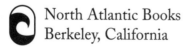

North Atlantic Books
Berkeley, California

Published by North Atlantic Books, P.O. Box 12327, Berkeley, California 94712.

Cover Art: Avalokiteshvara, Bodhisattva of Compassion. Twentieth-century Tibetan thangka from a private collection. Photograph by Roger Williams. Copyright © 1976 by Snow Lion Graphics.
Illustrations pp. 156, 157, 196, and photographs pp. 175, 197 by Stephen T. Butterfield.
Cover and book design by Paula Morrison.
Typeset by Catherine Campaigne.
Printed in the United States of America by Malloy Lithographing.

The Double Mirror: A Skeptical Journey into Buddhist Tantra is sponsored by the Society for the Study of Native Arts and Sciences, a nonprofit educational corporation whose goals are to develop an educational and crosscultural perspective linking various scientific, social, and artistic fields; to nurture a holistic view of arts, sciences, humanities, and healing; and to publish and distribute literature on the relationship of mind, body, and nature.

Library of Congress Cataloging-in-Publication Data
The double mirror : a skeptical journey into Buddhist tantra / Stephen T. Butterfield.
   p. cm.
  ISBN 1-55643-176-7
  1. Spiritual life—Tantric Buddhism. 2. Butterfield, Stephen T.
3. Trungpa, Chogyam, 1939–1987. I. Title.
BQ8938.B88 1994
294.3'923'092—dc 20
[B]
93–39497
CIP

1 2 3 4 5 6 7 8 9 / 98 97 96 95 94

Homage and grateful acknowledgment to all my teachers from the ten directions and the three times—without whom neither this book nor the dharma could exist.

TABLE OF CONTENTS

1. The Voice in the Closet ... 1

2. The Three Faces of Enlightenment ... 15

3. Meeting the Journey Master ... 31

4. Playing to an Empty House ... 45

5. A Pale Horse ... 59

6. Sending and Taking ... 73

7. A Jewel in a Heap of Dust ... 83

8. Great Eastern Sun ... 93

9. No Big Deal ... 103

10. The Protectors ... 119

11. Like a Body and Its Shadow ... 129

12. I Take Refuge: Prostration ... 143

13. Ordinary Mind: Purification ... 155

14. Blessings: The Sacred Mandala ... 167

15. The Guru Is the Buddha ... 177

16. Dancing between This and That ... 189

17. A Pack of Cards ... 201

18. Art and Dharma: Beauty Is Truth ... 213

19. Nothing Happened ... 227

20. Lotus Taking Root ... 241

Glossary of Dharma Terms ... 247

1

THE VOICE IN THE CLOSET

I T WAS LATE May in the north country. The winter storms had faded at last, and everything glowed with color: bright green leaves, white apple blossoms, lilacs, irises, dandelions.

The guru was dead. His body had just been cremated, after lying in state preserved by salts for fifty days. His disciples were sitting in rows in the orange-pillared shrine hall that he had designed, with its blue trim, gild, and polished hardwood floor. His throne still rested on its vividly painted dais, the seat occupied now by a photograph of the youthful guru wearing a gold-brocaded robe. "When the guru dies," he had once said, "there is still some warmth left behind." The posture we practiced, the visions and visualizations we evoked, the mantras we chanted, the dharma we studied, the whole life we had shared in this place, had been given to us by him.

In a high meadow surrounded by hills, we had just bidden him farewell as his corpse burned. All had been in accordance with traditional Tibetan ritual: a costumed procession led by stately horns and drums, prayer flags, and monks reciting liturgical incantations on a canopied platform. This Buddhist ceremony also included something Western: a smartly uniformed honor guard, standing at attention as a salute was fired from a hilltop cannon. The guru's ashes and bones were gathered together carefully afterwards and brought to the shrine hall to be blessed.

The clicking of the *mala* beads we used to keep track of our mantras echoed softly through the hall. We were doing a tantric purification practice: reciting a hundred-syllable prayer while visualizing a deity of peaceful wisdom seated in meditation above our heads, cleansing us with the milk of compassion. Millions of these prayers had to be recited in order to invest the ashes and bones with medicinal powers.

A group of senior students sat in a circle near the back, on a carpet of newspaper spread out to protect the floor. They were grinding the guru's bones in mortars with pestles, preparing to mix the powder with jewel dust, the work lit by a living room floor lamp that resembled a stage prop for a T.V. sitcom. Here and there were rows of little gold statues waiting to be filled with small amounts of this mixture and sent to different locations around the world as protection against evil spirits, ill fortune, bad dealings, and disease. The rows of solemn meditators with half-closed eyes, thumbs rising and falling to count off the clicking beads, the heavy grinding of the pestles pulverizing the bones—by turns, the scene struck me as outrageously funny, deeply moving, and more than a little macabre. It was all the things Chogyam Trungpa had been in life, sitting on his throne, receiving our devotional prostrations while reeking of saké, mixing bolts of lightning with dubious profundities like, "we must learn how to sit on our potties." His skull was preserved as a crowning relic for the gigantic stupa under construction in Colorado.

In the European Middle Ages, hardly a major town or church did not have its fragment of the true cross, fingerbone of a holy apostle, milk of the Virgin, or burial cloth of the Savior, all good sources of income from the credulous pilgrims who came to be cured of what ailed them by contact with these sacred relics. As usual, my mind was a jumble of such thoughts; my reality system was being torn down and rebuilt, and the "before" and "after" pictures lay superimposed.

"Do not intellectualize overmuch," warned the guru, "just do the practices, and their cumulative wisdom will become apparent as you go along." I had tried to follow his advice. Although never able to silence my questions, nor find satisfactory answers to them, I had traveled the Buddhist path anyway, without demanding that it make sense. My inspiration came as much from John Keats and other Western poets as from the Buddha; Keats had written about "negative capability," the power to remain with "uncertainties, Mysteries, doubts, without any irritable reaching after fact and reason." Such power, in his view, was an essential quality for a poet. My questions did not die, however, but went underground, ruminating and coiling into inarticulate forms; from there they fueled my journey, and perhaps one day they would also kill it.

As the smoke from the guru's cremated flesh perfumed the meadow that morning, I was filled with a bittersweet sense of gratitude and loss. I felt that I did not understand anything he had taught until after he was gone. In life, he had been a threat, a demand that I distrusted and needed to resist. I did not want him controlling my mind, or taking my money. But now he was simply heat from a fire, a salt smell on the wind. He was powder in a little statue. He was the teachings and practices he had given us, down to the colors and design of the meditation cushions we sat on. His message had always been that our nature is emptiness, and death had made him truly nobody. There was nothing to resist anymore. So I began to burn too. The cremation flames reached out and ignited my heart. During the next three years I did the practices he had taught us more intensely than in the previous nine. The whole world was burning, burning, all the time—shifting, changing, embers and seeds everywhere dying and being born. I was his ash and bone, ground by the mortar and pestle of practice into devotion, awareness, resentment, passion, peace. It was like walking around with the top of my head removed.

"Ordinary mind," said Osel Tendzin, the guru's American dharma heir, as we sat together in an airport bar watching a television talk show about AIDS. "Ordinary mind, that's what it feels like." Ordinary mind is the English translation of a Tibetan Buddhist term, *thamal gye shepa*, "mind without ego." The end of prac-

3

tice is to bring about this state, which can also be induced by the presence or death of a great teacher.

Osel Tendzin was the preceptor who had given me my Buddhist vows. Before he met Trungpa in the early 1970s, he was the yoga student Narayana, formerly Thomas Rich, an Italian from New Jersey. In 1976, Trungpa empowered him as his successor to the "crazy wisdom" tradition of Buddhist tantra. His title was "The Regent," and within Vajradhatu, Trungpa's church, he had his own staff, limousine, headquarters, itinerary, power base, personal attendants, and personal mystique. During the cremation, Tendzin had sat on the V.I.P. platform with the high lamas of Tibet, doing their complex chants and gestures, accepted by them as a fellow dharma king. Our meeting in this airport bar was pure auspicious coincidence: he was flying somewhere, and I was flying to Europe; we were waiting for different planes. In a few moments the entire setting would vanish.

A guest on the talk show was arguing that dolls should be manufactured with genital organs, so children can learn about sex and how to take precautions against AIDS. Then a commercial came on the screen: a haggard young woman said she got AIDS from her bisexual husband, who was having affairs with men. "I never knew about any of them," she said.

"This program is trivial," Osel Tendzin said. "It's cheap." I would have thought that warning people about AIDS fulfilled the Buddhist idea of compassionate activity. I had the urge to ask "Why do you think so?" but pretended instead to agree with him. He was the Regent and I was the disciple. If somebody had missed something it was probably me—and I didn't want him to know that I had missed it. I wanted to be important, like him, and to understand the world as he understood it.

In the guru/disciple relationship, this self-conscious longing for acceptance, regarded as a form of devotion, operates to intimidate the student into deference, when it would be far more valuable to look like a fool and speak up. Here was a priceless, fragile, short-lived opportunity, filled with uncontrived symbolism. If I had asked the right questions at that moment, I would have learned a great deal about the causes of the tragedy that was about to unfold around him, and around the presentation of Buddhist tantra in America. But I was paralyzed. Although I knew that I had as much power as Tendzin, I could not act from it. The meeting communicated anyway, on a level much deeper than my questions, and still does.

Perhaps he meant that AIDS is another form of cremation, in which the self gets reduced to ash and ordinary mind is liberated. "The sad skeleton turns," wrote Rosemary Klein; "Black rags dance the universe ... /To what song /Do we owe this dance. Where does the light go /when the light goes out." Alongside vision like that, the talk show was indeed cheap; it was drowning the subject in the jargon of "concern," and treating it as a Controversial Topic, always a boost for ratings.

Another commercial came on: a young woman held up a hypodermic needle and said "I got AIDS from using this."

I said "In the next commercial we'll see a guy holding up a dildo: 'And *I* got AIDS from using *this*.'"

Tendzin laughed. My question did not surface. I had glossed it over with a frivolous joke. He smiled and left, waving goodbye. There was a bond of sorts between us, formed during our dialogues at his dharma talks. He was gay, I was not, but I had fallen for his charm, his sense of humor, his quick wit, and his incisive and helpful answers.

I later had one more opportunity to question his whole act, putting myself at risk of being a fool in front of a hundred people, but of course I didn't take it. He was giving a program for advanced students of tantra, in which he said that if you keep your commitment to the guru, "you cannot make a mistake." I thought, "You are going to get into trouble believing that, my friend; that's hubris. All the people in the written history of the world who believed they could not make a mistake sooner or later got into trouble." Yet I kept silent, intent only on uttering sentiments that would please him.

Then I dreamed that I met Tendzin in a spaceport. I had always

5

liked his face—it was kind, but ravaged, the nose a little too thick—
probably from drinking. Both he and Trungpa were alcoholics. In
the dream I was waiting for a rocket to another galaxy, and so was
he. I knew neither of us would ever come back. I wanted to get
out. When I woke up, I feared the dream was a warning that I
would die in a plane crash, and I said protective mantras and made
a will.

A year later, I learned with the rest of the world that Tendzin
had AIDS, kept it secret, and infected one of his many unknowing student lovers. He knew he had AIDS while we were sitting
in the bar. The subject had surrounded us like the jaws of a croc-
odile, and we had sat on its teeth and laughed. Unlike him, I had
not known we were sitting on real teeth.

A lot was said after this about Osel Tendzin as a Buddhist example of the cult guru who seduces his students into self-destruction.
Trungpa's entire organization was splitting apart over the issue.
Almost overnight, devotion to gurus became politically incorrect,
a way of enabling the drunken elephant in the shrine room, as
author Katy Butler implied in an article for *Common Boundary*. Asked
by *The Sun* magazine to write about Tendzin, I refused in my essay
to judge him; others were already doing that. I did not need to
warn anyone against him; publicity had taken away his power to
cause further harm. The one thing missing in all the controversy,
the one thing I thought I could contribute, was how this, or any
disaster, could be used as a vehicle for teaching dharma. This was
the theme I had failed to explore with Tendzin in the bar. Whatever his sins, if the dharma is valid, then it should be applicable
when the excrement hits the fan, even, and especially, when the
fan happens to be the teacher. I wanted to honor what Tendzin
had given me by applying it to him. I also wanted to detach from
his bad example, and avoid being drawn into a vortex of meaningless recrimination and blame. The essay worked, as far as it went,
but it was not yet all that needed to be done.

The system of practices I had entered led me inexorably toward
Vajrayana, the most intense and controversial vehicle in the Bud-

dhist menu. From a Vajrayana point of view, passion, aggression, and ignorance, the sources of human suffering, are also the wellsprings of enlightenment. Afflictions like AIDS are not merely disasters, but accelerations toward wisdom, and opportunities to wake up. They can be transformed into buddha-mind. Trungpa was a Vajra master who had empowered Tendzin to guide students on this path. Since Tendzin had been my preceptor in two previous initiations, I had always assumed he would be the one to give me *abhiseka*, the gateway into Vajrayana, which includes a ritual of blessings, empowerments, and further teachings. But he was too sick to perform the ceremony, and Trungpa's Tibetan teacher, Dilgo Khyentse Rinpoche, instructed Tendzin in any case to go into retreat. So I was initiated by Jamgon Kongtrul, a Tibetan.

The abhiseka took place in a huge outdoor tent. The initiates lined up like passengers entering a spaceship. On the night of the ceremony, Tendzin lay dying in a hospital thousands of miles away. When the ceremony was finished, so was he. In a sense, he and Trungpa had been the booster fuel for the rocket. During the night there was a terrific electrical storm and I felt as if the top of my head had come off again.

Kalu Rinpoche and Dilgo Khyentse Rinpoche, senior masters of Tibetan Buddhism, died around the same time. Two of the last living representatives of Tibet's ancient culture, as it was before Communist China turned its broken remnants into a tourist attraction, had passed away. My sense of loss was compounded. I was bereft of my guides. Both had given initiations, Vajrayana transmissions, and empowerments that I had attended, and both were also my teachers, though I had no direct personal contact with them.

Jamgon Kongtrul died soon afterward, in a bizarre automobile accident. The official story said that his chauffeur slipped on a wet road while swerving to avoid a flock of birds. The unofficial gossip, which I picked up from sources outside the Vajradhatu network, said that Kongtrul's death was not an accident, but was connected to a power struggle going on around the installation of the Seventeenth Karmapa.

The Karmapas represent an unbroken line of oral Tibetan Buddhist transmission going back to tenth-century India. Within that tradition, they were thought to be continuously reincarnated, each one leaving instructions to selected disciples at the time of his death as to where and when he would take his next rebirth. The Sixteenth Karmapa, Trungpa's teacher, had died of cancer in America in 1981. His principal disciples, Kongtrul among them, were responsible for finding and installing the young Tibetan child who became his successor.

Vajradhatu, the church, or *sangha,* to which I belonged, published the official version of Kongtrul's accident with no hint that it represented anything more disturbing than confirmation of the orthodox Buddhist teaching of impermanence. Since the Tendzin scandal, the Vajradhatu press had put on a "smiley" face, excluding controversial stories about Buddhist leaders. I could not be sure whether the background of the Kongtrul story had been omitted for lack of information, or from a policy of printing only what would further the movement.

The Indian press reported on a conflict between two groups within the Sixteenth Karmapa's line of succession. One group accepted the Tibetan child, Ugyen Thinley, as the authentic rebirth of the Karmapa, and the other rejected him. The Winter 1992 issue of *Tricycle,* an American Buddhist journal, aired some of the details of this conflict in Keith Dowman's essay, "Himalayan Intrigue." Among other things, Dowman pointed out that the Sixteenth Karmapa's original letter of instruction about his next rebirth was vague. A rivalry existed between Tai Situ and Shamarpa, two of his regents, and Kongtrul had tried to mediate between them. Tai Situ had produced a second letter fairly late in the controversy, much more specific than the first, which he claimed had originated with the Karmapa and which supported Ugyen Thinley, Situ's candidate. Shamarpa did not accept the authenticity of the second letter. On one occasion, matters had almost come to blows. The stakes included control of the Karmapa's multimillion-dollar estate.

Dowman tried to report these events in a way that would still leave room for faith in the Tibetan Buddhist tradition, but his article nonetheless provoked an angry reaction from loyal Buddhists. In letters published in *Tricycle's* Summer 1993 issue, he was accused of being "disrespectful" to the high lamas, "distorting" Tibetan culture, relying on "hearsay" and promoting "claptrap."

Vajradhatu eventually got around to noting the existence of the Karmapa altercation in its quarterly journal *The Shambhala Sun*, in June of 1993, a year after Kongtrul's death. But the article did not raise the fundamental questions implied about Tibetan dharma: if the Karmapa was really omniscient, as our practice chants had been repeating for twenty years, why were his instructions not made sufficiently clear from the beginning? Did the child himself not know how to establish who he was? To what extent had the quarrel been fueled by competition for control of the estate, and the power and privilege of belonging to his court? Did even masters of dharma contend for such prizes? If so, what did this indicate about the effects of Buddhist training on behavior? What exactly happened to Jamgon Kongtrul? If his accident had been somehow arranged, and if even Buddhist masters were capable of foul play in power struggles, then why serve and fund them, and practice what they taught? How were they any different from the Catholic Church, the Mafia, or the Chinese Communist Party?

I no longer knew how to reconcile my inner experience of the dharma, which had been nothing less than life-giving, with my distrust of its outer organizational forms. "I don't matter," said Osel Tendzin at one of his talks, "what matters is the message." This was good advice at the level he gave it, but in Vajrayana, the teacher, the message, and the organizational form are held to be one and the same. Selective coverage of Buddhist events is propaganda, not dharma, resulting in a credibility gap between the public face of the Buddhist institution and its hidden undercurrent.

I stopped practicing.

Then all my questions came back—the ones I had ignored, the ones without answers, the ones I had stepped over carefully so they would not block my forward movement, and the same questions that had inspired the journey by refusing to die. Many were so elementary you never asked them of any teacher for fear it would seem as if you had made no progress at all and still did not know what you were doing. Some revealed pride and resistance. Why was I doing these practices, anyway, why should I continue doing them, and what did they have to do with enlightenment? Is Buddhism a vehicle, or a crutch? Or perhaps a shell, useful only until you hatch from it? Does it even exist, apart from the activity of minds using its frame of reference? Would I be happier if I quit?

The robed and suited people on thrones to whom I had bowed and prostrated, and helped support year after year, were they any more enlightened than anyone else, or were they just skillful at putting on a good show? And if they were not enlightened, then who was?

I wanted to write about my whole relationship with this path, to take stock of what it had done for me, and to me. But a strange, creeping guilt froze my intention repeatedly before it could flower. Vajrayana students had always been discouraged from trying to evaluate our personal journey. This was looked on as a form of egotism, an attempt to make a big deal out of our practice, to use the teachings as a cosmetic for the self.

"Your journey is not important," said a senior administrator who reviewed one of my manuscripts. "You should write about Trungpa's journey, not yours." You are the disciple; he is the master; I am the elder. Stay in your role.

Trungpa, in one of his homely metaphors, told us that we needed to boil in the pot of practice like vegetables, until we looked like any other vegetable, and could no longer stick our heads up and say "I'm a carrot, see how orange I am?" The master's job was to say, "Too orange—keep boiling," and push you back down into the pot. Trungpa's sense of humor always made me want to stay there and boil, because suddenly the whole world seemed to be a stupid, repetitive circus of arrogant carrots, bumping and shoving and trampling and backstabbing each other to proclaim their colors. And we all have the same colors: passion, aggression, ignorance, envy, and pride.

In the Vajrayana our choices were narrowed to two: accept the path as given, or fry in hell. Entering the Vajrayana is like a snake crawling into a bamboo tube, said the lamas: there is only one way out—straight ahead. If you don't go through the tube, you suffocate. We were admonished as well not to talk about our practice. "May I shrivel up instantly and rot," we vowed, "if I ever discuss these teachings with anyone who has not been initiated into them by a qualified master." As if this were not enough, Trungpa told us that if we ever tried to leave the Vajrayana, we would suffer unbearable, subtle, continuous anguish, and disasters would pursue us like furies. Heresy had real meaning in this religion, and real consequences. Doubting the dharma or the guru and associating with heretics were causes for downfall. In Tibetan literature, breaking faith with the guru must be atoned by such drastic measures as cutting off your arm and offering it at the door of his cave in hopes that he might take you back.

If this was the consequence of merely leaving the organization, what supernal wrath might be visited upon me for publicly questioning or discussing my experience in it? I wasn't sure I would have enough severable appendages for the magnitude of atonement that might be required, especially since two of my toes had already been amputated for medical reasons.

In the beginning I wanted to study the effects of Buddhist practices on consciousness and health, with my own experience as example: what about anger, what about being alone, betrayed, robbed, attacked, or afflicted by disease—did I handle these burdens any better for being a meditator? Did others? Never mind how we *should* handle them, what was the truth? Then I wanted to probe the whole issue of why Americans would take on a reality system so different from their own. I needed to see the path again from the outside, so that I could ask and think through the unthinkable kinds of questions I felt too intimidated to raise with Tendzin, or Trungpa, or any high lama, the questions that senior discussion leaders and officials ignored or politely squelched.

It was possible that I had been programmed by a powerful and highly sophisticated cult, one which is no less a cult for being sanctioned by revered tradition and great antiquity. If my questions were coming back as a result of not practicing, then maybe practice had simply repressed them.

I already had some experience with an American-born cult, the Amway system, which claims to be a road to spiritual happiness as well as a business, and is in reality a right-wing sociopolitical indoctrination process disguised as a network marketing enterprise. Like most cults, Amway exalts leader figures, cloaks them with an aura of charismatic mystery, separates its members psychologically from the outside world, converts them into servants of higher authority, takes their money and their labor, and holds them together with propaganda, ideology, repetition of secret rituals and gestures, and the hope of advancement toward a higher status within the group. Cults are means to achieve power. Leaders have it because cult members give it to them, in the belief that they themselves are inadequate as they are, and must be made over into something else. In the depth and beauty of its message, Buddhist tantra is to Amway what a rainbow is to a bottle of snake oil. But as cults there are some disquieting resemblances.

To write and speak freely as an individual is a difficult, precious act, one which is generally devalued by religious and political orthodoxies. But the individual voice keeps faith with a moral code greater than any other commitment: to make an authentic response to our world. However much we may fall short of it, the challenge of this code is constant, day by day and moment by moment. It does not come from any guru, therapist, or church, and it can never be surrendered to authority without a kind of unspeakable mental enslavement. Living this challenge is the essence of what I always believed I was trying to do as a Buddhist. My intention here is to continue doing so, under the guidance of the skeptical intelligence we are all born with—otherwise known as the great guru, Mother Wit. No organization or set of teachings claiming to offer spiritual truth should be insulated from her scrutiny.

A more basic question, one that I had to address before I could write, is whether you can make a Buddhist journey and yet stand outside the experience and study it. Who is studying, who is commenting, and why? The object of the journey is to achieve ego death. "Oh, really?" says the ego. "Ego death? Apotheosis? Let's go for it, I'm getting bored anyway, this will give me something new to put in my diary; I always wanted to attend my own funeral." Examining the journey may thus become a way of defeating its purpose.

But this does not ultimately matter. The journey cannot even occur unless we examine it, and the purpose is already accomplished from the beginning. The speaker is always buddha-mind, broadcasting with degrees of clarity, according to how well the equipment is tuned. The ego is not there anyway; it is just static in a jumble of signals. You can attend your own funeral, *and* join the festivities, like Finnegan at his wake. Otherwise, Buddhist meditation itself would be impossible. In the *Heart Sutra*, Avalokitesvara, the bodhisattva of compassion, is asked how a son or daughter of noble family should train on the path. He declaims, "There is no path, no wisdom, no attainment, and no nonattainment." The Buddha smiles with approval, and there is a cosmic wake: "that whole assembly and the world with its gods, humans, *asuras*, and *gandharvas* rejoiced and praised the words of the Blessed One."

Go, little book; join in that rejoicing.

2

THE THREE FACES OF ENLIGHTENMENT

O N FIRST GLANCE, Buddhist meditation seems as if it should be an easy and relaxing pastime: you sit on a cushion and do nothing. Chogyam Trungpa said it should be done like wearing a suit while holding a spoonful of water. Generally, for me it was more like wearing a straitjacket while standing on one foot juggling marbles in a roomful of mad grasshoppers.

"I tried it," said a novice, "but nothing happened." This is a well-loved joke among Buddhists, and was made into a bumper sticker; because, of course, nothing is exactly what is supposed to happen, and exactly what makes it so difficult. People try meditation for any number of reasons, but what drives someone to take it on as a regular discipline is a strong combination of push and pull. The push is confusion and pain.

At the time I began Buddhist sitting practice, a marriage I had tried to make workable for years was falling apart. I found myself drawn again and again into cycles of defense and mutual abuse that I could not unravel. I was terrified of emotional rejection, which I nevertheless arranged to receive as a matter of routine. In addition to emotional turmoil, my physical health was also seriously impaired, and I had not even reached the point of daring to find out what was wrong, much less what could be done about it. Some part of me knew that my life was intolerably absurd, a blind alley, a waste of energy, and could be changed.

Buddhists call this state of affairs the *revulsion for samsara,* and it is the impetus and basis for the journey. It is a pervasive disgust for the world and one's own part in it; for human stupidity, ineptitude, and corruption, for the eternal round of hustling, spending, and laying waste, for the inability to do even the simplest things properly and thoroughly. Generalized revulsion is not particularly a Buddhist phenomenon. The poet John Donne expressed it when he anatomized the world as a "cripple," a "cinder," a "ghost," a "carcass," a "withered and worn strumpet." No special talent or intelligence is required to feel this revulsion: the drunken criminal played by Al Pacino in the movie *Scarface* lurches to his feet in a restaurant and starts demanding to know whether the point of his whole career has just been to sit there and get a big belly. The essential element is to be revolted by the absurdity of one's own life. Without revulsion for oneself, disgust for others is no more than egoism, and leads only to further degradation. Genuine recognition of samsara is when you see it in the mirror.

Samsara is bewilderment, experiencing life through a filter of self-centered hope and fear, enacting a cycle of grasping, aggression, and ignorance. Samsara is the plot of the drama starring ourselves that we invent moment by moment, coping with threats, conquering or being subdued by obstacles, pursuing happiness or avoiding hell, dancing over pits or falling into them. Grasping, aggression, and ignorance are known as *kleshas,* or "stains," and these are the basic elements of the drama, the primary colors that make it up. We grasp at happiness, attempt to combat or evade threats, and ignore whatever has no potential to give us either pleasure or pain. The deep ignorance supporting the whole cycle is our forgetting that we are its author. We compose the plot, step into the story, and act it out, ignoring that it is an artificial reality, a show, and not a very satisfactory one. Happy endings never last, obstacles are never permanently subdued, the story does not stop or change direction when we want, episodes repeat themselves, and the gulf of anxiety underlying it all does not recede.

The analogy of drama or film has a distinctly Western flavor and history: "All the world's a stage," said Shakespeare, "and all the men and women merely players." Each of us is at the same time player, audience, and lighting. The *dramatis personae,* the identities, the egos, are just shadows, colored patches, directed to move according to a certain script. The light that illuminates the screen and makes the drama possible does not in any way depend on what happens in it, although the members of the audience may forget this in their identification with the characters. The world as imagery projected on a screen is an ancient metaphor, going back to Plato's allegory of the cave in *The Republic.* The components in his version are not projectors and films, but cave walls, shadows, puppets, and firelight. Adjusting for changes in technology, it is the same idea.

The favorite Buddhist metaphor for samsara is the wheel. In visual representations of the *bhavachakra,* the wheel of life, the three kleshas, symbolized by three animals, rooster, snake, and pig, appear in the hub. Between the spokes are scenes depicting the six kinds of dramas created by the kleshas; heaven, hell, stupidity, ambition, desperation, and the rational quest for pleasure. These are psychological mind-states or life-styles, solidified patterns of illusion held together more or less continuously by discursive thought. Around the rim of the wheel are the twelve links, or *nidanas,* in the chain of karma, the process by which the fixation on self keeps getting generated out of the ground of confusion and dissolved back into it. The metaphor of the wheel emphasizes that samsara is cyclic and repetitive; it keeps on spinning. Karma is an endless series of real headaches produced by imaginary hammers. All this described my failing marriage with ruthless accuracy.

Most Western forms of psychotherapy have various kitchen-sink methods of helping clients get unstuck from dysfunctional cycles. The Buddhist approach differs from these by seeking to penetrate entirely beyond the notion of self. From the Buddhist point of view, self *is* the problem. Any cycle created by it is dysfunctional—a needless perpetuation of suffering. The cycles function to solidify and protect self, an unattainable goal, for self is always being

The bhavachakra, the wheel of life

18

swept away—by old age, disease, death, change, unforeseen events, bad luck, floods, droughts, or badly timed indigestion.

I did not try ordinary Western psychotherapy, because the understanding I sought was more radical than insight into a particular result, such as how I set myself up for emotional rejection. Psychotherapy would have given me one branch of the matter, not the root. I wanted to see the space around the film, and to know more about the light that projects characters and dramas on the screen. I wanted to find out what is the ground of cyclic existence itself, and whether there was any possibility of living from entirely different ground. As revulsion for samsara is the *push*, this longing for fundamental understanding is the *pull*.

Jacob Needleman, in *The Heart of Philosophy* (Knopf, 1982) and elsewhere, makes a distinction between "concepts" and "ideas." A concept is a term such as "Buddhism," "ego," "samsara," "spiritual path"—useful markers that we push around in sentences in order to gain control of an intangible subject. An idea is a gravitational pull from the deepest level of our being, a longing to *know*, a source of energy that magnetizes concepts without being contained by them. Borrowing from early Greek philosophy, Needleman uses the term "Eros" for the deep urge of the human psyche to understand the ground of its own existence, even if it must sacrifice the ego to gain the truth. Arising from Eros, ideas make us question ourselves. Their authentic formulation "has the effect of bringing a man to silence, of stopping the mind." Ideas enter and transform the psyche; concepts cannot do this. Two examples of ideas are Justice in Plato's dialogues, and Duty in the philosophy of Immanuel Kant.

Socrates and his pupils talk all around the theme of Justice without ever being able to define it, although they agree that it exists. The fact that Justice eludes definition is a clue that it originates outside of conceptual mind. The master's method is to examine and reject, by careful inquiry, all the things that Justice is not. Then he begins to approach what it is by the metaphor of a just Republic. Some light beyond comprehension operates to arrange his details into a coherent pattern. This light is an idea. It is to the normal perceiving self what the sun is to the prisoners in the cave.

Buddhist enlightenment may be understood in this sense as an idea, and also as Eros itself, the source of ideas. It cannot be defined, yet has compelling moral force. It does not in any way depend on empirical self-interest. It brings us to silence, stops the mind, and makes us question ourselves.

Buddhist sutras amplify the nature of enlightenment with adjectives such as "supreme," "unsurpassable," "complete," "great," suggesting that it is the quintessence of all ideas, the end of the energizing process, and that every other longing for truth, beauty, good, or justice is therein fulfilled. The mantra in the *Heart Sutra* expresses that enlightenment "should be known as truth, since there is no deception." In Sanskrit this mantra is "*Om gate, gate, paragate, parasamgate, bodhi svaha,*" which means, approximately, "whole, beyond, beyond, further beyond, crossed over, awake, so be it."

The *Sutra of the Noble Three Jewels* describes the awakened being or Buddha as "learned, virtuous, unsurpassable, the knower of the world, the supreme teacher, the tamer of beings"; the Buddha is "virtuous, patient, and without disharmony; his actions are timely and appropriate; he is the king of noble ones" who possesses "immeasurable wisdom," "inconceivable confidence," "pure speech," "incomparable form." He is "completely and utterly liberated" from suffering and from all traces of egoism.

Contemporary Buddhist masters speak of enlightenment as being completely without problems. Chogyam Trungpa, in one of his many comic images, said it was "much, much better than Disneyland." Trungpa was careful to distinguish between enlightenment and "the realm of the gods," which is one of the mind-states on the wheel of samsara. The realm of the gods is a blissful, spaced-out, self-centered peak of ignorance in which nothing matters but the happiness of the ego. A member of the god realm has the temporary illusion of being without problems, but sooner or later the bliss erodes. When it does, the ego is plunged into a struggle to maintain itself on the pinnacle of happiness, and goes on to experience the darker, more haunted realms of desperation, aggression, and paranoia. Enlightenment, by contrast, is permanent, irreversible, and without extremes. Paradoxically, the self cannot go there. An "enlightened self" would be a contradiction in terms.

The absence of self is called *anatman* in Buddhist dharma, a term which is usually translated as "egolessness." This is the most difficult quality of enlightenment for the conceptual mind to understand. If there is no one to enjoy enlightenment, then how can it exist? And what good is it? If there is no self, then how could my fingers compose sentences, and how could anyone read them? Western students of Buddhism sometimes complain that the idea of egolessness teaches us to discount our perceptions and feelings as illusions, that the concept itself belongs in a foreign culture and cannot be understood by us, and that the ideal enlightened being would be a cabbage.

Like revulsion for samsara, there is nothing uniquely Buddhist about egolessness. It was also discovered by the eighteenth-century British philosopher, David Hume: "When I enter most intimately into what I call *myself*," Hume wrote, "I always stumble on some particular perception or other, of heat, or cold, light or shade, love or hatred, pain or pleasure." Hume could never find a *self* distinct from perceptions, and went on to conclude that such an entity did not exist. He granted that perceptions must be bound together according to some principle of connection, but confessed that he could not explain it.

Western philosophy had once before approached the idea of egolessness on a line of development independent of the Buddhist world: the ancient Greek philosopher Democritus saw the universe as constantly assembling and dissolving densities of tiny "atoms," or indivisible particles. Consciousness and identity were to be explained as modes of interaction between these particles. Beyond them, nothing existed but the empty space of the Void. For two millennia after the refutation of Democritus by Plato and Aristotle, the West retreated from the materialist analysis of identity, locating it instead in the mind or soul.

The early schools of Buddhism also analyzed the self into component perceptions, tiny processes called "dharmas." Democritus had to imagine his atoms as hard little lumps that combined and separated by the force of their collisions. But a process could be imagined as flashing on and off, like successions of light reflections in water. These processes clump together in heaps to form the illusion of a self. The precise pattern of their organization is described in the *Abhidharma*, a classic early Buddhist text in which the self is analyzed into five such heaps, or *skandhas:* form, feeling, perception, formation, and consciousness. I will question the validity of these terms later on.

The difference between Democritean atoms and early Buddhist dharmas illustrates the difference between East and West on the subject of ego and egolessness. The term "ego" is used here in its Greek and Latin sense, to mean "I," or self. The qualities of a self include wholeness, individuality, indivisibility, existence, and distinction from other selves. We tend to see reality as a field of discrete objects that have these qualities. Democritus removed ego from his large entities by showing that they could be resolved into small ones, but the ego retreated into his atoms: they were solid, eternal, whole, indivisible, and individual.

The dharmas, by contrast, are light, airy, colorful, transparent, changing, and vanishing moment to moment. Having resolved the self and the world into such ephemeral phantoms, it was an easy step for the Buddhists to declare next that the dharmas were no more real than the larger entities which they made up, but were simply displays of Buddha-mind. Driven by the urge to grasp some absolute certainty, we might then insist that the self is really Buddha-mind, whatever this term could mean. The maddening Buddhist answer to this is "No, Buddha-mind is just a concept. Who's asking, anyway?" We are thus led to, or left with, the idea of emptiness, or egolessness. Proclaimed in the *Heart Sutra,* this became the foundation of the Mahayana.

In the schools of Buddhism that emphasize practice, philosophical analysis is considered useless without the actual experience of no-self. The practitioner allows the experience to manifest through sitting meditation. After thousands of hours in which "nothing happens" other than the usual chaos of phantom lights and shadows displayed on the screen of the mind, we may come to realize that this chaos is all the self there is. The light and the awareness, strictly speaking, cannot be regarded as a self, since they are the same in everybody—and in animals too, so far as we can determine by interacting with them.

In the Buddhist view, once the concept of self is genuinely exposed, penetrated, and dismantled, then the root of samsara has been cut. The organizing principle, the source, of all future dysfunctional cycles has been unraveled. The enlightened state is now free to manifest. From the beginning we had the possibility of enlightenment, like treasure buried under the living room floor or plant bulbs stored in the garage, like an unfertilized womb or blindfolded eyes. The Buddha did not possess any special quality missing in everyone else, nor does the teacher give the student anything that the student does not already have.

The spiritual journey, then, consists of digging the treasure up from the living room and refining it, planting and cultivating the bulbs, fertilizing the womb, removing the blindfold. To use Plato's allegory, we would crawl up out of the cave and get used to life in the sun. Literally, what happens is that we listen to Buddhist teaching and apply it to the experience of practice, so that teaching and practice constantly amplify and clarify each other. After seeing through the illusion of self, we must then understand how the light and the awareness which created the illusion become convoluted into the shapes of ego. Without such understanding, the insight of egolessness may succumb again to the play of shadow.

This insight does not necessarily banish particular dysfunctional problems, such as alcoholism or drug addiction. These still require specialized treatment. But the context of the treatment, the attitude behind it, and the total outcome, might be quite different if we do away with the initial assumption of a sick self that must be cured.

The idea of enlightenment, in one form or another, inspires all the world's great philosophies and religions, as well as our highest artistic achievements. In the sayings of Lao Tsu, the Tao, the inner unifying harmony of nature and human, is beyond all description. For the third-century Western philosopher Plotinus, enlightenment is the One from which proceed Mind and Soul; these mirror the One throughout infinity in an endless proliferation of created forms. In the Christian gospel of *John*, enlightenment is the Logos, the Word, the universal plan, the incarnate Love and Light which brings grace and truth to humankind walking in darkness. In the synoptic Christian gospels, enlightenment is "the kingdom of heaven within you"; it is "like a grain of mustard seed, which a man took, and cast into his garden, and it grew, and waxed a great tree"; it is the "leaven, which a woman took, and hid in three measures of meal, till the whole was leavened." (*Luke* 13:18–21). The kingdom is attainable by the simplifying practice of unconditional charity, by regaining the innocence of a child, by renouncing greed and aggression, by behaving toward our fellow beings as we would like them to behave toward us; it grows from humble beginnings and is found in the ordinary conditions of life.

The myths of the ancient pagan world, those that are more than pretty stories, take on vitality and power because the idea of enlightenment is present in them. For example, read the tale of Cupid and Psyche, as narrated by an old woman in *The Golden Ass* of Apuleius, a second-century novel from the Roman empire. Psyche, the youngest of three sisters, is so famous for her beauty that the goddess Venus, the mother of life, is enraged with jealousy, and vows revenge. Following an oracle of Apollo, Psyche's father abandons the girl on a cliff to be married to an ugly serpent, but the soft west wind ushers her into a gorgeous palace where she is wed to an anonymous bridegroom on the condition that she never look at his face.

The two lovers sleep together in the dark. Eventually her envious sisters convince her that her husband must be the foul serpent of the oracle and they persuade her to light a torch while he is sleeping and dispatch him with a knife. But when the torch is lit, she discovers the beautiful, sweet, gentle face of Cupid beside her on the couch. Swooning, she drops the knife and begins to make love with him as he sleeps. Awakened by a sputtering drop of oil from the torch, Cupid realizes he has been betrayed and flies away, leaving Psyche begging and weeping on the ground.

Determined to punish Psyche for her presumption, Venus offers her the chance for atonement by a series of impossible tasks. Psyche must separate hills of different seeds, pluck wool from mad golden sheep, fetch a vial of water from the bubbling spring of Cocytus, and journey to hell, ask for a scrap of Proserpine's beauty, and bring it back. Daunted by these tasks, Psyche is on the verge of killing herself several times, but she is helped by ants, reeds, eagles, towers, and finally by Cupid himself, who is unable to forget her. Cupid brings her an exilir from the god Mercury. Made immortal by it, Psyche is able to enter heaven, having now been transformed into a fit bride for a god.

Apuleius understood this story as an allegory of the spiritual journey. Cupid is Eros, the idea of enlightenment, the primal urge for truth, the child of the goddess of passion, the mother of all life; Psyche is the human soul; the serpent is ignorance, or samsara; the sisters are forms of ego. Seduced by ego to doubt and attack Eros, Psyche allows her connection with him to be severed. She can only repair it by making herself a doormat for passion, whose demands drive her to the brink of despair, sending her finally beyond death, to beg beauty from the goddess of hell. In the end, Psyche cannot succeed by her own efforts, though these are necessary; Cupid has to rescue her with the pagan equivalent of Divine Grace. We can marry enlightenment, then, but we need help to do it.

At the same time, our secret doubt is that no such goal can ever be found. Classical Buddhist texts describe the beauty and splendor of enlightenment in the most extravagant language. When the Buddha achieved his victory over illusion, the gods arrived to strew flowers, the earth shook like a woman in ecstasy, light pervaded myriads of universes, and heavenly beings anointed the Enlightened One with jars of water from the oceans of the world, singing cosmic harmonies of conjured choruses. If enlightenment could be induced by Buddhist poetry, we would all have vanished long ago into the void. Ordinary meditators may be edified by these texts, but still find themselves facing traffic jams and coming home from the store to pay bills and taxes. Enlightenment then seems a mirage, a myth, a pie in the sky, a magic rabbit on a stick, which we pursue like greyhounds for someone else's benefit, and which, if attained, would be entirely lacking in food value, a huge disappointment.

We pursue enlightenment in the first place because we do not accept what we already are, and approach the spiritual path as a means to change ourselves into something else. From the start, our own desire makes us vulnerable to being cheated—by fraudulent masters and by ourselves. The act of seeking, the idea of a spiritual journey, is both a help and a hindrance—a help because without it we would never be motivated to begin, a hindrance because it defines us at the outset from the standpoint of poverty mentality: we lack something and must search to obtain it. We humbly beg at the feet of the masters for the wealth, power, and self-respect that we believe they have and we don't. It would be a lot simpler to accept what we are from the beginning and let enlightenment take care of itself. We seek because we are not able to do this. But if we kill the idea of a journey, there would be no help at all. Confusion and pain do not vanish on the mere assertion that the kingdom of heaven is already within us. The fact of suffering is profoundly indifferent to our thoughts about it. Our whole quest is never free from contradiction and double value. It is both true and false. It is fate, faith, and fraud.

Buddhist masters address this dilemma: Chogyam Trungpa taught that what matters is not the goal, but the journey; there are no credentials that establish enlightenment, and on one level the whole thing is a fool's errand. Enlightenment is a peg on which to hang our hope for a higher, more pleasurable, more secure field of expansion. Zen master Shunryu Suzuki told his students to let go of enlightenment and just practice. If enlightenment happens at all, it is not sudden, like a bolt of lightning, but gradual, like walking in a mist and discovering after a while that you have gotten wet by degrees. The act of sitting practice is itself enlightenment; any hope for more just perverts meditation into a labyrinth of ambition.

A good teacher, then, tries to distinguish between genuine enlightenment and the realm of the gods, between a fruitful journey and a spiritual ego trip. Buddhists readily grant that enlightenment cannot be understood by the conceptual mind, and that whatever we might say about it is not the real thing. The deeper doubt insisted on here is that there may be no real thing either. If sitting practice is enlightenment, then so is eating cereal, going to the toilet, getting dressed, or hailing a cab—an assertion already made by many Zen teachers. To say this, however, destroys the idea. When enlightenment cannot be distinguished from anything else, then as a term of discussion, it is rendered meaningless. It becomes nothing but a sound—perhaps the sound of one hand. In that case there is no dharma, and no need for meditation.

Doubting enlightenment is listed in the Tibetan Buddhist texts as a cause for imprisonment in the lower realms of samsara. It is unthinkable. Insisting on this doubt is a sign of arrogance. It means we are saying that Buddha, Jesus, Lao Tsu, the Karmapas, Gurdjieff, et al. were only brilliant teachers whose disciples inflated their reputations to the level of myth. They may have had just as much potential for being irrational and power-hungry as anyone else, and perhaps there is no special reason to worship them, or defer to their authority. They may have been little more than creations of their students. Chogyam Trungpa wrote that Marpa, the tenth-century Tibetan guru, "lost his temper and beat people." Marpa is also considered an incarnate Buddha, the spiritual father of Tibet's greatest yogi Milarepa. Maybe his beatings were compassion in disguise, but it is hard to understand why the same argument could not be made for the drunk who abuses his wife and children.

A common method of spiritual teachers to handle this kind of doubt is to make a joke at the questioner's expense, agree with all the objections, and laugh hilariously, as if the teacher understands the whole issue on a higher level which the disciple can only attain by surrender. Maharishi's trademark was his high-pitched giggle; Gurdjieff played innumerable pranks on his anxious followers; Chogyam Trungpa's teaching style depended on getting his audience to laugh at themselves, and each other; Don Juan, the fictional guru of Carlos Castaneda's books, is always slapping his thighs and mocking his pupil. Western psychology might see here a classic case of mixed messages: "Of course you are right, seeking is useless, counterproductive, and absurd; I see you are making some progress. Good; keep seeking." Far from being resolved later on, the mixed message is intensified by further practice.

Sometimes laughter functions to loosen up our self-importance and sweep away obstacles; but derision also intimidates. Its unstated message is that we are schmucks who haven't "got it" yet. Nobody wants to be outside the circle as an object of ridicule. The voice of doubt whispers that the knowing laughter of the master is little more than a manipulative trick, and spiritual seeking is a perfect field for games of one-upmanship. The rules are slippery, the object is undefinable, and the stakes are unlimited. You lose by daring to presume that you do not need to be enlightened, by trusting your own wisdom when it contradicts the master's, by showing negative emotions, or simply by asking too many questions. You lose grandly by calling attention to the game. A cardinal principle of one-upmanship is not to admit when it is being played. If you are inept enough to say that your opponents are playing it, then they can give a concerned and sympathetic smile, touch you on the shoulder, and ask if they have done something to make you angry. You win back a little bit of face by admitting that you are neurotic and confused, but that your neurosis is "workable," that is, it need not prevent you from being accepted by the teacher and submitting to the path. We may not believe enlightenment exists, but most of us certainly want to appear as if we are making progress in that direction. The initial doubt is soon abandoned as naive.

When it comes back, it is treated as the resistance of ego. Trungpa called it "rat shit."

Far from being rat shit, fundamental doubt—of the teacher, the dharma, the sangha, and the goal—ought to be fully present in the mind at all times, given a place of honor along with prayer, confession, and the thought of death. This doubt should not be allowed to kill the journey, or prevent us from learning; but without it, the path becomes the trail of a slave crawling up to kiss the feet of a king. Enlightenment has at least three faces: if one face is the revulsion for samsara and the second is the longing for realization, the third is this rebellious devil, this insolent child wearing a cap and bells, who is always ready to observe that the emperor has no clothes. All the faces are equally necessary. Together, they multiply awareness by a factor of three. Doubt is also enlightenment—which turns out to exist within the space of its nonexistence.

In order to avoid being defeated by these paradoxes, or seduced into playing with them forever, one must simply begin. We cannot judge the recipe unless we taste the food.

3

MEETING THE JOURNEY MASTER

THE TIBETAN BUDDHIST curriculum brought by Chogyam
Trungpa to the West is divided into three main stages. These
yanas, or vehicles, are called Hinayana, Mahayana, and
Vajrayana—the narrow or individual vehicle, the great vehicle, and
the indestructible vehicle. At certain times and places, the yanas
existed independently of one another as separate and distinct schools.
In the Middle Ages, Tibetan monks integrated them into a single
progressive system. You begin with a ground, advance through a
path, and attain a fruition. This threefold logic breaks the journey
down into cumulative phases and gives the intellect something to
chew on. The folds do not necessarily proceed in strictly linear
fashion, nor does the student graduate from one to the next. Tibetan
teachers compare them to the foundation, structure, and roof of a
temple. The foundation is never put aside; it is always fully present in the completed edifice.

The general purpose of Hinayana (a Mahayanist term) is to tame
the mind, to detach from the grosser forms of passion, aggression,
and ignorance, to simplify goals and desires, to withdraw from participation in the games of samsara and attain the insight of egolessness. The object of awareness in this vehicle is personal confusion:
its textures, transformations, and themes. Hinayana is individual in
focus, narrow in scope, simple and direct in method. It is like cleaning your house. Mahayana, the "great vehicle," seeks to expand

attention outward, to the rest of the world. The experience of no-self, which is the fruition of the first yana, becomes the ground of the second. The objective now is not only to relate with personal confusion, but to develop compassion for all beings, and to extend oneself to them in wise and practical ways. In Mahayana, you might help others clean their houses, inspire them to do it themselves, or accommodate their mess, depending on what they need.

The Tibetan path is distinctive within the Buddhist world for its "crazy wisdom" vehicles, the Vajrayana and a fourth stage called Maha Ati. These are secret teachings available only to initiated students. Tibetan dharma is passed orally from master to disciple in a lineage of transmission. The four major Tibetan Vajrayana lineages—Kagyu, Nyingma, Sakya, and Gelugpa—have different styles and methods, but their common Buddhist goal is to speed up the process of attaining enlightenment and condense it into a single lifetime.

In Vajrayana, the separation between samsara and enlightenment, between good and evil, is regarded as an artificial convention. The poisons of samsara, the neurosis, the passion, aggression, ignorance, envy, and pride, are not rejected, but experienced instead as forms of buddha-mind. Confusion is wisdom in disguise. The mess is now regarded as a stage filled with creative possibilities. Vajrayana respects social conventions, but is not bound by them. It is therefore, inevitably, a highly controversial vehicle, even among other Buddhist schools. It could be highly dangerous too. The actual practices of Vajrayana are not especially exciting; most of them are as sedate and tedious as anything else in the Buddhist menu. The danger comes from within ourselves, from the energy of our own minds, which is the energy of the universe. Vajrayana invites us to open up this energy, to enjoy and work with it directly, instead of keeping it under lock and key. If we are unprepared for the task, we hurt ourselves, or somebody else—like monkeys playing with loaded guns.

On their initial contact with Vajrayana, Westerners tended either to sensationalize it as a phenomenon of the "Mystic East," or to misinterpret it as a corruption of pure Buddhism. In the integrated three-yana system, it completes the other vehicles, and relates to them as higher mathematics does to algebra and arithmetic. Vajrayana cannot be understood without a thorough grounding in the first two systems.

Each of the yanas has its own practices, purpose, characteristic experiences and view. Together they form a continuum in which the teachings and practices of one level are carried over into the next, and are there understood in a more expanded way. The basic Hinayana practice is sitting meditation. This is the most important practice of the entire journey; it is never abandoned but continues throughout all the stages as the matrix for everything else that follows. Introduced at the very beginning, it is the end as well. Sitting meditation grows the crop that the higher yanas merely harvest and market. When Chogyam Trungpa introduced Tibetan Buddhist dharma to Americans, he was insistent that they learn to sit for years before he would teach them any practices from the Vajrayana.

Tibetan dharma places great emphasis on the role of the teacher. Without the teacher, there is no dharma. In the Hinayana, the teacher is a preceptor and a physician, the person who administers the refuge vow marking your formal commitment as a Buddhist, and gives you practice instructions like a doctor prescribing medicine. These offices are often delegated to senior students. In the Mahayana, the teacher is imagined as a spiritual friend and guide who walks beside you on the path; although in actual fact, the teacher is usually surrounded by a wall of limousines, closed doors, and guards, and is walking beside you only in a metaphoric sense; this role, too, is played by proxy. In the Vajrayana, the teacher is the guru, who is also the Buddha, the embodiment of the dharma, the path personified. All Buddhist schools offer the triple refuge, the ceremony in which the student takes refuge in the three jewels: the Buddha, the Dharma, and the Sangha. In the Tibetan system the guru is a fourth refuge, the key to the other three. Meeting and connecting with the guru is the most important single event of the practitioner's life—of one's whole existence, we could say, for one prays earnestly that the effects of this meeting will continue through many lives in the future, and believes that it was prepared for by many lives in the past.

Chogyam Trungpa was born in Tibet around 1940, a generation before the Chinese invasion. From infancy, he was marinated in the three-yana system. His teachers acknowledged him as a *tulku*, the eleventh of the Trungpa line. A tulku in his tradition is someone who reincarnates with the memories and values of previous lives intact. By the time he was in his late teens, he directed the monasteries of the Surmang region of Tibet and was a lineage holder in both the Kagyu and Nyingma traditions. He was considered a master of Vajrayana and Maha Ati. His career in the West began in the early 1960s, after he led a party of several hundred refugees over the mountains into India, befriended some English relief workers there, and went to Oxford University on a fellowship to study comparative religions. By 1970 he was fluent in English and started teaching in the United States. He was the first and the most Westernized Tibetan Vajrayana master who succeeded in making this vehicle available to American students.

The American ground had already been prepared for Trungpa's work by the consciousness expansion movement of the 1960s. As a young graduate student in literature, I had heard of the *Tibetan Book of the Dead*, the *Bardo Thodol*, through users of psychedelic drugs. The *Tibetan Book of the Dead* purports to describe the stages of the *bardo* or after-death experience, but LSD trippers were claiming that it presented a paradigm for understanding the psychedelic journey. Eager to discover what they were talking about, I was soon perusing a copy of the Evans-Wentz edition of the *Bardo Thodol*, first published in 1928 with an introduction by Carl Jung.

Between 1967 and 1973 the *Book of the Dead* was mentioned frequently in movies and newspapers and on television talk shows. One movie from the period, *I Love You Alice B. Toklas*, included a scene in which a "flower child" reads portions of the *Book* to a crying hippie during an acid trip. A collection of poems against the

War in Vietnam featured a "found poem" that juxtaposed quotations from the *Bardo Thodol* with Viet Cong body counts and fractured news from the *New York Times*. American generals were compared to "the shapes of the Lord of Death," uttering "from their mouths the sounds of STRIKE SLAY." They lick brains, drink blood, and tear heads from bodies, and hearts from ribs. Containing both peaceful and terrifying visions, the *Book* instructs the listener to remember that these are the dying person's own projections.

The Victorian-era theosophists believed and taught that great Himalayan spiritual masters were guiding the consciousness of the planet upward to higher levels, preserving secrets of ancient wisdom until the time was right to reveal them to the world. These masters have highly developed supernatural powers: they can disappear, read minds, practice thought-transference, leave footprints in solid stone, and exist without bodies, independent of space and time, in a realm inaccessible to ordinary people. They had established a perfect society in a remote mountain fastness of central Asia, and then vanished into other dimensions.

British and American attraction to Tibet was expressed in film and fiction during the first half of the twentieth century. The idea of masters with supernatural powers, preserving a secret tradition of wisdom in a remote mountain kingdom somewhere over the Himalayas, was the basis of James Hilton's popular novel, *Lost Horizon*, first published in 1933. In this tale, four Westerners are kidnapped from an airfield in India and flown to a valley dominated by a cone-shaped mountain, and completely surrounded by impassable peaks. The "lamasery" of Shangri-La cannot be found on any map. The snow-peaks, "utterly majestic and remote," seem to float "upon vast levels of cloud." The gaily colored building which stands at the head of the valley clings to the mountainside "with the chance delicacy of flower petals impaled upon a crag." Hilton's descriptions were clearly intended to suggest a Tibetan Buddhist monastery; but the High Lama turns out to be a Capuchin monk from the West who has lived in Tibet for three hundred years.

In Shangri-La, time slows down, and people live for centuries, although eventually they pass away. Anyone who tries to leave grows old immediately. The inhabitants devote themselves to lives of music, art, contemplation, study, and wisdom. They admire Western composers, especially Mozart. Social and religious authority is vested in the High Lama, but government in the ordinary sense is not necessary. When conflicting passions arise, people just make space for them. Religion is neither Buddhist nor Christian, but combines the devotional and contemplative features of both: *"Te Deum Laudamus"* and *"Om Mani Padme Hum"* are heard equally in the temples. Shangri-La has Tibetan lamas, but takes recruits from all races. The purpose of the kingdom is to preserve the enlightened heritage of the world against a coming storm of violence that "will rage till every flower of culture is trampled, and all human beings are leveled in a vast chaos." Among the newcomers, only Conway, the consul, has the "passionlessness" to appreciate Shangri-La. He is chosen as the heir to the kingdom's destiny. But his loyalty to a friend forces him to leave, and he spends the rest of his life trying to return. Shangri-La becomes a symbol of the lost horizon of his mind.

Hilton's novel went through seventeen editions between 1933 and 1936, and another sixteen by 1954. In 1934 it won the Hawthornden Prize, an English award for an imaginative work by an author under the age of forty-one. *Lost Horizon* was made into a movie, and is still imitated in popular fiction. The novel has no compelling drama, and the characters are flat and lifeless; yet the wide reception of this book suggests that its theme appeals on a deep level.

As a romantic fantasy, *Lost Horizon* was enormously successful; but it was something more than that. There was an actual tradition in Tibet of an enlightened society, the kingdom of Shambhala, whose ruler was supposed to have received special teachings from the Buddha on how to integrate meditation with secular life. According to this tradition, everyone in Shambhala became enlightened, and no one else could enter the kingdom except by developing the awareness needed to see and appreciate it. Tibetan lamas say that Shambhala exists on the planet right now. Hilton was therefore working from a real basis in history and legend. Millions of Westerners were drawn to the idea that Tibet might contain something of special importance to the happiness of humanity, some quality of wisdom, some secret teaching, that would be capable of fulfilling the universal human longing for a saner, more peaceful and beautiful world. These wise old lamas, Carl Jung wrote, might "after all, have caught a glimpse of the fourth dimension and twitched the veil from the greatest of life's secrets."

W. Somerset Maugham's 1943 novel, *The Razor's Edge*, portrays a spiritual seeker, Larry, who travels to the Himalayas to meditate. Returning to the West, he is imbued with expanded compassion and mysterious healing powers. Maugham's work, also popular, was made into a movie in the late 1940s, with Tyrone Power in the lead role. Although Maugham's book, unlike Hilton's, had three-dimensional characters in credible dramatic conflict, Hollywood maintained the "lost horizon" romanticism in the image of Larry's teacher, a white-robed saint with a long beard, who calls him "my son" and radiates angelic light. In a second version of the movie, which appeared in the early 1980s, with Bill Murray in the role of Larry, the teacher is clearly a Tibetan Buddhist lama. No special effects are used to give him an unearthly appearance, and he lives and dresses according to the customs of a real tradition. Perhaps the change in the image of the eastern guru between these two films measures how much our knowledge of Tibetan Buddhism had matured in the intervening forty years, from vague fascination and longing to genuine experience. The one led to the other.

Thomas Merton, the Trappist monk who inspired a resurgence of interest in contemplation within the Roman Catholic Church before his death in 1968, helped prepare the American ground for the reception of Tibetan dharma in a different way. Strongly rooted in the Christian tradition, Merton had nothing to do with drug trips, theosophy, and romantic fantasies of lost kingdoms. His interest was energized by the profound parallels between the experiences of Christian and Buddhist meditators. He thought that the

Buddhists had developed meditation to a higher level than the West, and he wanted to learn from them in order to reawaken the sources of life in his own religion. Westerners who approached contemplation from a Catholic direction were open to Buddhist teachers partly because of him. His *Asian Journal* records details from his encounter with Tibetan dharma, which may have produced radical changes in his work had he lived longer. His meeting with Chogyam Trungpa in India was remembered well by both men, and germinated the idea for the Naropa Institute, Trungpa's Buddhist college in Colorado founded in 1974.

Like others of my generation, I was interested in all these cultural currents, and in anything that might provide an alternative to the deadening corporate materialism of American society. I studied the theosophists, explored my consciousness with psychedelics, read Thomas Merton, D. T. Suzuki, and Alan Watts, tried to make sense out of the *Bardo Thodol,* and practiced yoga. Traditional Christianity did not appeal to me; it required belief in too many theological doctrines. I was not satisfied that God even existed, never mind that He was really three gods, or that a virgin brought forth His Son.

Trungpa's first American students included large numbers of counterculture dropouts, refugees from the collapsing New Left, student mystics, poets, amateur yogis in rebellion against the materialism of their parents, and hippies who liked the idea of gathering in a remote rural farmhouse to grow vegetables and be weird. By the time I met these students, Trungpa had changed them into ordinary citizens wearing suits and ties, or dresses. They did not shave their heads or wear robes. They drank, smoked cigarettes, and ate meat. They were unimpressed by my claim that I could see auras. Their meditation instruction was exactly the opposite of what I had been doing for the previous two years—I had been trying to use my breath to raise the serpent power coiled at the base of my spine, hoping vaguely that Tibetans would show me how to generate psychic heat, so that, like the legendary yogi Milarepa, I could levitate naked in the snows of Mount Everest and not even shiver. According to Chogyam Trungpa, breath was just breath. It had no mystical meaning at all.

The book recommended to me was Trungpa's *Cutting Through Spiritual Materialism* (Shambhala, 1973). I opened the pages at random and read: "It is important to see that the main point of any spiritual practice is to step out of the bureaucracy of ego." This meant dropping the ego's desire "for a higher, more spiritual, more transcendental version of knowledge, religion, virtue, judgment, comfort, or whatever...."

He nailed me with his very first words.

"Spiritual materialism," a term Trungpa invented, is a major contribution to the vocabulary of religious discourse. It cuts away the endless fog of "human potential" speculations by which we put off being simply who we are. The term describes any form of spirituality that is practiced for personal gain and self-improvement, whether through money, power, attention, purity, or bliss. Trungpa identified the commercial mentality behind the hope for some kind of payoff at the end of the path, and correctly related this to the materialism that permeates our whole society. He did not reject business methods as such. For him, the important point is whether we open up, or continue to center on ourselves by means of spiritual techniques.

Reading this book, I realized the irony: the very fascination that drew me to him was an obstacle. I sat down and laughed. Somewhere in this world, someone understood my experience, with a sense of humor and no condescension or moralistic judgment. Not only that, he could reflect it back to me so I could understand it too. I was both disappointed and relieved. I no longer had to pretend anything. Here was a Tibetan master saying that my goal of a higher, more spiritual, more transcendental version of knowledge, religion, virtue, judgment, comfort, whatever, could not be accomplished. And even if it was accomplished, although I might impress my family, lovers, and friends, although students might gaze up at me, envious of my serenity and willing to pay fees to hear my words—the person who had written this book would not be fooled. He would see through my whole game, and both of us would know it was still nothing but a game.

I had to lay eyes on this person. As winter melted into spring, I continued sitting and listening to his tapes. Trungpa was to give a public talk in Boston on June 1, 1978. On that day, I drove from my home in Vermont south toward Massachusetts, imagining that Trungpa, at least, would be dressed in robes, and fantasizing that he would immediately recognize my high level of realization and take me on as his dharma heir.

Circling Copley Square, my grand spiritual quest was reduced to the search for a parking spot and a toilet, as I fretted about the lateness of the hour and glanced again and again at my watch. I went first to the wrong address, but at last I found out that he was speaking at the Arlington Street Church. I arrived forty minutes late, all in a dither, convinced that I had missed the talk. He didn't show up for another hour. My humorless anxiety about time looked like something from a cartoon. I relaxed and waited. Why not? There was nothing to lose. He had established an atmosphere of meditation without even showing up.

The church was jammed to the walls. Every seat, every foot of aisle and balcony space was occupied. I squeezed into a corner of a balcony that gave me a view of the dais. My fantasy of being noticed by him in any way was pulverized.

Trungpa limped in with his attendants, wearing glasses and a dark blue suit. No robes. He had given them up ten years before to marry a sixteen-year-old English girl. He looked happy. He looked like he had just told a wonderfully dry joke, and was waiting for everyone to get it. All the people in the church rose to their feet. He was helped into his chair. Behind him was a banner decorated with a huge red dot. One one side was a table, set with flowers and a decanter. We waited until he was seated before we sat down.

He gazed at us very seriously and drank from a glass. He looked at the students, the intellectuals with scarves, pipes, and tweed jackets patched at the elbows, the ministers in clerical collars, the professionals in business suits, the old ladies, the hippies in ragged jeans wearing jewelry displaying astrological signs, sprawling in the aisles, heads resting on backpacks. He looked at the young man in yoga costume, complete with beads and headband, who was perched in the lotus posture on the balcony railing where everybody would notice him, thumbs and forefingers in circles, backs of hands resting on knees, and eyeballs turned upward to gaze at his third eye.

"Good evening, ladies and gentlemen," said Trungpa. "It's good to be back in Boston." He cleared his throat several times. "But all of you are cowards."

He said we lacked the courage to meditate regularly, open ourselves, give up our territory, and drop our ego defenses. He said there is only one way to drop defenses, and that is to do it—"Just," he said, popping a fan, "like that." He said ego is wanting to take everything in, to hold onto it and hold onto it: he mimed the act of pulling the world into his stomach, gritting his teeth against the microphone. Everyone laughed. Enlightenment means that you drop your cowardice—he popped his fan—"just like that." He said enlightenment was possible then and there, on the spot, for everybody in the room. He said we all have basic intelligence which is crowded in by defenses; if the defenses are dropped, basic intelligence can function without being blocked. "It is a very simple thing. You just do it, here and now." He told us to cheer up.

He was simple, silly, goofy, and physically frail, but he radiated warmth and wisdom. His least gesture commanded the attention of the whole huge vaulted churchful of spectators, including the ones who couldn't get in the door. People leaned over the balcony to catch a glimpse of his face. The old woman next to me closed her eyes and bent forward, listening intently, half smiling, as if in prayer. The woman behind me whispered "Could you move a little? I can't see him."

He opened the floor for questions. Someone asked if, when you drop your defenses, the job of defense is taken over by basic intelligence. Trungpa asked "What? What?" A staff member rephrased the question in his ear. He said "Oh. Good heavens." There was general laughter. He paused, and said "Why do you want to know that?" The audience laughed again. "No, it is not a question of defense at all," he said. "Basic intelligence is what is revealed after the defenses are let go."

A woman asked, "Rinpoche, do you want to take a question about ego, or do you want to restrict the topic to cowardice?"

He sipped his drink and said "It's up to you, sweetheart." She laughed. His response relaxed the audience and loosened up the tightness of our reverential awe.

The question was about people with weak and insecure egos: wasn't it necessary for them to build up a strong ego before they could let go of it? He said that ego itself is weak and insecure, always needing to be defended and built up, because ultimately it does not exist. Genuine strength is discovered by letting go of that need.

He cut off the questions after about fifteen minutes, repeating his assertion that enlightenment was possible for all of us, "right now." He opened his fan and displayed a large red dot. Everyone applauded. He said we were a fine group of people, and he loved being with us, but we must drop our cowardice and cheer up; not cheer up to be happy, not to make the world a better place, just cheer up. "On the spot." And we must meditate. On the way out, he took the people nearest the door by the shoulders and kissed them.

There was nothing spectacular about Trungpa's message or his technique. He just touched people where they were soft, made them laugh, and invited them in. He could establish a rapport that was immediate and direct, like recognizing in the mirror for the first time the face you had before you were born. He told the truth, with no attitude that it was either fascinating or terrible; it was merely the truth. He inspired a spark of trust, and the heart opened.

Like many other Americans, I was predisposed to listen just because Trungpa was a Tibetan, because he was the authentic product of that world of lost horizons and mystic masters. Before I saw him, he had already made me realize something I knew but did not want to admit: that without the teacher, there is no way to step out of the bureaucracy of ego; instead, it ends up directing the quest.

I liked the sensuality of Tibetan dharma: the deep maroons and yellows of the robes, the golds and blues of the temples, the haunting sounds of the horns, drums, and gongs, the pungent smells of incense and saffron water, all draw the longing, wandering mind and heighten its experience of beauty and splendor. The curriculum, however, is presented through a hierarchy of forms that intensifies the mixed message behind seeking what you already have: enlightenment credentials are meaningless, said Trungpa, but you should definitely respect mine, and here is a graded process for acquiring them. Although he deflated, and his students scorned, the ego's desire for a higher, more spiritual, more transcendental life, the whole Tibetan style lured me on with the promise of a higher, more spiritual, more transcendental life.

The system of the three yanas has an inherently elitist appeal. It triggers our desire to join the big shots, do the secret rituals, and find out what the masters really know. In my first contact with him, Trungpa undercut this elitism; he presented enlightenment as something anyone can have, right now. His message was too simple for intellectual analysis: you can do it, don't be a coward, cheer up. Any sensible country schoolgirl could have said the same thing. Yet he wore expensive suits and jewels, rode in a chauffeured Mercedes, had servants, designed and awarded pins to symbolize levels of attainment in his programs, and was known to offer secret tantric instruction to selected disciples. Since he was telling the truth about my own motives, I believed that if he did offer me something transcendental, it would be the real thing, not some plastic manipulation. But the ego, which supposedly did not exist, was both deflated and fully engaged. The impetus behind the journey came as much from the desire to earn one of his pins and hold a title in his organization as from a genuine longing to wake up or an altruistic wish to benefit sentient beings.

4

PLAYING TO AN EMPTY HOUSE

THE SITTING PRACTICE taught in Tibetan dharma is called *shamatha*, which means "abiding in peace." Shamatha is good basic Buddhism, common to most traditional schools. The best place to do it is in a clean, well-ordered room where one can sit for several minutes at a time without being disturbed. The seat should be a firm but pliable cushion that will elevate the body several inches off the floor, so the legs can be crossed comfortably in front. The back should be straight, preferably unsupported, with the knees at or below the level of the hips, and the head and shoulders erect but not stiff. If the knees are too high, this will put strain on the back muscles. The hands rest lightly, palms down, on the thighs. The posture is awake and relaxed, expressing the body's natural vulnerability, strength, and presence. The eyes are left open, the gaze resting vaguely on the floor, about three feet away. Then a slight effort is made to bring awareness onto the outbreath. This attention may be relaxed as the breath comes in. The meditator should not force deep breathing, or alter the natural rhythm of the breath, but just feel it going out.

Thoughts and emotions are noticed and allowed to pass away by themselves. In meditation they are just waves in the mind, nothing more. Trungpa's instruction for noticing and letting go of them was to say, mentally, "thinking," whenever they occur, and then return attention to the breath. There is no need to struggle against

45

thoughts, or attempt to favor some and get rid of others. It does not matter whether they are stupid, brilliant, painful, blissful, nasty, or sweet, whether they come in trickles or floods. Thoughts are a natural occurrence, like ripples, clouds, and the sounds of wind in the leaves.

After a while, a rhythm develops between awareness of the out-breath and immersion in thoughts. You could be right with the breath for a few seconds, and then realize ten minutes later that you have been planning the menu for dinner and making up a dialogue with your boss. This is a common experience for all meditators and is nothing more than mental flow; it does not mean that you are doing anything wrong. No one can keep attention focused at all times. The rhythm between awareness and forgetting is a process of "touch and go." You feel the breath, gently and silently notice your thoughts, then let go of that awareness, touching back to it again and again. There should be no attempt to try and fixate on awareness as a goal. You will not necessarily be better at it after ten years than after the first five minutes. When the attention wanders away repeatedly into daydreams and preoccupations, you bring it back to the breath like a kind and patient mother feeding a baby who wants to look at everything but the spoon. If your body gets tired and cramped, or you feel overwhelmed by a sense of confusion and struggle, a good remedy is to take a break, loosen your posture and start fresh, or quit for the day.

When done exactly as described, shamatha embodies the essence of the Buddhist path: it does not divide reality into means and ends—they are the same. Keeping the eyes open but only vaguely focused expresses simultaneous awareness and detachment. Nothing in the mind is either rejected or held; it is noticed and allowed to vanish. There is no aggression toward ourselves or the world, and no attempt to produce a specific result. Awareness of the out-breath has a decentralizing effect as the attention is constantly opening outward, toward infinite space, instead of centering inward on some imaginary self-core. The body posture tends to transmit its qualities to the mind: upright, awake, open, vulnerable, gentle, relaxed, firm. As these qualities manifest, mind and body are synchronized. The word "thinking" repeatedly cuts our identification with the contents of thought, allowing us to remain entirely outside and beyond the images on the screen—all the dramas of elation and sadness, love, lust, and pain. We just watch them pass.

Practicing mindfulness of our thoughts and emotions is a process of making friends with them. True friends do not demand that we live up to their expectations; they accept us as we are. Sitting meditation extends this acceptance toward ourselves. Whatever comes into the mind is permitted to appear, and dissolve, according to its own laws. It is neither condemned nor praised, acted out nor suppressed. Shamatha is a kindness, a willingness to make room for any mind-wave that comes along, no matter how threatening, seductive, or absurd it may seem.

There are subtle differences between shamatha and the forms of sitting and *vipassana* meditation taught in the Zen and Theravadin traditions. Teachers in these Buddhist schools may tell their students in some stages to count breaths, or to be aware of every phase of breath, both coming in and going out, and to watch every thought and bodily sensation. Shamatha is a somewhat looser technique which allows more gaps in the attention span. This approach does not bewray a lack of precision, but reflects a valid philosophical orientation that is extended and developed in later stages. Gaps permit ignorance, but they also make room for the experience of emptiness without reference point. The two are inseparable. The general attitude of shamatha is to trust the gap, rather than try and haunt every thought, breath, and muscular twitch. If awareness is too demanding, it turns into aggression. The spacious, unfocused quality of ignorance has a place in the total system. In Hinayana, it is invited into the field of practice as a general background of neurosis; in Mahayana, ignorance, as emptiness, becomes a ground for compassion.

After five hundred hours of sitting, the subtle differences among Buddhist meditation techniques tend not to matter. The shamatha student is more than willing to count breaths, watch grasshoppers

47

jump through mental hoops, recite poetry, or sort individual grains from a mountain of rice, if it will make the time pass. The whole idea of technique itself keeps evaporating, like a cup of water in the middle of a prairie.

The effects of sitting practice depend on how long and how often we sit, and how we handle the obstacles that inevitably arise. The first thing I noticed is what a traffic jam the mind really is; when I took ten or fifteen minutes to sit and do nothing, my head was flooded with internal noise. I had the impression that meditation was impossible for me, that I would never be able to concentrate long enough to clear out all those voices, and I wanted to fall asleep. But by merely noticing this chaos, I was doing exactly what I was supposed to do. Meditation is not a transcendental realm of thoughtless tranquility; it is nothing at all, really, other than what we are at any given moment. The only features added by meditation are awareness, which sees, and space, which accommodates. The secret of the practice is more in what it does not do. Normally, we suppress, grasp, exploit, ignore, and identify with the contents of mind. Meditation detaches from these responses, and then boycotts them entirely. Shamatha has no purpose for them.

Doing shamatha five or ten minutes a day begins to create an atmosphere of peace and relaxation. Just that much is precious, especially if we are afflicted by chronic tension; but the peace is unlikely to have any permanent effects unless our practice encounters the deeper levels of confusion that we customarily shut out. This requires longer periods of sitting. Trungpa recommended minimum sessions of fifty minutes at a time.

During longer sessions, I became acutely aware that I wanted to stop sitting. Here is the first real threshold, the first level where practice either falls apart or starts to turn into a genuine discipline. For a while there is physical pain in the back, legs, and shoulders. The body complains about being asked to do something new. I took breaks, made small shifts in my posture, and attempted to treat pain like any other thought: labeling it "thinking" and letting it go. Physical pain, however, is more demanding than thought. In some cases it signals a health problem requiring specialized attention, like scoliosis, but usually it is little more than a form of resistance. Sitting is like a mirror—all our neurosis will be reflected in it. Looking in a mirror can be uncomfortable. If we have a problem with authority, for example, it will be transferred to the instructor or the practice itself, and we may find ourselves filled with the aches and pains of our private battle.

Children in my family were sometimes punished for wild behavior by having to sit in a corner and stare at the wall. I would fidget, swing my legs, wipe my nose on my sleeve, tie and untie my sneakers, pick my fingernails, think about all the games I wanted to play, silently exhaust my slender vocabulary of curses on my father, pity myself, make the time pass by remembering books and comic books, and then at last hang my head penitently so I would have a better chance of being released early. Yet when I finally got up, all that usually happened was that I went and sat in another spot.

As an adult meditator, I often relived memories like these on my cushion, chuckling or weeping, according to how they struck me at the moment. A tragic mood of identifying with childhood hurt might bring the tears rolling down my face, and then I would giggle at the stupid irony that I was still making myself do what I used to dread and hate. I was reminded of a man I heard about who spent part of his childhood in a concentration camp, digging ditches. When he grew up and bought a house in America, he always had some yard project going that involved digging ditches and putting up barbed wire. Without the wire and the dirt piles he was homesick. Then I would reflect that all of life is a prison, etc. and entertain myself with mental pornography shows—adult comics.

In between the shows, meditation is extremely boring. Meditators make this discovery fairly soon, often in the first half hour. Trungpa taught that if meditation were not boring, it would be without value. Many Americans treat practice as a form of cross-cultural tourism, he said, and will brag about how they visited Buddhist sites in Asia and sat in a Zen monastery for a month. They might show slides of the grounds to their friends, giving the impression that it was a wonderful time. In actuality, practice does not begin until our fascination with it as an exotic artifact has been eroded in boredom. If the tourists really gave themselves a chance to experience practice, he said, they would tell their friends to stay away from it.

The phenomenon that we call boredom has several stages, as different from one another as rivers are from brooks, or lakes and ponds from bogs. "Hot" boredom is the restless caged feeling that drives one to pace back and forth, call up old lovers, raid the refrigerator, smoke cigarettes by the pack, turn on the television, or go out to bars. This type of boredom is most likely to be a problem during the first hundred hours of sitting, and it takes the form of obsessing over itches, aches and pains, surreptitious glances at your watch, and temporal disorientation—you are convinced that ten minutes must surely have been sixty. New meditators are identifiable by the audible sighs and frequent posture shifts emanating from their corners. The cure for hot boredom is extending the length of the sit, by spending entire weekends or weeks at a retreat center, beginning each day early in the morning, with scheduled breaks for walking and natural functions, and continuing into the night.

It is fairly typical to be distracted by feelings of restlessness, panic, joy, and bliss. We would like to use the practice to escape irritation. In shamatha, on the contrary, irritation blooms and swells, but is then fully experienced, and dies. Boredom simplifies confusion. It softens the habit of trying to shut out disappointment, and brings us down to the immediate present. Eventually the hot boredom cools off, mellowing into a steady undulation of impatient waves and peaceful troughs. We learn to ride the waves. If we embrace boredom, it turns into an equilibrium in which we are freed from the craving for entertainment. Our need to grasp onto happiness and fight discomfort is gradually relaxed.

Taming boredom into an acceptable cool flow of equanimity has tremendous benefits in and of itself: it means we do not need constant entertainment, nor do we have to use or depend on any-one else for it. Lovers often go through anxious phases where they ask each other, "Are you bored with me?" For a person immersed in shamatha, this question changes meaning, or becomes humor-ous. A shamatha practitioner regards boredom as a positive expe-rience. Boredom is the whole background of human existence; we spend so much effort to escape it, unsuccessfully, that it is no exag-geration to say it enslaves us. Samsara is created by the effort to escape boredom. Because we cannot accept boredom, we have an out-of-control advertising industry, drugs and drug cartels, ava-lanches of polluting products, television and air waves filled with constant inane chatter, desperate seeking for all kinds of stimula-tion, street gangs, even wars. For meditators, boredom is good news. Its presence means that we have made genuine contact with the basic anxiety of our lives.

Ordinary details, such as wildflowers clustered around the reflec-tions of light on broken glass, become so engaging and alive that we lose the need for the imagined dramas of the video industry. Our appreciation for everyday sense impressions is heightened: we notice the configurations of lines on faces, the patterns of rain-drops hitting the surface of a pond. The face of the person asking "Are you bored with me?" could reveal hitherto unknown and unap-preciated depths of beauty and tenderness. After five days of sit-ting, a bowl of rice looks like a royal feast. Emotions pass through one's being as ripples that have textures, transformations, valleys and peaks. They are full of display. They die and return, impossi-ble to hold.

In the boundless space created by the boredom of shamatha, the mind begins to empty itself of its former conditioning. When this stage is reached, it is good thing to extend the length of the sit even more. Begin to sit two hours a day, and go on a month-long practice retreat in a Buddhist center with a schedule of all-day meditation sessions.

It is important to have a qualified teacher who has gone through this process, for without proper guidance, the obstacles that arise during extended practice distort our view. It might take a long time to give up the idea that we have some kind of defect that must be cured by meditation. We might imagine that we have too many thoughts, or the wrong kind of thoughts; we might like to get our lives together, become highly evolved, and then suffer from the disappointment of failure when we realize that sitting practice is not going to achieve these goals. We might suffer tremendous guilt for allowing ourselves to be here without expectations and requirements.

All these hopes and fears belong to a de-repression process, which continues until the mind has gone through its attic of old scripts. An instructor can help us past any tendency to fixate on our triumphs and trials. In the absence of a guide, a generally effective antidote is to take ourselves lightly and humorously, practicing in the same spirit in which we brush our teeth—attaching no special importance to any meditative experience, whether good or bad.

Sitting at a retreat center is more reliable than withdrawing alone into a corner somewhere, because neurosis is most clearly displayed in relational situations. Alone, we do not have the opportunity to witness things like how we seduce others into our territory, or how aggression toward ourselves is triggered by certain patterns of interaction.

When I sat my first week-long retreat, meals were taken in silence according to a formal Japanese ritual called *oryoki*. This demanding and precise eating practice requires heightened mindfulness of detail and choreographed movements that must be synchronized with those of others. Immediately I made contact with my chronic fear of doing it wrong. Everything I did felt painfully inept. My recent marital separation was still raw at this time, and I went from aching over wrong moves in oryoki to a sense of guilt and sin reaching back thirty-five years into my childhood.

If I had gone to a psychotherapist, perhaps I would have been encouraged to spend many hours of talk eviscerating my guilt and studying the entrails for clues to my depression. In sitting practice, I simply relived it with full consciousness, deliberately letting one memory trigger the next to see how far back they would go. Talking about it would only have insulated me from the emotion itself. I sat in silence, with meditators on either side, letting the memories roll off in my head and the tears trickle down my cheeks, and every now and then I repeated, mentally, "thinking," and came back to the breath. That's all it was, all that guilt, all the imagined and genuine sins, all those years of defending myself from imputations of wrong—it was "thinking." It was no more important, ultimately, than the cramp in my leg. When I straightened my posture, feeling the strength of its inherent self-respect, the miserable burdening memories moved away toward the horizon like huge masses of clouds before the wind; and when I rose for walking, the vibrations of the gong penetrated them like sun rays. My point of view shifted from the clouds to the sky. This personal revolution was accomplished inside my mind, privately on my own cushion. But without the relational environment of the center it could not have happened.

Still, it was only a beginning.

Dysfunctional cycles of behavior are built up by the same process as any behavior; they are conditioned into existence by patterns of punishment and reward. The ability to explain the conditioning process is one of the achievements of behavioral psychology, and I believe its language may be useful for clarifying what happens in Buddhist meditation.

Operant conditioning works by reinforcement: the dog brings the newspaper because he gets a biscuit along with praise, and eventually will work just for the praise. The child does the chores to get an allowance or the approval of his parents, and will eventually do them just to feel like a responsible member of the family. Dysfunctional behavior is conditioning that causes harm: the delinquent vandalizes property to get the approval of her gang or the disapproval of authority figures; the husband and wife may abuse each other in part to experience the rush of passion and forgiveness that follows; children throw tantrums to gain control over their mothers; the corporation controls its workers with employee-of-the-month badges instead of paying them a living wage.

To extinguish unwanted conditioning, we must stop reinforcing it, and build up new behavior that is incompatible with the old. The gang members must be given better sources of approval, the husband and wife must find an alternative way to arouse passion, the mother must reward the child for socially appropriate responses, the workers must stop competing for badges, organize, and demand what they really need. When awareness is added to the conditioning process, the whole game is changed. We may be controlled by the hope for a merit badge until realizing that the authority dispensing it is manipulating us, against our own best interest. This new awareness dissolves the reinforcing value of the badge.

Meditation extinguishes conditioned cycles in three ways: lack of reinforcement, incompatible behavior, and awareness. In the terminology of Western behavioral science, these are classic methods. The cycles turn and play in the mind, through fantasy, memory, images, and words, but during shamatha they are disconnected from any environment that could nourish them, either punishment or reward. They are like actors playing to an empty house. The disconnection is done with that simple but uncompromisingly sharp label, "thinking," which keeps cutting their umbilical cords and leaving them to abort. The incompatible behavior is the sitting itself: as long as we are on the cushion we cannot do dysfunctional deeds. Eventually we have to get up and participate in the world, but the three-yana journey provides an alternative pattern to business as usual, a way of continuing and consolidating what meditation begins. Awareness makes it possible to altogether boycott the cycles, which can only flourish in ignorance. When we observe them, the cycles cannot repeat themselves in the same order and no longer have the same effects.

The chain that kept pulling me back into my personal round of passion and abuse was my own desperate clinging: my partner could use my jealousy and dependence to gain her version of power over me, which I would then resist with tricks that were equally damaging. One day, after my chain had been yanked, instead of chasing her, I went straight to the cushion and sat there all night. I had realized that no matter what she did, the key to my health was in this practice, and as long as I was doing it, my mind was free. Thoughts of who she slept with, or how she had rejected me, were exactly the same as any other thoughts: they were "thinking," that's all, just like the memories of wrongdoing and the cramps in my leg. When the abandoned child having these thoughts finally collapsed and wept, because I had detached from his demands, I could hold my seat and give him love. Shamatha at this point had undercut the dependence, the clinging, and the ignorance that permitted the cycle to go on. I held my seat and the universe fell into place. It moved in a natural order that required no interference from me.

Boredom, then, establishes a space for deconditioning to occur. When the deconditioning is far enough advanced, the mind is resensitized to its own perceptions. The resulting panoramic vision and appreciation for detail, called *vipashyana* in the Buddhist vocabulary, feels like recovery of lost innocence.

The appreciation for detail cultivated in sitting practice can be applied to any activity, such as washing dishes, pulling weeds, and hammering nails. Chores are made burdensome by wanting to be somewhere else, by dwelling in a realm of fantasy far removed from the task at hand. Through meditation I developed a love of carpentry and home improvement work, which had never interested me in the past. I liked drawing lines on boards, making precise cuts, framing a space, or laying a slate floor. I liked imagining how the completed job would look while I lay in bed at night, and then shaping the materials gradually to embody the idea. I found humor in the fact that carpentry visits swift punishment on any lapse of mindfulness: a wrong cut ruins wood, disorganized routine misplaces tools, ill use of hammers and saws leads to injured hands. With vipashyana, the steady feedback between mind and body heightens ordinary work into an artful dance. Laying slate is no less inherently creative than playing a piano concert.

In the conventional world, many people feel deprived of a sense of fulfillment. "Only bullfighters live all the way up," said Ernest Hemingway. The desire to be turned on, to live on the edge of vivid sensations, drives us to dangerous and aggressive sports, damaging love affairs, drugs, and criminal behavior. We crave the quick fix of violent emotions, but there is also a real need in our craving for full presence in the here and now. Vipashyana fills this need from the inside.

Clients and counselors involved in drug and alcohol treatment will see parallels between deconditioning the mind through shamatha and detoxifying the body through withdrawal and twelve-step rehabilitation programs. Samsara is like an addiction; drugs are like dysfunctional cycles created by the ego and its distorted view; vipashyana is like the mind's original state of health, before toxification. The analogy, however, is not exact. Drugs and alcohol are ingested into the body from outside, whereas passion, aggression, pride, envy, and ignorance are part of our basic makeup from birth. Shamatha does not assume that there is anything inherently wrong with this makeup, nor is it an illness requiring a cure. The approach is not to destroy or conquer samsara, but to understand it. The world of samsara is not separate from the experience of enlightenment.

This point is illustrated by contrasting how we normally regard thoughts with how a meditator regards them. Thoughts usually appear to us as the judgments and opinions of the self interacting with other selves. To a meditator, however, they resemble a continuous vista of cloud forms in the sky of awareness manifested as a perceptual field. The self is made of these forms. In the world, we want to know things like whether the problems that thoughts present to us can be solved, and whether our opinions and judgments are right or wrong. A meditator is more interested in the discoveries that can be made about thought itself as a phenomenon—how, for example, no thought ever occurs twice in exactly the same pattern, how feelings and perceptions are defined and supported by thoughts, and how every fantasy is a process that begins from a previous thought, goes through a life-cycle, and decays, its energy carried over into the birth of the next fantasy. Questions of whether a thought is "right" or "wrong" are just more thoughts. In a sense they are always both right and wrong: they bear a relation to their objects, but also create their own universe. What they are is true; what they say is selected, or fictional.

The stages of relaxation, boredom, de-repression and deconditioning may be accompanied by laughter, tears, anger, and silliness. The reliving of past memories may be accompanied by depressed silence and deep inward focus. The increased clarity of detail brings a raw emotional sensitivity, and intensified libido, which may be accompanied by sexual acting out. After two weeks of group practice, the atmosphere in a shrine hall is vivid with lust. Spalding Gray, in his article "Impossible Vacation" in the Summer 1992 issue of *Tricycle*, described how he saw on the blank wall of a zendo "giant disembodied erect cocks with balls and little fluttering wings," penetrating "deliciously swollen, pink, puckering vaginas" that looked like "fleshy butterflies in flight." His instructor told him to keep sitting.

With gains in empathy, flexibility, and sense of humor, there is less worry about getting our own way, and greater willingness to give up fixed opinions. Later stages include heightened appreciation for beauty, erosion of ego boundaries, and increased sense of spaciousness. These effects do not result from any active manipulation of the mind—they just happen. Shifting the emphasis from identifying with thought to observing it creates a setting where they can unfold.

5

A PALE HORSE

SHAMATHA AND ITS post-meditation effect, vipashyana, have been minutely analyzed in classical Buddhist texts. The *Satipatthana Sutta* outlines four foundations of mindfulness: contemplation of body, feelings, consciousness, and mental objects. The general idea is to know what is going on in all four areas by attention to direct perception. Chogyam Trungpa simplified this text a great deal by describing it as tuning in to life: "It is not a question of forcing the mind back to some particular object," he said, "but of bringing it back down from the dreamworld into reality." He defined mindfulness as the act and the experience happening at the same time. "You just do it, with absolutely no implication behind what you are doing, not even mindfulness."

Tibetan dharma describes nine cumulative techniques for resting the mind in shamatha: simple resting, extended or continuous resting, literal or naive resting, thorough resting, taming, pacifying, thorough pacifying, one-pointedness, and resting evenly. There are likewise four progressively deepening categories of vipashyana: discriminating between processes, or dharmas, fully separating them, completely comprehending, and completely investigating.

I always had difficulty matching such lists of categories with what actually took place on my cushion. They might be products of the mind's concept factory, or simply invitations to pay closer attention to consciousness. Perhaps I was vacant or obtuse, but I could never distinguish "pacifying" from "thorough pacifying," or "resting evenly" from "simple resting," nor did it seem important to do so. All dharmas flash and flow together like sparkles on the rippling surface of a lake. One may as well try to investigate completely the paths of single bubbles as they race down Niagara Falls.

Complete comprehension might be something like tracking the sound of ice falling from a roof. The sound develops its own trajectory phase by phase: rumble, slide, clunk, smack, shatter; then the mental echoes go on vibrating in the memory for several minutes, fading and fracturing as they resonate with impressions of new sounds. I wished sometimes that I could analyze and digitally recombine these trajectories with a recording computer, they were so elegantly complex, multifarious, precise, and mathematically graceful. But my own mind was all the synthesizer I needed, and my whole environment was nothing less than a mighty, variegated, continuous display of this beauty, like flutes in raindrops, crystals reflecting gardens, fields of singing crickets, and fugues played from golden pipes in the clouds.

For me, a better paradigm to describe the effects of meditation is the dying process outlined by Elisabeth Kübler-Ross. Her classic study of death and dying lists five stages encountered by a person with a terminal illness: denial, bargaining, anger, depression, and acceptance. Bargaining is the effort to buy back life by giving up something else: I will give all my money to the church if I can only get well, I will beat my suffering by turning it into a lesson if only God will grant me more time, I will stop smoking if only I have the chance.

These stages also occur in meditation—indicating that meditation is a form of death. What dies is the old life, the old way of looking at the world, and the old patterns that depended on this way. Meditation has consequences. It can start, end, or reform relationships, cause relocations and career changes, dissolve long-standing blocks, or alter personality traits. In extreme cases, when improperly practiced by someone who is unskilled or ill-prepared, it can be a catalyst for suicide. Its least effect on me was to bring about deep shifts of attitude resulting in a much-needed divorce.

My denial was a rejection of the path in favor of a business activity that seemed less threatening. Next I attempted to bargain with the practice by deciding that I would manipulate it for my own goals. When I saw that this attitude was a barrier put up by the ego, and that meditation would not work unless I moved past it, I was by turns furious and depressed. Finally I felt that nothing I did made any ultimate difference, and I might as well sit forever, until my bones were festooned with cobwebs. At this point I understood the applicability of Kübler-Ross' five-stage paradigm.

Trungpa compared shamatha to the process of taming a horse. The mind is like a wild horse. First you give him a large pasture, and let him jump around in it until he gets tired. You don't try to control him; you just watch. Eventually he calms down and gets used to your smell. Then you make friends with him. You slip a longe-line on him, let him run around in circles, and draw him in slowly, until he is standing near you, fanning his ears back and forth, waiting to see what comes next. In the end, you can ride him and keep your seat, playing your flute. This image is borrowed from the Ch'an Buddhist ox-herding pictures, in which the meditator is compared to a boy learning to play a flute while riding an ox. Trungpa substituted a horse for an ox, probably because he and his wife were interested in the art of drusage. What I drew in on my longe-line was the pale horse of death, which had circled me for years waiting until I got up the courage to let him approach.

This may seem a morbid depiction of meditation, but it touches the heart of the Buddhist journey. I heard of a young man who went to a Zen master and asked to be accepted as his student. "Are you ready to die?" the master asked. "I came here to study Zen," said the student, "not to die." "If you are not ready to die," said the master, "you can't study Zen."

Tibetan liturgy includes the reminder, "death comes without warning; this body will be a corpse." The practices of tantra include real or imagined meditations in charnel grounds, where one may indulge in artistic admiration for bone piles and wisps of hair clinging to skulls. Tantric drums, cups, and trumpets are symbolic representations of skulls and thigh-bones, and some archival sets are actually made of these materials. In the *Bardo Thodol* and the *Kalachakra Tantra*, death itself is seen as a magnificent practice opportunity. The humorist might imagine a cartoon of Dr. Kevorkian, the Michigan physician who assisted some patients' suicides, enthroned as a high Buddhist lama, wearing a miter hat and shaking a skull drum. The function of meditating on death is not to encourage suicide, however, but to remind ourselves of how little time we have, how all things are impermanent, how fragile is the ego's clinging to existence, and how the message of enlightenment comes through far more vividly in suffering and change than in security and bliss.

It is instructive that in the *Heart Sutra*, the famous Mahayana Buddhist doctrine of emptiness, or *sunyata*, is expounded not by the intellectual Sariputra, but by Avalokitesvara, the bodhisattva of compassion. Dying to every concept of existence is the basis of unconditional love.

Those who witness death and suffering often feel intuitively the connection between compassion and emptiness. A moving scene in John Irvin's 1987 Vietnam War film *Hamburger Hill* features a group of black veterans, one of whom has just witnessed the violent death of his friend and is on the verge of a breakdown. The others draw around him in a circle and slap each other's hands over and over, chanting "It don't mean a thing, man, not a fuckin' thing; it don't mean a thing, man, it don't mean nuthin'," until he begins to laugh and cry. This absence of meaning is sunyata, and from it emerges compassion in the form of laughter, tears, and a group ritual, almost religious, that reaffirms their bond.

The same words and actions might also constitute rejection and denial, the attempt to detach from grief by refusing to acknowledge its reality. But everything in the path, from beginning to end, has this double value. Both possibilities emerge together. Even if we take this scene as denial, the form it assumes here still expresses compassion and sunyata, as if denial itself were made of these ingredients—which it is. Ultimately, there is nothing else to make it from. Of course, it makes a difference whether we know the true nature of our denial, and if it is merely an attempt to avoid grief, then we are only delaying and prolonging the pain.

In Buddhist teaching, the very essence of liberation is found by opening to the reality of death. From my own experience, I know the truth of this. Each time death has come near me, some limit was broken through, some old preconception was dispelled, some area of darkness illuminated, some fixation discovered and let go.

When my grandfather dropped dead of a heart attack, I began to review the entire history of my relationship with him. I thought about his faith in Christ, his competence as a machinist, his love for the Bible, his bad temper, his sense of humor and his warmth. I remembered how pleased he was that I loved Handel's *Messiah,* and how he used to come up behind me in the kitchen and tickle me. I found myself repeating some of his habits. In later years I would go and lie down on his grave and tell him about my broken marriages and spiritual discoveries. I was never so close to him in life as I felt after he was gone. His death was my passage to adulthood. It woke me up in some way to who he was, and how thoroughly his life inter-twined with mine. His death made me look closely at his values, and therefore, at my own. Most important, I knew then that my whole family would die, and that I would die, too.

The most intimate and meaningful conversations I ever had with my mother happened three weeks before she died. At the moment of her passing, our whole connection, from the prenatal stage on, swept through my mind in waves of powerful images, and I saw the world as if I had just been born. I learned from her death something about how mind transcends and outlasts body, and how we interact and communicate beyond space and time.

Then my father sank deeper and deeper into Alzheimer's dis-ease, and I watched how his loss of memory and coherence slowly unwound from him the painful agony of his past, and all his con-flicts, until he, too, looked on the world as if he had just been born, and there was nothing left I could share with him except sense impressions and a smile. All our disagreements had dissolved. We had saved the best for last.

As my own body functions break down from the effects of disease and age, the expansion is carried still further. All the aspects of my being, all my dreams, hopes, fears, and memories, flare into life and make their claims before passing on, leaving a shell of flesh and bone which is melting back into earth.

To be mindful of thought is to notice death—my death. I started to die the moment I was born. Dying and living are alternate perspectives of the same event. Anabolism and catabolism, the building up and breaking down of cell structures, happen all the time in our bodies. We are consuming and expelling ourselves constantly. The body is a moving, changing flame, maintaining its shape only so long as the harmony among its different parts is preserved and the fuel going in balances the energy and waste coming out. In the stream of consciousness, all manner of ideas and concepts form and dissolve, moment by moment. The truth of emptiness is the understanding that everything—the body, the consciousness, the world, the self—is like flame. There is no entity of a "flame" apart from the constantly dissipating light, heat, and gas, which arise each second from the changing conditions of temperature, fuel, oxygen, and wind. It is no more possible to maintain a self in this conflagration than it is to preserve a log which fire is converting into embers and smoke.

The death of someone close to us opens a gap in the fabric of our lives. One could say it is a gap in our ignorance, for ordinary life is made up largely of routines, habits, memories, beliefs, hopes, fears, plans, and prejudices—all of which are based on ignoring the truth of emptiness. This fabric is woven by thought, but we ignore its source. Nothing in it has any real substance. Believing in the reality of our constructs, we seldom question them until some catastrophic loss disrupts their functioning. Because the gap is there, we can see through it and while it lasts, we have a wider view. We can see all the ways in which our lives interconnected with and depended on the person who died. We think about how much time we have left, and what anything means. But in the grieving process, we close the gap and return to our normal habits, urged to do so by those around us. Expansion happens, but is soon ignored.

Paying attention to the death process in ourselves, on the other hand, opens a gap in the fabric of thought that cannot be closed. The practice of meditation deliberately seeks to widen that gap, look through it, and make it a regular part of experience. And so meditation is a pale horse.

All suffering, from irritation at the weather to lifelong anger toward an abusive parent, is rooted in the belief that we are a separate being: I am here, the environment is there. I interact with my environment by grasping, attacking, avoiding, ignoring—keeping this, rejecting that. I suffer by losing what I want and getting what I do not want. Discomfort does not become suffering until it is personalized by this duality—until I perceive the discomfort as specific to *me*. From this perception follows a kind of personal wretchedness, and a conditioning history built up around grasping pleasure and avoiding pain. The belief in separateness is deeply rooted in our whole language and culture; it is so deep that Buddhists maintain we bring it with us at birth from past lives, and, indeed, is the reason we are born at all.

Buddhist meditation aims to expose and cut the belief in separateness, in the exact moment of its creation, here and now, every instant. Doing so is the equivalent of a conscious death. As a side effect, the personal wretchedness of suffering, along with any sense of being trapped in it, is brought to an end. Ironically, however, this has long ceased to be the goal.

Words like "death" and "emptiness" are provocative to the Western reader, sometimes leading to confused notions that without feelings, desires, or perceptions, a buddha must be little more than a smiling vegetable. On the contrary, a buddha is simply abiding in the condition of wakefulness. The person of a buddha is a form taken by the environmental field. The mind of a buddha is the intelligence and compassion of the field, in skillful dialogue with ourselves. The feelings, desires, and perceptions of a buddha are those of the field. When we look at a field of dandelions, for example, without the reference point of the separate observer, the event may be experienced with equal truth as the mind contemplating its own ability to perceive yellow, and as the color yellow enjoying itself. The enjoyment is not destroyed by the erosion of separateness, but rediscovered.

Willingness to die cheerfully, right now, that is, to live fully, to give in to the fluid, uncontrollable emptiness of experience, opens a way out of the prison of the separate self. Death, too, is empty. We speak of summer passing away, but there is no such thing as summer. There are changes in temperature, in the relation of the earth to the sun, in the activity sequences of plants and animals; we reify these into an abstract entity, with a life cycle and a name, "summer." Outside this reification, summer does not exist. The same can be said of all its components, and of any event or object whatsoever.

I never knew my dead family members, I only knew my images of them. For that matter, I doubt if they ever knew themselves; they too knew only images of themselves and wove these together into the fabric of a world, as I have done. When I say they are dead, this can only mean that whatever spoke to me through their bodies no longer speaks through those bodies. A closure has occurred in my experience of their voices, faces, and gestures, but their effects on me have exploded into unforeseen realms. Like summer, they cannot end, because they never were. But, also, like last summer, they really happened, and will happen again in different forms.

From the viewpoint of the total environmental field, nothing can die; this would be like saying that the New Jersey Turnpike goes through Newark at noon and arrives two hours later at the Delaware Memorial Bridge. The concepts of arrival and departure do not apply to the field, they apply only to the traveler. From the viewpoint of the traveler, there is a journey, but as far as the field is concerned, there is only one place, or none, and the traveler never left—or was never born.

While these discoveries about death have power to free the mind from suffering, they did not make me any more eager to welcome the cessation of vital signs in my own body. I still wanted to be around so I could enjoy not being here. After four months of intensive all-day practice, I decided to go to a doctor about my lungs. They were seriously impaired; I wheezed all the time, and could not run or climb a flight of stairs without gasping like a beached fish. I approached the problem a little too heroically perhaps, almost expecting to hear a death sentence. The sound of that wheezing became the voice of the grim reaper sitting on my shoulder. The possibilities included emphysema, cancer, severe damage from environmental toxins, and a host of other potential killers with complex names.

My condition was diagnosed as sarcoidosis, a disease capable of killing but which is usually not fatal. It gradually swells and scars the delicate lung tissue, the alveolar membranes, that take in oxygen and give out carbon dioxide, destroying their ability to exchange gases. If the disease progresses unchecked, you suffocate. There is no cure, although its symptoms can be arrested with the corticosteroid drug prednisone, which shrinks the swollen air sacs and prevents them from scarring. Unfortunately, if you stop taking this drug, the lung tissue swells up again and the disease tends to resume its old course. Possible side effects of prednisone include leg pains, weight gain, eye and liver damage, depletion of calcium from the bones with consequent increased risk of fracture, diabetic symptoms, and weakening of the immune system, depending on dosage. The choice is difficult but clear: the drug buys time, and no matter what else happens, you have to breathe.

Meditation first gave me the courage to look at this disease, and then transformed my attitude toward it. I was keenly interested in all its symptoms and effects—what limits it imposed on my life, what it brought to my experience, what it could teach me, and how it may connect with, or express, states of mind which eventually solidified in the body. I regarded the disease the same way I had learned in shamatha to regard thoughts. I detached from any preconceived idea that it was bad, invited it into my field of awareness, made friends with it, and studied the totality of what it is. This approach cut through self-pity and despair.

Inviting the disease into the field of awareness is a healing technique that can be applied to any form of negativity. It works especially well with negative emotions, such as fear, jealousy, rage, depression, and grief, that we would normally prefer to suppress. We often think of negativity as something that should be conquered or shunted aside by a "positive" attitude, as if a smile were the only acceptable facial expression and human personality could be weeded of "negative" elements like a showcase patch of tulips. In meditation, negativity is neither indulged nor rejected, and instead noticed and fully lived.

For example, suppose I am representing a client at an important hearing. My fear feels like a bat stuck in my esophagus, and at first I would like to get rid of it. But then I find it motivates me to prepare thoroughly, reflects how involved I am in the need to win, or keeps trying to show me something that is drastically wrong with my case or my client. The emotion itself turns out to have a complicated texture, alternating with thoughts of escape, defense, longing, and revenge. I might discover that I am afraid because I care about my client, my family, and my work, or because I cling too hard to my reputation. Listening to the fear becomes a way to tune in to the total reality of my life. If it will not disappear, then I let it nest in my shirt while I go through my day's activities. Eventually it turns into a form of tenderness. Like negativity, disease can also be a mirror, a motivator, and a friend.

Sarcoidosis restricts all physical activity, including walking, hiking, dancing, playing, shoveling snow, pushing wheelbarrows, doing chores, and making love. None of these activities is entirely impossible, but they must be done slowly and carefully, timing breath with movement. Propelling 200 pounds of flesh requires oxygen, which is in short supply. When the expenditure of effort exceeds the amount of air available to support the combustion, you feel as if you are being buried alive, breathing through a thin straw that reaches up to the surface. And the straw, your only connection to survival, keeps filling up with phlegm. You cannot hurry anywhere for anything, nor can you forget the ratio of energy to breath even in your most trivial motions. A stroll around the yard or a trip up the stairs must be counted out slowly in mindful steps.

I achieved carpentry board by board; I opened and transported shingle packs to the roof piecemeal; I gently walked sheetrock sections across the floor, raised them to the ceiling or wall one end at a time, and slid them onto braces that held them in place until I could fasten them home; I rolled concrete blocks to their destination on wheels. Engaging the body for any task necessarily involves the mind as well. I learned great economy of effort, and ingenious solutions for getting mass from one place to another. I learned to allow plenty of time for a physical job; rushing is impossible, so I was relieved from the pressure of haste. It always required mindfulness of body, and mind over matter; I had no choice, if I wanted to do anything besides sit in a chair and wheeze.

For a few months my condition was so serious that I did little more than this. I had a liquid oxygen tank in my bedroom, from which I could replenish the portable unit slung on my shoulder. I crept around with plastic tubing up my nose, gasping at every exertion, wondering if I should be collecting tombstone brochures. Finally I tore off the tubes in a rage and sent the unit back; the extra oxygen it gave me had to be used just to carry it around, and anyway I preferred dying with tools in my hands. Mindfulness of how I moved in relation to breath was a better solution, and gave me more freedom.

I could see clearly that my physical condition had emerged from a ground of clinging to samsara, and was aggravated by ignorance. Because I could not accept boredom, I had smoked marijuana for fifteen years. In fact, back then I could hardly accept myself unless I was stoned. I had held the smoke in my lungs after each toke in order to economize on expensive weed—a precise physical metaphor of stinginess, of holding on, tightwad-fashion, despite the fact that what I held in was hurting me. Temporary marijuana-induced relaxation and euphoria reinforced this behavior. The basic dysfunction arose from trying to grasp pleasure and avoid pain, and lack of awareness perpetuated it. I had always known there was something wrong with all this, but denial can keep a bad cycle going for a long time.

The anxiety and terror of imminent suffocation, both physical and emotional, pushed me toward dismantling the behavior that sustained the disease. Then I could turn the light of meditation on the disease itself.

One approach to self-healing is to try and use meditation techniques as a cure; to stroke my chest, for example, and talk soothingly to the inflamed tissue, focusing attention on where it hurt and attempting to relax the swelling with "good vibrations" and positive thoughts. These methods might include visualizing the swollen membranes gradually shrinking and turning back into healthy air sacs. The danger of this approach is that if it doesn't work, we are left with a sense of moral failure, a feeling that we are being punished for having a weak mind or a bad attitude. Meditation can help in two ways: it may improve the condition, or it may show how the disease can be used as a doorway to expanded awareness, when improvement is not always possible. In those circumstances, the most healing course of action may simply be to cultivate compassion for ourselves and experience fully the mortality of all living things.

In general I found that my mind does not directly heal my body, nor make it sick. The connection between mind and body is mediated by a whole environment of intervening factors. Clearly my decision to hold in smoke, my clinging to pleasure, my psychological conditioning, my ignorance and denial of symptoms, my indifference toward self-harm, were all aggravating mental events, but the physical effects required physical or physiological agency: smoke particles, previous lung ailments, and perhaps a gene for respiratory weakness. I have practiced many healing visualizations, but none of them even comes close to the reliability of a prednisone tablet. I felt the power of the mind to heal more in its ability to change the environment around the disease: to insure, for example, that I stay away from smoke, that I eat well, that I get enough exercise, that I pay attention to feedback from afflicted body parts, and that I refuse to sit in a chair all day with tubes up my nose unless I really and truly have no other choice.

The second way I have used meditation for healing is to explore the disease itself, to see whether it had to be regarded necessarily as a handicap. Although I would not wish it on anyone, sarcoidosis is by no means all bad. It slowed me down, heightened my appreciation for small moments, intensified my love of life, awakened my compassion for myself, brought me again and again from mind-wandering to the immediacy of the next breath, motivated me to make better use of my time while I still had some, revealed my kinship with the disabled, elderly, and chronically ill, and ushered me to the threshold of emptiness. If it offered so much, then perhaps it was not a disease at all. Perhaps this affliction could teach me to ride my pale horse.

I had dreams in which my whole body was diaphanous, except for a hard knot in my chest—my inflamed and scarred lungs. The light pouring through my translucent form stopped there, casting a dark, mountain-shaped shadow. But the mountain was Mount Meru, the gravitational center of the Vajrayana Buddhist universe; the disease was really Mount Meru growing in my chest. In the manner of dreams, Meru turned into Kailash, the home of the Kalapa Palace, the capital of Shambhala. I did not have to search for the mountain any longer; in fact I could hardly avoid it. When I had ridden my horse to its summit, I would enter the kingdom.

6

SENDING AND TAKING

MEDITATION AND POLITICAL activism are sometimes thought to be incompatible, for they appear to point in opposite directions. In fact they complement and complete one another, although to a political ideologue, a meditator may seem an untrustworthy and uncommitted ally, or a vacuous fool.

The constant habit of detachment which is formed by meditation works to insulate the mind from ideologies. Opinions rolled off my brain as if it had been sprayed with a concept-repelling varnish. Religious and political fanatics would likely find it difficult to indoctrinate Buddhist meditators, in whom beliefs do not easily lodge. The reference points that could serve as anchors for fanaticism are gradually softened up and flushed away. Rulers who maintain power by imposing ideological conformity have generally preferred to slaughter Buddhists rather than try and convert them. We must keep asking, however, whether the loss of reference points leaves Buddhist disciples vulnerable to exploitation by their own teachers.

Meditators are sometimes accused of regarding the world as illusion, and being so detached from it that they cease to care about political issues. Like many stereotypes, this one is essentially false, but also contains a grain of truth. The capacity for caring is enhanced rather than diminished by Buddhist practice. I was sensitized by it to the suffering inherent in all conflict and could point easily to the greed, aggression, and ignorance, the self-interested hope and fear, that lay behind the posturings of a great many moralists and politicians. My sensitivity, however, did not translate into a solid conceptual position, nor did it necessarily respect the conventional humanist hierarchy of values. I wept as easily for an abused dog as an abandoned child.

There is no general agreement in the Buddhist world about what political positions a Buddhist should support. Some Buddhists are fully engaged in the social issues of their countries. Others warn that taking part in political struggle defeats the purpose of the dharma to attain release from samsara and develop compassion and mercy for all beings. Identifying too closely with any one side abandons the middle way, the golden mean, and hooks us again into a cycle of aggression.

As a meditator, I believed everything and nothing: I was willing to let in any point of view to see how the world looked that way; but all concepts were just phenomena to be watched, like thought, neither wrong nor right. Meditation can lead to political passivity, even indifference. We are surrounded by immense social problems demanding attention and action: environmental catastrophe, urban decay, alcohol and drug addiction and the invasion of drug cartels, government bankruptcy, the dictatorial powers of multinational corporations, the escalation of violence. As we expand the list of issues, their collective weight becomes so overwhelming that we might wonder if any remedy is possible. Meditation provides an easy retreat from a pervasive sense of helplessness. We can become absorbed in personal transformation, dismiss social responsibility as "thinking," and let it go.

The detachment of Hinayana achieves a great deal; it opens another level of consciousness that keeps flashing through the mind like a sudden shift to a wide-angle lens. Certain mystics have written about opening the third eye and tuning in to new colors of the spectrum. During my naive yoga adventures, I used to wait for some such perceptual zap to occur in the middle of my forehead.

Later on, I wondered if this kind of language was only a metaphoric description of the sense of melding into the waves that touch every shore. A birdsong might draw me outward along ripples of awareness toward the realm of feathers, beaks, and wings, so that for a few minutes I was no longer centered inside my head, but expanded to the wider arc of meditator-hearing-bird. Close attention to the precise modulation of the song blended me into the bird, as if awareness could beam along the vibrations from one entity to the other. The sensation was not like becoming the bird, but rather spreading into a larger entity that included both the bird and myself. It was like being inside and outside my body at the same time. This experience resembled lucid dreaming, but was much more firmly grounded in the tangible reality of my backside on the cushion and my breath sliding through my nose. If such experiences become a ground for further journeying and not places to hide, they have definite political implications.

Buddhist dharma has a much richer and more active range of responses to the world than revulsion and detachment. Many Buddhist centers support community service programs. All schools accept the Hinayana eight-fold path, which includes the Buddha's teachings on right action and right livelihood as the basis for activity in the world. Buddhists take part in AIDS and hospice counseling, care for the elderly, assistance to the homeless, support for animal rights, and charitable fundraising, and many Buddhists are drawn toward the helping professions. Their general aim in society is to be good citizens, obey the laws, avoid extreme views, refrain from causing harm, and do what needs to be done. The pursuit of happiness is not an issue; if you walk humbly in the dharma, cling to nothing, and help those who need, happiness will take care of itself.

In the Mahayana view, the expansion of consciousness achieved by shamatha is worthless unless we offer it to others. Getting unstuck from the limited reference point of self only prepares the way for a wider field of action. The sensitivity and compassion discovered by sitting is called *bodhicitta* in the Buddhist vocabulary, which means "awakened heart." The Mahayana developed the ideal of the *bodhisattva,* the sage who is motivated by awakened heart to give up nirvana and manifest enlightenment by working actively for the benefit of others. A bodhisattva vows to care for all sentient beings and remain in the world of samsara until every last person, dog, frog, blackfly, and shellfish has been liberated from suffering.

The role of the bodhisattva is to serve and teach, to be a bridge, a boat, a highway. This role must be based on the ground of egolessness established in the Hinayana, the discovery of no-self that insures we do not impose our private agendas on people under the guise of helping them. The expansion achieved by detachment is not limited to birdsong; it is a vital basis for developing the skills of perceiving the background environment of a problem, listening to conflicting interests, sharing blame, and finding solutions that benefit all sides. Without the insight of no-self, the Mahayana, like many Christian missionary efforts, could degenerate into evangelism, charity, harboring contempt for the objects of our charity, and finally, coercing their agreement.

To carry out helping programs on a broad scale requires coordinated effort. But in all organizations, there is a tension between the need of the organization to maintain itself and its purpose in the world at large. If a union, church, school, government agency, or political party consumes too much energy in maintaining itself, its larger purpose gets lost, and it becomes a self-serving bureaucracy. This danger applies no less to Buddhist organizations and is particularly acute in those groups having a strong guru principle, such as Vajradhatu, where the habit of deference to authority is built into the entire system. Most Buddhist centers operate on shoestring budgets and seldom provide much income or power for anyone except the top leaders. Nevertheless, even volunteer organizations can acquire enough unhealthy weight to settle into themselves.

In presenting Mahayana, Chogyam Trungpa's disciples and successors tend to equate bodhisattva activity with teaching their sequence of dharma programs and giving money to their network. If the programs are good, and the network keeps to the larger purpose, this is indeed bodhisattva activity, and we cannot help admiring the staff members in Buddhist centers who give up lucrative employment to carry out their largely thankless roles. Nevertheless, the Vajradhatu version of Mahayana may be at risk of converting the "great vehicle" into a self-serving mechanism for supporting Vajradhatu. Such risk is inherent in meditation itself, and in the nature of organizations, but it is aggravated by the guru principle.

Political engagement, for the most part, is left up to the individual. At times it has been overtly discouraged. Even on the pressing Buddhist issue of opposing the Chinese destruction of Tibet, the Vajradhatu press was late to speak out or take a position, although its coverage of the political persecution of Buddhists in Asian countries improved during the late 1980s. Osel Tendzin was scornful of the "liberal conscience" of American Buddhists who resisted the corrupt, shortsighted policies of the Reagan administration in Central America. And Trungpa, in his Seminary talks from the 1970s, often referred pejoratively to political demonstrations and acts of civil disobedience, using them as examples of a false, aggressive heroism whose purpose was more to affirm the ego of the demonstrator than to do anything constructive about the problem. While he may have been right in some cases, his views always reflected his dislike of democracy. Proposals for membership control of his own organization were squashed; he once referred to them as "democratic farts," and walked out of a meeting in disgust when a student suggested that the audience vote on how late he could keep them up.

A major Buddhist political teaching is that meaningful change has to begin at home. We cannot set a very helpful example for others if we do not even bother to pick up our own dirty clothes. A woman who thinks all men are enemies of the earth goddess will not be able to communicate very effectively with them. A man who needs to nail his opponents to the wall makes a poor choice as a negotiator. Anyone who has ever taken part in a union or political movement knows what happens when untamed egos compete for attention at the same planning session. Underlying all social injustice, according to Buddhists, are the problems of self-clinging and self-inflation, which prevent us from seeing or caring about the consequences of our stupidity. We cannot address this problem in others unless we have first addressed it in ourselves. The history of the world is full of successful revolutionaries who conquered their enemies, only to turn their murderous principles afterwards on their own followers. The fundamental social oppression is not patriarchy, racism, or class rule, but the dictatorship of the ego.

The Mahayana trains the student in six ego-transcendent virtues, called *paramitas*. Literally, this word means "crossing to the other shore." The paramitas—generosity, meditation, patience, discipline, exertion, and wisdom—can be imagined as spiritual ferryboats. Buddhist generosity is giving without a giver, opening the clenched hand, saying "Yes, I will help," rather than "No, I don't have the time." Patience is the practice of accommodating impatience—your own or that of another person. Discipline is the willingness to stay open to learn from any experience, especially if it is boring or negative. Exertion is essentially cheering up, without requiring a reason or reward for doing so. Meditation is applying mindfulness to relational demands, not taking sides for or against. Wisdom is the deep and comprehensive insight that is free from personal agendas. The paramita of wisdom prevents meditation from turning into paralysis—a bodhisattva should act swiftly and ruthlessly if it is a question of preventing harm.

The substance of Mahayana teaching consists largely of how to practice the paramitas, and what they imply. In a sense, the paramitas are like six rays of light from a single sun. Patience, discipline, generosity, exertion, and wisdom are different terms for how meditation works in the relational world. If we split buddha-mind with a light prism, or spread it out like a mercator projection on the map of time, it would yield the paramitas, and perhaps the entire threeyana path.

The essence of Mahayana is conveyed by its primary meditation practice, called *tonglen*, "sending and receiving," exchanging self for other. To do tonglen, you must first have sat for dozens of hours in shamatha. You begin a tonglen session by sitting for a half hour or so, to click into the realization of emptiness, which Zen teachers sometimes refer to as Big Mind. Then you imagine the suffering of a person you love unconditionally, such as your mother or your child. The suffering is visualized as a smoky cloud. On the inbreath, you take this dark cloud into yourself through all your pores. On the outbreath, you visualize equanimity, wealth, health, and love as clear white light, and exhale this light from all your pores, giving it away to your subject. The smoky cloud dissolves into emptiness; like thoughts and opinions, it cannot stay inside of you, because there is no place for it to adhere.

After the rhythm of taking in suffering and giving out peace is established, the next step is to visualize that you are doing this for people you do not love as well, or not at all. Finally, you visualize that you are doing it for those you hate. Tonglen must come from an experience of egoless compassion. Otherwise it can easily be perverted into an exercise in martyrdom, or you end up bloating yourself with the misery of the world.

Theravada Buddhism has a similar practice, called *metta*. After sitting for a while to make contact with your own tenderness, you visualize those persons you love, and wish that they be free from suffering. You send that wish toward them as an active thought form. You repeat this process for those you like, those you neither like nor dislike, those you dislike, and finally, for all beings everywhere.

In Mahayana one does tonglen for five or ten minutes at a time; in Vajrayana, the tonglen sessions increase in length and frequency. Trungpa's requirement for entering Vajrayana was fifty half-hour sessions of tonglen.

Like many other Buddhist practices, tonglen recalled for me the innocence of childhood. It gave me a feeling of essential purity. We can take in bad and give out good, because we are basically good from the beginning. Tonglen reminded me of my childhood bedtime ritual in which, after I had said my prayers, my Christian grandmother would prompt me to repeat, "God bless mommy and daddy, God bless my brother and my aunts and uncles, God bless grampie, God bless everybody." Ending my day like this meant letting go of all sense of injury, making peace with everyone, and returning to the unity of the family just before sliding away into the alpha state.

The practice of Mahayana makes it easier to function in threatening situations. As a union grievance officer for fifteen years, I frequently had to work directly with stress and adversary conflict. I represented teachers in grievances against their employers, and my job entailed enforcing the union contract, processing violations through the levels of the grievance procedure, negotiating settlements where possible, and preparing for hearings.

I was accountable both to my union and my client, whose interests did not always agree. As a teacher myself, I was also accountable for my academic performance to the same employer that I often sued on behalf of my union. Hidden agendas, grasping, manipulation, duplicity, distrust, anger, and pressure were typical working conditions. Tonglen, done for myself as well as the total circumstance, was an effective way to relax and focus. When I made mistakes, I found that I could admit them openly instead of wasting effort covering them up. I could then let go of any need to defend myself, and continue working. Ego needs are unnecessary impediments. An opponent filled with ego who moves into your space prepared for a struggle is sometimes baffled, even won over, by non-resistance. Tonglen sometimes pacifies antagonists the way shamatha pacifies bristly and irritating thoughts: by inviting them in and letting them play to an empty house. The job required a delicate balance between caring and detachment that I could not consistently achieve, but there was no better preparation for it than Mahayana.

On one occasion, tonglen may have saved me from being mugged. I was touring Stockholm, Sweden, on June 21, a rowdy holiday in that country, similar to New Orleans' Mardi Gras. Walking alone back to my hotel at midnight, I got lost in a public park. A gang of four young hooligans surrounded me to cut off my retreat. The tallest approached to within a foot of my face and said something to me in Swedish. "I don't understand your language," I replied; "Do you speak English?"

"I said," he repeated, "do you have a cigarette?"

"No, I'm sorry, I don't smoke."

They argued among themselves for a few minutes, probably about what to do with me. I had been saying mantras silently in walking meditation for the last half hour, and now I began the tonglen practice. For some reason I felt no fear, although with my lung impairment, I could neither run nor fight. My mind was in the wide-angle lens mode. The speaker blocked my path again. "I won't hurt you," he said, "I swear." I stood silently with my hands in my pockets, looking into his eyes.

"Forget that you saw us," he said. "My friends and I have no money. We are going to cut some crazy capers tonight." He waited for my response. When I made none, he asked, "How long have you been in Stockholm?"

"One day," I said. "I arrived this morning."

"English?"

"American."

"So. You are a tourist from America. So we are not going to harm you. Have a good Midsummer's. But do not walk alone in this park at night, it is very dangerous." He gripped my arm. "All right? Do you understand?"

"Yes, all right," I said, "Thank you."

He let go of me. "Some others, they are not like us, they will hurt you. Do not walk here. Okay?"

"Okay. I'm leaving now."

They turned and ran. Immediately, the force field that had surrounded me collapsed, and I was terrified. I slunk toward the lighted street like a hunted cat.

They had a clear motive for robbery, and their initial behavior of fanning out to cut off my escape suggested that they had something in mind besides wishing me a nice holiday. But instead they ended up helping me. Maybe they found it difficult to attack someone who behaved as if he had no reason to fear them, or maybe the fact that I was a tourist in the wrong place touched their code of hospitality. Whatever the explanation, I'm certain that without my practice, I would have been in serious trouble, although I would never test its protective power by deliberately putting myself in danger.

The purpose of Mahayana, however, is not to protect ourselves, but to extend ourselves to others in whatever way is needed. This is a grand and powerful idea. To me it seemed only a logical extension of egolessness: self-clinging is the root of samsara; if we give it up, then we are no longer here just for ourselves. If we are not here for ourselves, there is no other reason to be here, except to help "those who have not yet crossed over." Generosity is the bridge, for us as well as for others.

The wide-angle lens mode is the experience of being the universe, embodied in a particular form. To the extent that I practice generosity and mercy, I perceive the universe as being endowed with these qualities. I am the raw material through which they flow and work. The sun is generous and merciful, but it can speak human language only through a human being who has been fed and nurtured by the sun, and therefore is made of it. The human Mahayanist can walk around on the surface of the planet and nurture in rooms of reality where the physical sun cannot go. So I am both child and emissary of the sun, the moon and stars, the wind and earth.

Doubt shakes the bells on his cap and laughs. "Take a close look," he warns, "at the people who taught you this grand and powerful idea."

7

A JEWEL IN A HEAP OF DUST

M Y FIRST INTENSIVE dharma program was about generosity. Vajradhatu meal chants proclaim that generosity is the stairway to the higher realms and produces peace. I learned that holding back is stingy, and that we can afford to give because we are already inherently, inexhaustibly rich with bodhicitta. After three days of sitting, I was so soft and mushy I wanted to give away my clothes. Then Osel Tendzin appeared and asked everyone to pledge a thousand dollars a year to Karme-Choling, the center hosting the program. Sitting there on his throne with his mustache, his suit and tie, and his lackeys who knelt to remove his shoes, he looked to me like a mafioso who had sweet-talked his way into a fantastic new Buddhist scam. Pledge cards were distributed throughout the audience. Not to sign one meant that you had missed the point of the weekend. I had already paid a program fee, which entitled me, between sitting hours, to clean old bottles and boxes of trash out of the Karme-Choling barn so Tendzin would not be offended at the unsightly disorder if he should happen to walk that way.

"I don't like your suit," I told him.

"*Now* you're in trouble," he said.

"I'm angry at everything," I continued. "Anger is one of the stages of dying; to be a good Buddhist you have to be dead. That five hours of meditation tomorrow should do it."

"Well don't write about it until you get there; otherwise we'll put on your tombstone, 'Here lies so-and-so, who almost went to meditation practice.'"

Having become skillful at trying on different points of view, I could easily construct a defense for him: an organization like Vajradhatu represents Trungpa's Buddha activity. It was founded and built up to establish a setting in which the dharma can be learned; the dharma is the means to achieve liberation from the suffering of samsara, and is therefore the most precious gift that could be offered to anyone. Nothing could be more generous than giving the dharma. Without a proper organizational setting the dharma could not be given. To fund and work for the organization, or *mandala,* as it is called by insiders, could be considered the quintessential bodhisattva journey, for if the mandala disappeared, the activity of the Buddha could not manifest in the human realm.

Generosity is the foundation of Mahayana. It is better to give than to receive. We learn generosity by giving our time and money to the folks who taught us how noble it is to serve them. As a bodhisattva, the teacher is giving you more by allowing you to help him than by helping you. So the more I give to the guru, the more he is giving to me. I should thank him for his great compassion while writing my check.

Sometime during that weekend, I had felt inundated by the experience of cosmic generosity: the earth was generous by giving us air, the sun was generous by giving us light, the wind was generous by carrying seeds, the plants were generous by supplying us with food, my every breath was generous by giving nutrients to the atmosphere, cows were generous by giving milk and manure, farmers were generous by feeding them hay, death was generous by enriching the soil and making room for more life. Generosity was a ceaseless flow of energy coming in and going out. We did not really have to cultivate it as a virtue; we cannot help it—we ourselves are made of generosity. The act of our coming into existence is a gift from our mothers, and the act of our going out will be our own gift to the earth. The only problem is the little ego, standing in the traffic, interfering with the flow, yelling "What about me? I'm betrayed! You took advantage of me!" And when the ego is seen as just another worm trying to get a meal, not even that is a problem. "Here, little worm," I wanted to say, "don't worry, you belong to me; you shall be fed." With this vision, a thousand dollars a year seemed like nothing, a cheap price for awakening that continued without limit.

Trungpa warned his Mahayana students against the error of "idiot compassion." In general, this error consists of trying too hard to be nice. Your practice of generosity and patience enables parasites to exploit you, when they would benefit more from a generous kick in the backside.

"Tell me about the Mahayana," said an alcoholic mother of four to a new Buddhist. "Well," said the Buddhist, puffing herself up, "in the Mahayana, you learn to serve others." "Do you really believe that?" said the mother. "Of course," said the Buddhist, "and I practice it too." "Good," said the mother, "you can babysit my kids tonight while I go out. Do you have twenty bucks?" The mother used her free time to hit the local bars and get drunk. Idiot compassion lacks the wisdom to set limits. Genuine compassion might have been to refuse the alcoholic mother's manipulation and respond instead to her actual needs: "No, I won't babysit your kids so you can go out to a bar, but I would help you get daycare for them so you can go to a twelve-step program or take a class."

Mahayana students were not taught, however, that it was legitimate to set limits on their teacher. These limits invited a different set of value words: "neurosis," "ego obstacles," "personal territory," "arrogance."

In an ancient Indian Buddhist text that we studied during a Mahayana class, the teacher cannot speak to the people because evil spirits have created dust storms. There is no rain, and no water to lay the dust, so a loyal bodhisattva offers to lay it with his own blood. In another text, a bodhisattva throws himself off a cliff so a starving tigress can eat his body and feed her cubs. These exempla of generosity led me to wonder if "idiot compassion" was less a perversion of Mahayana than a description of it.

Entry into the Mahayana was marked in Vajradhatu by the formal ceremony of the bodhisattva vow—a ritual which goes back for centuries in Buddhist tradition. It is customary for those taking the vow to make a gift to their preceptor. Even if the gift is a corpse, wrote Chogyam Trungpa, it should represent "your sense of attachment, your basic attitude of clinging." Bodhisattva candidates gave works of sculpture and art, old blankets, wedding rings, lamps; by the time I took the vow, staff members were bluntly informing new vow takers that the guru had a whole barnful of such junk, and the most appreciated gift would be money. No more corpses allowed.

An aspiring bodhisattva who had given up her grandmother's heirloom brooch later found her commitment severely tested when she saw one of the guru's lovers wearing the brooch at a cocktail party. But I could spin out a defense for this action, too, if one is required: a brooch is a brooch is a brooch; a material object handed over by the student as a symbol of offering her attachments, and subsequently loaned or given away by the guru as a symbol of—whatever. For the student to see it again in that context was a poignant reminder that she had not really let it go, or let go of its meaning which was inextricably woven into her autobiography, her sense of self. In case this argument is not completely convincing, we can always say that the loss of a precious object confirms the truth of impermanence.

A bodhisattva, wrote Trungpa, invites all sentient beings as guests; they are all our family members. Bodhisattvas cannot reserve personal privacy, privilege, or pleasure just for themselves. "We have been sold to sentient beings, merchandized. Sentient beings can plow on us, shit on us, sow seeds on our back—use us like the earth."

In moods of black humor, I occasionally rejoiced that I had found a way to commit suicide without upsetting anyone else, and while still preserving a body in which to enjoy being dead. Trungpa joked that there were analogies between Mahayana and masochism. "Aren't we fools?" he would add, grinning mischievously. The laughter he provoked among his students dissolved resistance and created a field of belonging, an in-group atmosphere, the clique of Buddhist fools who were doing something so extraordinarily simple and ridiculous that only members could understand it. Who else but fools would pay money to sit somewhere and bore themselves to tears, and then learn to give themselves away? But Trungpa himself had done this all his life, supposedly, and now he was selling it to us. That field of belonging was my first experience of mandala, the network of bodhisattvas drawn into relationship around a center of value that in the world of ego has no value at all.

Like everything else in dharma, the mandala principle can cut both ways. On the one hand, the field is an essential support for practice; it is the sangha, the third jewel of the triple Buddhist refuge. On the other hand, a knot of disciples gathered around a teacher with a common in-group experience that no one else can understand is the beginning of a cult. Unless the field of belonging is extended unconditionally to the rest of the world, you are inevitably separated by it from the reality system of the mainstream society. You depend on the cult for self-worth, validation, direction, even law. If the cult starts to get weird, you tend to adjust your own perceptions to fit its weirdness, like someone in a movable room that is gradually tilting to one side; instead of taking your cues from gravity, you keep trying to adjust your posture to the tilting room, until finally you fall over on your face.

Members of the guru's inner circle say that Trungpa literally was never alone, that he did not even go to the toilet without making himself available to others. In the early years of the mandala, students could just walk in and talk with him. Yet I found Tendzin and Trungpa more difficult to gain an audience with than the Pope. Like any powerful figures, they were surrounded by screens of guards, whose job was to make sure that random sentient beings did not get close enough to plow on them, shit on them, or sow seeds on their backs. I heard the folklore of stories about the many times and many ingenious and funny ways that Trungpa risked his life to push someone further along the path. These stories are probably true, and no doubt there were routes of access to him that I never discovered. But in my experience, the way to have personal contact with Trungpa and Tendzin was to request that you be allowed the honor of serving them. That is, you could get near them on their terms, not on yours. If you were chosen, your service might consist of dressing up in a suit to serve cocktails at their midnight court parties—which would exempt you from washing dishes. Or perhaps you might be granted the rare privilege of holding their coats, removing their shoes, delivering meals to their suites on silver platters, pouring their liquor, or driving their limousines. This arrangement was said to express their great generosity toward their servants.

Things are never what they seem—or perhaps they are nothing else but what they seem, and their seeming is different for each observer. The only way to understand a reality is to experience it yourself. Early in 1983, I was asked to help clean up the site of a retreat that Trungpa and Tendzin were planning to do together in Dublin, New Hampshire. A wealthy friend of the dharma had donated an estate for this purpose, a huge mansion on a hill, with a grand staircase, servants' quarters, a private library, long corridors, expensive hardwood interiors, wall hangings and art works that reminded me of sets for old Vincent Price movies, a terrace, glass-paned doors opening onto acres of landscaped grounds—the kind of place I might visit as a tourist if it were open to the public. Trungpa's students arrived in force with buckets, rags, sponges, brooms, mops, vacuums, cleaning compounds, and squeegees. Our mission was to get the house in shape so that our teachers could have a pleasant retreat, to which we were not invited. It is probably not necessary to add that none of us got paid; bodhisattvas give without expecting a reward.

I took on the job quite deliberately in order to study my resentment of the rich in the context of dharma. As a union activist and a Socialist refugee from the New Left, whose father was a union member and a blue-collar worker, I relished the irony that I had actually chosen to wash windows and scrub floors for a pair of Buddhist celebrities to drink and revel in what they considered "an uplifted atmosphere." I enjoyed not being controlled by my proletarian outlook; at the same time, I thought, "your game does not control me either; if you need a place like this for your retreats, then both of you are slaves. I know exactly what this is; and when I've seen enough of it, I will walk away as free as I came in, and the hell with you." This so-called arrogance left me smiling, cozy, and comfortable—just cleaning glass.

Voicing such thoughts to leaders made one an object of solicitude: "Oh, won't it be nice when you can drop all that burden of paranoia?" "Oh, that's your neurosis, but that's fine, it's workable." Or the laughter. The ubiquitous smile. "How are you doing with your anger, are you okay? Cheer up."

Loyal students told me that Trungpa would have been happy meditating in a cave, and that the only reason he was here was to help us. I did not see him in a cave, however; the place I helped prepare for his meditations was a small palace. Maybe he had put in enough time in caves already, and was tired of them. When I got near him again, his chosen corps of personal retainers waited on him hand and foot, in the finest suite of the Bedford Springs Hotel in Pennsylvania. I was in the kitchen, washing pots and pans—paying him to be there. He was paralyzed on one side of his body, and needed attendants, but that was not the reason he had servants. He had them anyway, as did the Regent, the top members of the hierarchy, and other Tibetan gurus who were unimpaired.

In his talks and answers to questions, Trungpa himself did not condescend to his audience. Tendzin often did. "Sir," I asked him once—all utterances addressed to the Regent or the guru had to be prefaced with "Sir"—"Some people criticize Buddhists for not respecting family attachments. How would you reply to that?"

"In the Mahayana, everyone is your family," Tendzin answered; and then he added, *"As a student of the Mahayana, you should know that. I'm surprised at you."*

Put on a dunce cap and sit in the corner.

Amazingly, I complied. I accepted his sneer as a deserving judgment on my ignorance. He was on the throne, and I knelt on the floor. He had been scheduled to meet with us at nine o'clock, and I had waited for him until nearly two in the morning, so that I would not miss this precious opportunity. He was an important person, I was not, and what's more, I was nobody. That message was built into the whole structure of the event.

Trungpa drew his students deeper into his curriculum by means of a three-month Seminary of practice and study.

Enlightened labor at Seminary was performed by the ROTA system, a work rotation plan that assigned about twenty-five hours of chores per week to each person — except staff members, leaders, personal servants of the guru and his favorites, and their favorites, who were exempt. While I never quite understood the hierarchy of exemptions, my place on the bottom of it was utterly clear to me. All work is a form of meditation, and relating to work was a necessary part of the Seminary training; so there was no reason to be unhappy if you spent five sweaty hours mopping floors and scraping burned rice off pans, while the exempted elites delicately stepped over your mop on the way to the refrigerator and lectured you about snacking on the dainties being saved for the parties in the Court. The word "court" here is not ironic: Trungpa's suite was called the Kalapa Court, and you needed an invitation to go there.

One of those parties asked me to come and provide a background of guitar music. I went, a minstrel summoned from the scullery to play for the king. And as any servant in the presence of nobility, I was appreciated for what I could do but remained otherwise invisible. No one here seemed any more enlightened than the people at the weddings and social gatherings of the samsaric world where I had played for money, although, at least in this context, these Buddhist aristocrats had power.

"Kings!" I snorted. "I thought we got rid of kings in 1776." It may have been partly this kind of clash with Yankee history and Yankee contempt for royalty that led Trungpa to relocate the center of Vajradhatu to Halifax, Nova Scotia.

The ROTA was a good system, actually, but its flaws mirrored those of the Tibetan Buddhist class hierarchy that was central to Trungpa's vision of enlightened society: insufficient value was assigned for inherently unpleasant jobs, and privileged people were exempt from them. But one had only to compare Trungpa's centers with those of other Buddhist teachers to realize that the idea of rotated program-participant labor is thoroughly sound. I stayed for several days at a Buddhist center in France run by disciples of Kalu Rinpoche, who did not have a ROTA system; the work was done by staff members and young monastic novices. Paying program participants did not clean up after themselves; they expected to be waited on, while staff members were stressed, overworked, and inattentive to the most basic chores. The whole place was a mildewed chaos that I could hardly wait to leave. When I returned to Trungpa's mandala after that experience, I could see how the gravitational force of his hierarchy imported order, clarity, and cleanliness to his system, and held it together as a supportive practice environment, even though individuals within it might be irritated and provoked.

One of my jobs at Seminary was serving oryoki in the main shrine hall, a duty I particularly resented at breakfast if we had stayed up half the night practicing elocution. Oryoki servers must conduct themselves elegantly: hold the bowl up high as if it contained diamonds; at the sound of the wooden clapper, walk briskly to your aisle, bow to a quadrant of seated students, who return the bow, kneel, rest the bowl near your hip, and begin serving to the person nearest the shrine. Trungpa would switch sometimes to Western dinner service, which he modeled on the etiquette of formal banquets.

One night I dreamed that I was serving rice to a hotel dining room full of important Vajradhatu leaders in suits and ties. Outside were rows of naked, starving children meditating perched on the edge of a garbage pit. "Hold your head up," said the head server, directing me to the tables of the elegantly dressed leaders, decorated with pins to symbolize their rank, resembling South Amer-

ican generals. "Remember, this is an offering to the three jewels."
At the sound of the clapper, I disobeyed the directions of the head
server, walked briskly outside to the children, and bowed. The children bowed. Their ribs were showing, and they had the spindly
bodies, huge heads, and sunken, hollow eyes of famine victims.
But still they bowed, as they had been taught. Their palms were
pressed together at chest level while I dished rice into their bowls.
In the background I heard the classical music played at Vajradhatu
gatherings. Trungpa, dressed in a dark blue suit, sat on his throne
and smiled.

I did not know the meaning of this dream: whether his version
of Mahayana was a cruel, bourgeois mockery of service to others,
whether his monarchic politics were simply irrelevant to the real
problems of humankind, or whether the peaceful beauty and mutual
respect of the ritual itself were the only things that lifted us above
the level of garbage rats.

"Somehow bodhicitta has been born in me," chuckled Doubt,
wearing his motley clown suit, jingling his cap and bells, and reciting lines from the bodhisattva vow: "just like a blind man finding
a jewel in a heap of dust."

8

GREAT EASTERN SUN

AFTER HE HAD introduced his students to the three-yana curriculum, Trungpa unfolded his own approach to political activism: the Shambhala vision of the "Profound, Brilliant, Just, Powerful, All-Victorious Great Eastern Sun." The question addressed by Shambhala training is how to establish an enlightened society without the help of a religious outlook. The teachings are expounded in Trungpa's book, *Shambhala: The Sacred Path of the Warrior* (Shambhala, 1984), and need not be recapitulated. My purpose here is to debunk their political vision and to question their claim to enlightenment.

The foundation of the Shambhala version of enlightened society is sitting practice, which comes as no great surprise. The Shambhala programs have developed a rich panoply of offerings whose praiseworthy purpose is to integrate meditative consciousness and everyday life. The advanced levels, however, are stamped with the same attitudes of class hierarchy already seen in Trungpa's presentation of the Buddhist path. These levels have the flavor of British aristocratic bias that Trungpa found eminently compatible with his feudal Tibetan background. In the Shambhala setting, his self-assumed title was *Lord* Mukpo, the Dorje Dradul, heir of the ancient Rigden fathers and warriors, enlightened masters of the past. We saluted and honored the Rigden Fathers with special gestures and chants, and although I was never quite sure who they were, I knew that Trungpa was unquestionably one of them.

His elocution lessons at the 1984 Seminary convey a general idea of the Shambhala vision in practice. He had decided that our American speech was sloppy and imprecise, and did not command respect. He tried to remedy this defect with elegant Oxonian diction, which he insisted on teaching at one o'clock in the morning when I could barely mutter my name. His method was to school volunteers in the Oxford English pronunciation of word lists. Mastery of this diction would give our utterances a crisp, enlightened, uplifted quality. In between the pseudo-British accents practiced by the disciples around me, I could sometimes hear the honest, unpretentious, good-humored dialect of the blue-collar Pennsylvania workers hired to maintain the building. Their speech was like a breath of fresh air wafting into a madhouse.

Trungpa's elocution project was based on the premise that working-class speech is ignorant and inferior. I could not reconcile his narrow preference with the expanded and precise appreciation of diversity that shamatha practice develops for all dialects—for the details of their regional peculiarities, and the way they express the occupation, upbringing, and personality of the speaker. Oxonian dialect expresses education, privilege, and wealth, and these were among the reasons Trungpa admired it enough to take as a model. It was not apparent to me why his class bias had anything more to do with enlightenment than mine.

Shambhala training is currently subdivided into undergraduate and graduate levels, culminating in a two-week event called the Warrior's Assembly. These programs deliver a Buddhist-inspired political vision in a secular package. Their virtues are those of the Buddhist path generally. Their faults may be traced to the feudal outlook of Tibetan dharma or the way Trungpa adapted it to the Western context. The structure of the Shambhala programs, at every level, discourages any serious critique of its substance, at least by participants. Its format is elitist and intimidating, its social analysis is simplistic and mythological. The view fosters an inhospitable condescension toward working people. For me, the quantity, content, range, and depth of Shambhala practices were insufficient to achieve the perceptual breakthroughs that I experienced in the more traditional Buddhist curriculum.

In the format of a Shambhala program, assistant coordinators wear semi-formal clothing. The schedule usually begins with a Friday night talk by the head coordinator, whose chair at the front of the shrine room is chosen according to that person's rank in the mandala. Trungpa and Tendzin had thrones. Lesser entities had elegant polished chairs, flanked by tables decorated with formally arranged flowers. A whole ritual of protocol determines the sequence for opening and closing a talk. You bow from the waist on entering and leaving the shrine room. The main speaker's arrival is preceded by attendants, and when that person enters, all participants stand up. The speaker's importance can be gauged by whether or not they wear shoes into the shrine hall. Generally, shoes are removed outside, but the highest members of the hierarchy wear their shoes up to the chair and seat themselves; attendants then kneel to remove the shoes. In the advanced levels of Shambhala training, the talk is opened and closed by group chants, recited in a kneeling posture with heads bowed. Questions and answers are taped. At mealtimes, the leaders sit at a head table, eat from conspicuously superior plates and utensils, and are waited on by servants.

The formalism of many Shambhala events is far more elaborate than what I have described. The whole effect can be quite beautiful aesthetically, and I often enjoyed blending with the atmosphere. Like the rigorous formality observed by the Japanese samurai or the knights of King Arthur's round table, the Shambhala forms are intended to arouse a wakeful state of mind and a dedication to warriorship. But they convey a definite authoritarian political outlook, elevating the leader above the follower, and silencing heresy. While "confusion" is allowed, challenge to the forms or the teachings is not.

I was never told the difference between confusion and heresy in so many words, but I got the idea by listening to the types of questions that are never asked. Transgression of these unspoken boundaries is painful; the audience laughs on cue, the staff members patronize you, and your every stammer is recorded for posterity by the microphone. In one question, I drew a comparison between Shambhala mythology and Christian theology, and was embarrassed into silence when the head of the program told me, in front of everyone, that I had said enough. I never quite understood why this was a forbidden subject, but the message was unequivocal: shut up and take these teachings as we give them, or go someplace else.

The basic ideology of the Shambhala program divides the world into two visions: Great Eastern Sun, which corresponds to enlightenment in the Buddhist path, and setting sun, which corresponds to samsara. The Great Eastern Sun realm is characterized by a willingness to be vulnerable, to step out and help others, to risk emotional pain, give up the shelter of routines and private occupations, and accept mortality as a condition of life. The setting sun realm is characterized by fear of death, grasping at pleasure, staying inside the shelter, celebrating neurosis, and working only to achieve limited personal dreams. Great Eastern Sun is accepting disappointment; setting sun is wanting to feel good. Great Eastern Sun is cheering up; setting sun is complaining and criticizing. Great Eastern Sun is elegant and rich; setting sun is sloppy and poor. To paraphrase George Orwell, "Great Eastern Sun good, setting sun bad."

At each major transition in the Shambhala program, students are awarded pins to mark their level of attainment. The undergraduate pin is decorated with a single yellow dot, the emblem for the Great Eastern Sun. The graduate pin, given at the end of Warrior's Assembly, is a round white setting about the size of a small cufflink, bearing the *ashe*, a stroke of calligraphy executed by Trungpa symbolizing action without the reference point of ego. This mark is also an object of meditation in one of the advanced practices. The final pin depicts the yellow dot flanked by four colored stripes, representing the four virtues of a Shambhala warrior: meek, perky, outrageous, and inscrutable.

The pins reinforce the hierarchy of the mandala. It could be said in their favor that they help to hold the organization together by rewarding loyalty to it, providing visible badges of attainment, rank, and group identity, like the Boy Scouts, the Young Pioneers, and the Armed Services. It was Trungpa's express purpose to absorb the organizational structures of military life—ranks, uniforms, and medals—neutralize their aggression, and turn them to the uses of peaceful warriorship. I found the pins and badges distracting and inhospitable to genuine dharma, yet another mixed message. On the one hand, we learned that enlightenment and meditation have nothing to do with the paraphernalia of social rank, while on the other hand, the point of the programs seemed to be the attainment of the next rank in the system. This is an incestuous mode of practice, drawing a line between who is in and who is out. Wearing the pins advertises that you belong to the in-group.

But all that was required, really, to gain membership in that group was to take the programs, pay your fees, articulate the Shambhala doctrines and buzzwords with reasonable facility, and support the mandala. In the Shambhala context, the pin gave you the authority of an elder, but it proved nothing about your genuine attainment as a warrior. You did not have to relate the training to the rest of the world through community service, nor demonstrate under real life pressure that you had absorbed the four virtues into your character and could apply them to the tasks of being a good parent, mate, or citizen.

The Shambhala mythology becomes increasingly complex and cultish in the upper levels. Where the introductory programs include only a simple dais with flowers in place of a shrine, the graduate shrine adds a calligraphy brush, ink, symbols of the five senses, incense, a poster reproduction of Trungpa's calligraphed ashe, and a ritual for beginning and ending the practices. Poetical texts in Tibetan and English, "revealed" to the Dorje Dradul—from the cosmic mirror, said the coordinators—provide a doctrinal basis for the cult. These texts may be elucidated by discussion, but cannot be revised nor can their authority be challenged. They are secret Scriptures, and the student is enjoined not to discuss them with anyone outside the program.

It is unnecessary to outrage this injunction by paraphrasing extensively from them here, although I would not hesitate to do so if they contained harmful or morally despicable material. The process of sifting their enlightenment pretensions with skeptical inquiry, however, is made more difficult by such prohibitions, which reinforce the line already drawn between the in-group and the out-group, and inflate the self-importance that attends those in possession of "secret" knowledge.

Some of the "Rigden fathers" are named, such as Ashoka, the first Buddhist king of ancient India, and Chinese and Japanese emperors. The original Rigden King has neither beginning nor end, a description analogous to that given the figure of the Guru in the Vajrayana and the Christ in the biblical book of *Revelation*. A mythology of images is built up around the principal exercise for developing the four virtues, the practice of drawing the stroke of ashe on art paper with a calligraphy brush. Drawing the stroke is compared to cutting the throat of ego with the brush, pressed in and down on the paper as if it were the knife in the Japanese ritual of *seppuku*, or self-disembowelment.

The four Shambhala virtues are further identified with totem animals: tiger for the quality of meekness, lion for perkiness, *garuda*, a mythical man-bird, for outrageousness, and dragon for inscrutability. Trungpa's verses pile adjectives onto their meanings: a meek warrior is friendly, merciful, mindful, and confident; a perky warrior is disciplined, uplifted, and joyful, "not caught in the trap of doubt"; an outrageous warrior is impartial, immeasurable, vast and great; an inscrutable warrior cannot be fathomed. As poetry, the text inspires contemplation, rich in images that open the mind to limitless possibility. As doctrine, it does nothing to train the student in the actual behavior that might accompany these adjectives. You can memorize every verse, for instance, and still not have a clue how to deal properly with exploitative bosses and prevaricating auto repair shops, or how to stop enabling the family alcoholic.

Yet the absence of specific instructions or commandments in the text is a virtue in comparison to the divine revelations of the-

istic religions. Shambhala revelation is unlikely to inspire theocratic dictatorships of the type that have been founded on texts
from the Bible and the *Koran*. But simply elucidating Trungpa's
utterances is not the same thing as enlightened political action.
This activity breeds a verbal relationship with the *idea* of being a
warrior, a "warriorship of the mouth." Its primary message and
behavioral result is deference to the revelation's author and his spiritual heirs, the "elders" of the Shambhala Lodge, mystified by the
Shambhala chant, the anthem, and the concept of the Imperial
Rigden.

Shambhala jargon projects the class biases of the program's view
onto the outside world in the guise of "enlightened" outlook. During an advanced Shambhala level training I attended, the director
of the program used a waitress's failure to supply garnish for his
meal as an example of "setting sun" vision. No doubt, "Great Eastern Sun" vision would have honored his importance by arranging
his plate more attractively and giving him better service. There was
no awareness in this example that the waitress might have been
overworked, had aching feet, missed her bathroom break, disliked
his attitude, disliked her job, or was worried about paying her bills.
The experience of being a waitress was omitted; she had importance and reality only in terms of her usefulness to him, an attitude no different than how bourgeois clientele regard workers at
expensive restaurants and hotels anywhere in the world. The label
"setting sun" mythologized and obscured the real nature of the
director's criticism: an inferior had failed to give him the deference
he thought he deserved.

According to his intimates, Trungpa related warmly with every
social class. When he flew on planes, for example, he would pretend to be an important diplomat or head of state, and would
instruct his attendants to ask the people around them, while point-
ing to his beaming Tibetan face, "Who do you think that man is
over there?" Outfitted in an elaborate uniform of his own design,
he would con the pilot, the crew, and even the control tower into
assuming that the Vajradhatu servants waiting for him at the air-

port in their suits were members of his private security force, or perhaps secret service agents. Flight attendants would lavish attention on him, thinking he was the king of Burma or Nepal visiting America as a guest of the State Department. His intimates tell these stories to illustrate the behavior of an enlightened being, the Dorje Dradul, the supreme warrior, the Rigden father who could magnetize a whole group of perfect strangers into a cooperating mandala full of warmth and good will. The stories themselves are plausible enough—I saw him do the same thing with his students. But they do not compel the conclusion that the person who did these things was enlightened; they could as well depict a man who took childish pleasure in being the center of attention, who needed to feel important and was happiest when he could get everybody to wait on him. P. T. Barnum, or Ferdinand Demara, the great imposter who assumed different identities, possessed similar skills.

To be part of Trungpa's inner circle, you had to take a vow never to reveal or even discuss some of the things he did. This personal secrecy is common with gurus, especially in Vajrayana Buddhism. It is also common in the dysfunctional family systems of alcoholics and sexual abusers. This inner circle secrecy puts up an almost insurmountable barrier to a healthily skeptical mind.

Of course, everyone has the right to privacy, and a brief experience of dealing with the public soon reveals how viciously aggressive and intolerant the mass of humanity can be toward those who differ even trivially from conventional concepts of how people should behave. Glancing at supermarket scandal sheets, I sometimes wondered why the media mogul doesn't go ahead and organize public banquets to cannibalize the bodies of his victims, since he has already done so with their lives. Public figures who succeed in evading this kind of predation are entitled to some respect for their skill in camouflage.

A Vajra master, however, is someone who has supposedly given up all privacy for the sake of others, and who demands of his students that they accept him as a buddha, an enlightened being. His actions and words are looked to as models of how enlightenment appears in the world. It seems reasonable to expect of a person making such a claim that he should have no secrets, that anyone should be able to test his pretensions by examining everything he does. But the vow of silence means that you cannot get near him until you have already given up your own perception of enlightenment and committed yourself to his.

A loyal disciple of the Vajra master might argue that some of his actions, like certain of his teachings, must necessarily be kept secret in order to protect them from perversion, misunderstanding, and attacks from the uninitiated. This question brings us squarely into the middle of a principal issue in the Vajrayana, and I will have occasion to come back to it in later chapters. The issue is trust: if there is a conflict between my judgment and the actions of the guru, who do I trust—the guru or myself? This is an especially poignant question if I have taken a vow of secrecy and the guru is doing something harmful, unethical, or illegal.

An interview with Trungpa in the Vajradhatu press quoted him as saying that hierarchy is important because it creates a setting for the development of compassion and devotion. In a good society, the upper class displays compassion toward their inferiors, and the lower class maintains devotion to their betters. Compassion goes down, devotion goes up. Without hierarchy, you could not cultivate these virtues. This version of enlightened society, then, is an idealized feudal monarchy, held together by the condescending noblesse oblige of the good duke for his peasants and serfs. I have a similar relationship with my German shepherd dog.

"And she loves it, too," says Doubt, laughing.

At least one practice, called "raising windhorse," taught in the advanced levels of the Shambhala curriculum is worth putting up with the sillier features of the system to learn. Based on the assumption that human beings already possess innate powers of brilliance, compassion, energy, and harmony, "raising windhorse" is a fast method of accessing these powers directly through a visualized meditation. The practice cuts immediately our habitual preoccupation with anxiety, self-doubt, and despair, as morning sunlight floods a dark room. Because it bestows unconditional confidence and cheerfulness, it is useful in almost any difficult life situation we could imagine, from having major surgery to going on a job interview. If "windhorse" could be regarded as a Shambhala term for enlightenment, then a successful method for tapping its powers presupposes that the teacher of this method knows what enlightenment is, and also knows how to convey that knowledge to students. The teachings on "raising windhorse," therefore, are strong evidence that the person who devised the Shambhala programs was—sometimes, at least—awake.

There is nothing wrong with recognizing and honoring wakefulness, as long as we do not succumb to the myth of the "enlightened being" as a sort of omniscient holy person who knows what is best for us and is always right. What matters, ultimately, is whether the teachings wake us up further, and by this standard they do more good than harm.

In truth, I appreciated the order, humor, gentleness, and respect for human possibility displayed in Trungpa's vision. His system embodied his mind, a mind shining with a splendid intelligence. Like a pilot in a small plane flying blind at night, you could find your way home on his beacon. But when you got there, you still had to decide for yourself whether you were in an airport, an ocean, a desert, or a swamp, and whether to stay or leave. In this task, somebody else's beacon is at best only a temporary help, however splendid it may be.

9

NO BIG DEAL

THE BUDDHIST EXPERIENCE changes personal relationships, perhaps in some cases for the worse. The very idea of detachment may be particularly annoying to a meditator's non-Buddhist lover or spouse. Most of us want to belong to someone, to love and be loved with passion, and to enjoy exclusivity as part of a couple. We may feel less than thrilled at the news that our bodhisattva partner has decided to take on all sentient beings as family members, or that our anger, jealousy, and insecurity have become the objects of tonglen.

The scenarios I lived through were repeated, with variations, in the personal lives of many other sangha members. One spouse begins to practice meditation and becomes a Buddhist; the other feels threatened, sensing that dharma leads to examining the whole basis of human interactions, with unpredictable results. If the couple is destabilized in the process, the non-Buddhist partner may blame Buddhism, or accuse the meditator of using detachment as a smokescreen for self-protection and escape. The irony of these accusations is that they are often true. As a further irony, instead of soaking into the mind, such challenges may bead up on the repellent coat of shamatha and run off, or get absorbed by tonglen and dissipate into space—an effect which tends to drive a threatened spouse nearly berserk from loss of power. Meditation is of great assistance in getting free from a dysfunctional bond, but it also opens the possibility of getting free from any bond at all.

The chances are good that most meditators will feel revulsion for samsara through the pain of romantic love. It occurs to you that this pain could be avoided by transcending possessive relationship entirely, by letting go of the need for bonding the same way you let go of thought. The agony and the ecstasy of romance come to seem like mere indulgence in the fatuous extremes of neurosis.

The Buddhist teacher Dr. Judith Simmer-Brown of Naropa Institute called romantic love "the primary symptom of cultural malaise, the central neurosis of Western civilization." Simmer-Brown condemned romantic love as an obsession with fantasy which fosters poverty mentality in ourselves, thrives on separation, and can only be completely gratified in death. Because we are always looking for an ideal type, we cannot appreciate the concrete reality of what another person actually is.

The tension between detachment and love is built into the nature of dharma—or the nature of mind, which dharma reflects. In a story from the respectably celibate monastic Buddhist tradition, a lay practitioner at a temple grew enamored of a Buddhist nun, and began telling her over and over that he had fallen in love with her beautiful eyes, and could not live without her. In vain she tried to convince him that her eyes were only an illusion, but he declared his passion for her all the more fervently. At last, she cut out one of the eyes with a knife and gave it to him. "Since you love them so much, you can have this one," she said.

Her dramatic demonstration of the bodhisattva's commitment to give everything for the benefit of others won him over. His fixation was destroyed. He then devoted himself to the dharma—presumably, after he stopped vomiting.

The tantric libertine possibility would have been to share passion with him, and then let go of him—or get rid of him. Either way, he is challenged to give up his fixation on romance. Sexual passion is permissible in Buddhist tantra because, like all authentic experience, it is nonconceptual and impermanent. It may be enjoyed for what it is without causing harm, as long as we do not try to turn it into a romantic fantasy. The pain of samsara comes not so much from passion as our fixation on its object. In both the celibate and the libertine approaches, romantic bonding has a bad name.

The ego would like to use relationship as a means to secure its own territory. Being desired confirms that I have power, importance, and appeal. When I fall in love, I may fear loss of power; I want to be cherished as a guarantee against this loss. Love may call up feelings of inadequacy, fear of abandonment, and the terror of looking like a fool. Love threatens to penetrate my defenses, so I try to convert it into romantic bonding as a means of rebuilding them.

Perhaps I become addicted to the agony and ecstasy of romance because extremes of misery and joy confirm that I exist. The problems of jealousy, betrayal, abandonment, and conflict turn into an occupation; they give me something to talk about with my friends and make me a subject of their attention and concern. As long as I am riding my emotional roller coaster of highs and lows, boredom and the fear of death are kept at bay. Or perhaps I develop a system of hanging onto my lover by pleasing and serving; I accomplish my goal of self-confirmation by seeming to efface myself entirely. This strategy may succeed so well that not even I can perceive its real intent.

To understand how Buddhist relationship may differ from these patterns, we need some affinity for the idea of egolessness. In the Hinayana, all forms of self-clinging are identified as the root of personal anxiety and pain. Self-clinging is not a sin, but simply a mistake. It is not as if we actually could cling to the self, and doing so is immoral; instead, we are trying to do something that cannot be done, like stealing Christmas, or keeping a summer day in a jar.

Once this insight registers, a longing arises to live differently. Buddhist practice interrupts and exposes the habit of using relationship as a form of ego-reinforcement. Feelings of inadequacy, insecurity, possession, and fears of abandonment are allowed to surface in a context where they need not determine behavioral choices. Instead, they occasion tenderness toward ourselves. We may wish to withdraw from love entirely at this point, but the Mahayana teaches that withdrawal is only another device of the ego to protect itself.

Love to a Buddhist is enlightenment, because it is inherently egoless. In the Mahayana, it is *maitri,* or loving kindness, and *karuna,* or unconditional, compassionate warmth. These qualities are aspects of an awakened heart, the soft, intelligent caring for all beings that is completely independent of ego, as the light from a projector is independent of the images it casts on the screen. Passion is filled with the color, beauty, sensitivity, and woundedness of awakened heart, until the ego intrudes with issues of possession and control. The ego may use passion as a kind of glue to draw in and hang onto its victims, but passion itself is pure.

In the Buddhist lower yanas, grasping territory is seen as a form of confusion to be transcended. All existence is marked by impermanence and absence of self. Partners in relationship cannot be possessed or controlled, for there is no one to possess, and the bond itself is passing away moment by moment, like everything else. The only proper ground for a Buddhist relationship is disappointment, emptiness, and compassion. In disappointment, we give up our fixation on the loved one as the answer to our problems, or our salvation from boredom, and prepare ourselves to appreciate reality. The experiential understanding of egolessness, gained through meditation practice, awakens maitri and karuna, which are nonterritorial, nonpossessive, and nonexclusive. Genuine love is given without asking anything in return.

For a Vajrayana Buddhist, tonglen is the enlightened basis of partnership. Instead of using the other person as territory, you give up your own territory. Instead of worrying about getting love, you give it away. Instead of demanding space for yourself, you give space to your partner. Instead of requiring that your needs be met and your feelings honored, you practice the paramitas. Instead of dumping your burdens on your partner, you take on the partner's burdens and offer in exchange whatever wisdom and equanimity you have.

At first blush, such a view of partnership may seem like impossible idealism. A couple who behaved this way all the time would never fight or disagree, and a marriage without conflict is hardly typical on planet Earth. Conflict is not denied or avoided in Buddhist intimacy, however, but allowed and even welcomed into the couple's conscious attention, just as negative emotion is fully experienced in shamatha. The Buddhist meditational practice of relating fully with the actual contents of mind trains us in extending the same principle to relationship. John Welwood, a Buddhist psychological counselor, explains in *Journey of the Heart* (Harper-Collins, 1990) how intimate relationship may be transformed into part of our spiritual path by deliberate meditative attention to conflict. Such attention opens us further by moving us beyond the limits of our individual needs for security and comfort. The original basis of the conflict manifests wisdom and sanity, even though the feelings brought up by it are momentarily painful.

In Trungpa's teaching style, sexual passion was accepted as a reflection of our basic goodness, and could even be a way of experiencing enlightenment. His favorite metaphor for giving in to the dharma was having an orgasm. "You just do it," he said, "all at once." He referred to arousing bodhicitta as tickling "the clitoris of the heart." One Shambhala coordinator in a program I attended told her students, "Be fearless—get it on." Trungpa and Tendzin were both notorious for the number of their sexual partners, or "consorts," as they were called.

Despite the appearance of corrupt self-indulgence, Trungpa's own conduct and his teachings about passion, were, so far as I could discern, consistent with one another and with dharma. They represented a coherent moral and philosophical outlook, drawn from the tradition of Buddhist tantra and grounded on the Mahayana principle of helping others.

The philosophical coherence came from the three-yana curriculum. Each yana has a view toward passion which expands that of the previous yana. In the Hinayana, passion is a klesha, an obstacle, a poison leading inevitably to jealousy and pain. This is straightforward recognition of how passion is used in the wheel of samsara: ego hangs onto people, things, or ideas to confirm itself. The Hinayana strategy for handling passion is to invite it into the mind, but do nothing about it. The student takes the five precepts against killing, stealing, lying, intoxication, and sexual misconduct. The precepts in Buddhist dharma are not moral laws imposed by a god-like authority, but devices to heighten awareness and avoid causing harm. Breaking them is not a sin, but a lapse from practice. There is no punishment other than bad karma, which can be neutralized by further practice. The broken precept is repaired by confession.

Unobscured by supporting systems of opinion and belief, passion is directly experienced as an emotional event. It is poignant, vivid, magnetic, energetic, pleasurable, and painful. We lust and long, but cannot get rid of these feelings by distraction, projection, or entertainment. They have to go through their transformations in full view of the watching mind. Lusting and longing are transformed into raw sensitivity, woundedness, tenderness, empathy—that is, bodhicitta. The supporting systems of opinion and belief are the ego. Disconnected from them, passion is egoless.

In the Mahayana, passion is a bridge to others, a way of opening the heart and venturing forth without conceptual armor. Passion does not have to be gratified. It has already become bodhicitta, the longing for transcendence of self, which corresponds approximately to the notion of Eros in Greek philosophy. Disappointment is a necessary precondition for the change, in the sense that the demands of the ego have to be frustrated before bodhicitta can begin directing our lives.

The paramitas of patience, discipline, generosity, exertion, and meditation describe the practices by which passion evolves into unconditional friendliness and warmth. The paramita of wisdom sharpens unconditional friendliness into sensible and effective action so that it does not remain on the level of a generalized mushy glow of good will. Sexuality, in the Mahayana as Trungpa presented it, is a school for the paramitas. Our most intense and difficult areas of neurosis are likely to be encountered in sexual intimacy: alienation from our bodies, insecurity about pleasing and being valued, jealousy, fear of abandonment and old age, self-concepts, fixation on fantasy. With enough time, disappointment here is certain. Sex is a perfect arena for the exercise of mindfulness, generosity, patience, sense of humor, meditation, wisdom, and unconditional warmth, and in few other places are these virtues appreciated so much.

Trungpa designed a Buddhist marriage ceremony that illustrates the differences between dharmic relationship and romantic love. In this ceremony, mutual attraction is recognized as an expression of our basic goodness, our enlightened genes. The couple do not vow to "love, honor, and cherish" till death do them part; instead they make offerings to each other so that they may learn to cultivate the paramitas. The basis of marriage is not possession, but generosity and space. The partnership is viewed as an opportunity for practicing dharma and bringing one's enlightened genes to fruition.

In the Vajrayana, passion is the universal creative energy; it embodies the cosmic yin and yang, the "male" and "female" principles of all existence. The balance of masculine and feminine principles transcends gender: gay sex makes use of both orifices and appendages, as well as passive and active roles. Even autoerotic passion implies that which rubs and that which is rubbed.

The abstract qualities of compassion, emptiness, skillful action and wisdom are symbolized in Vajrayana by male and female deities in copulatory embrace. Jamgon Kongtrul told his students that these symbols do not equate sexual intercourse with dharma. They are used in tantric practice to purify the five kleshas of ego and reveal their true nature as five forms of enlightened wisdom. The original nature of passion, aggression, ignorance, envy, and pride is the mind of the Buddha. The enlightened names for these kleshas are *padma, vajra, buddha, karma,* and *ratna.* Padma, the lotus, is passion. The lotus is a beautiful flower that grows in muck. Enlightenment thrives on corruption. The same insight appears in certain masters of English poetry: "Fair and foul are near of kin, and fair needs foul," said Crazy Jane, in a work by William Butler Yeats.

Passion in Vajrayana is not merely sexual; it is basic to all aspects of living, even sipping coffee and enjoying a book on computers. As padma energy, it is not especially shocking or scandalous; it may appear simply as the kind of hospitality that puts new visitors at their ease in a strange place.

There is nothing in Vajrayana that requires the student to have orgies, but neither is sexuality condemned. Some Vajra masters choose to be celibate. In his youth Trungpa was a monk, although he fathered a child before giving up holy orders. His method of practicing Vajrayana was to drink the poison—to take on the actions of samsara and bring them under the power of enlightened mind. Instead of separating himself from jealousy and lust, he turned them into vehicles of dharma. The spirit of Buddhist teaching is consistent with his approach, provided it could be shown that he did not contradict the Mahayana commitment to benefit all beings, or the Hinayana precept against expressing sexuality in ignorant and harmful ways.

Drinking the poison is highly dangerous, as Trungpa himself warned many times. His insistence on training his students thoroughly in Hinayana was precisely to discourage them from playing around with poison until they knew what they were doing. Yet Osel Tendzin, the man Trungpa chose for his dharma heir, knowingly putting many of his partners at risk of HIV infection without telling them. Tendzin violated both the Mahayana commitment and the Hinayana precept, which he himself had been administering to new Buddhists for a decade. This fact in itself does not refute Vajrayana, nor does it necessarily discredit Trungpa, or even Tendzin in his better years, as teachers. But it does show that the tantric Buddhist way of handling passion may lead to disaster, and Tendzin's actions reveal that no matter how much we have practiced or how great a master we become, the danger never disappears. Devoted Buddhists need to be reminded of what is for everyone else simply a common-sense truism: there may be no such thing as a being whose every action at all times is completely enlightened, completely transcendent of all weakness, ineptitude, ignorance, and error.

As in all human endeavors, theory is one thing and practice another. The questions we must ask are whether detachment is really compatible with loving, how our experience of love and friendship is really affected by dharma practice, and whether the desire for positions in a hierarchical mandala, contrary to its theoretical purpose, can obstruct our ability to accept and appreciate each other as we are.

Some Buddhists have told me that their friendships within the Vajradhatu community were unsupportive, superficial, and lacking in warmth. The desultory nature of my Buddhist friendships is due partly to my own reticence, and it is no doubt true that strong personal bonding exists between Buddhists. But after eleven years in the sangha, I often wondered why I preferred a non-Buddhist domestic partner, was seldom contacted by sangha members for any personal reason, did not especially miss the people I had met at Buddhist programs, and had never formed any lasting friendships with other Buddhists, except for the occasional maverick whose commitment to the mandala was even more desultory than mine. Surely there are reasons for this that go beyond my own laziness and reserve.

Chogyam Trungpa taught that we had to accept our fellow sangha members as brothers and sisters, we ought to choose our friends, lovers, and partners from among them, and we should not associate too much with "heretics," as he called those who rejected the dharma. Part of our role in relation to each other was to mirror neurosis and encourage practice.

I find it a barrier to intimacy, however, when friends or lovers try to "mirror" my neurosis and correct my deviations from orthodoxy. These kinds of exercises in guidance are precisely *not* accepting and appreciating "things as they are." The hypocrisy of cult friendships, typically, is that while they pose as unconditional love, they depend powerfully on loyalty to the cult. The Buddhist sangha does much better with this problem than other cults that divide people frankly into the saved and the lost. In a Buddhist world-view, these divisions are undermined, although they are still reflected in the hierarchical structures and attitudes of Buddhist organizations.

I liked my heretic friends because they did not have any motive of helping me to "work" with myself, nor did they think I needed more Buddhist programs to become a better warrior, bodhisattva, *tantrika, sadhaka,* or whatever. Outsiders did not understand my experience in the mandala as well as members, but in some ways I could talk more honestly and fluently about dharma with a so-called heretic than a fellow Buddhist, because there was no reason to censor my views. Sangha friendships are often conditional on participating in the social events of the sangha and on sharing the doctrine of the organization. What counts in such cases·is not the friendship, but the cult and the doctrine.

With a genuine friend, I could be a fool without having to feel like one. I could talk about my petty irritations, worries, griefs, and injured vanity, and not suffer guilt for wallowing in samsara or indulging in ego trips. Heretics did not expect me to live up to an ideal, be on the dot, assume a crisp, cheerful posture, or bring our relationship to the path. Especially, I did not have to be detached. I could slap mosquitoes, get angry when a thief broke into my home, and admit that I was hurt without losing face. If I needed the company and warmth of friends, I knew that heretics would spend time with me just because they enjoyed hanging out with me, not because they were practicing warriorship.

In a strongly authoritarian mandala, the "unconditional friend-liness" of maitri turns out not to be so unconditional after all. Renaming our conditions in a Buddhist vocabulary is different from dropping them, and they can be even more poignant and painful for being disguised. It is easy to pull rank in an organization where rank is given tremendous importance by practice levels, offices, and colored pins. When a senior student with a higher rank than your own betrays you emotionally or perpetrates some odious piece of arrogance, at which you express overt resentment and anger, the situation may then go over into the game of one-upmanship. The ranking "elder" calls attention to your resentment as though it were solely the result of an ego problem characteristic of your inferior practice level.

In the early years of the sangha, there was a lot of groping for alternatives to monogamy. Many American Buddhists reflected the general trend toward sexual freedom in the 1970s and early '80s, but tried to base their attitudes on the values of detachment and generosity. Multiple sex partners, drinking, and wild parties characterized the tone of the Vajrayana community, which emanated from the leadership. If a husband or wife had an affair, the spouse was more or less expected to regard the triangle as a practice opportunity: a chance to be spacious and accommodating, and to work with the "neurosis" of jealousy by doing tonglen. Demands for sexual exclusiveness were not respected. It was understood when you went to Seminary that you would probably have an affair with at least one other Seminarian, whether either of you were married or not. The Buddhist spouses that I knew in these situations went through just as much pain as anyone else, but perhaps they handled it differently. There was more willingness to live pain rather than disguise or reject it, and Buddhist practice was a common bond among sufferers.

Meditation can arouse libido, and this was part of the reason for the heightened passion at Seminaries. With large numbers of both sexes living and working in close proximity for weeks on end, things would happen in any case. Some Buddhist centers strictly discourage sexual acting out. Trungpa discouraged it for the Hinayana section of Seminary, and then in the Mahayana section took the lid off, in accordance with the way his teaching style sought to transform passion into a vehicle of dharma. For him, a broken heart was the awakening of bodhicitta. The combination of passion, marriage, and sexual permissiveness is a sure formula for heartbreak.

At Seminary, I swivel-necked back and forth like a spy in a nudist colony, pursued sexual partners with the desperation of the recently ravaged, and seriously annoyed a few people. Others around me were doing the same. The dharmic atmosphere dissolved sexual guilt and shyness and added generous doses of humor. Dharma practice mirrored whatever game you were playing, so that dissimulation was difficult. Here it was not even necessary. One man I knew of would approach women strangers in the corridors or in an elevator and say, "Why don't we go to my room right now and fuck? Don't be shy, you're beautiful." On the streets, such behavior would likely be met with a Mace attack. At Seminary it was at once comic, exciting for some, but also irritating and sad. That mixture is raw bodhicitta.

The class hierarchy of Trungpa's mandala carried over into the pattern of its love affairs. As it does in the samsaric world, passion flowed toward those who had power. The expression of passion could range from serving their drinks to sharing their beds. A position close to the guru conferred sexual perquisites, and I resented the fact that in the competition for lovers, a kitchen worker was at a serious disadvantage compared to a sangha celebrity. The figures who hold the aces in this game, typically, are the ones running the cult—in the Buddhist world as in any other.

After the public disgrace of Osel Tendzin, the leaders of Vajradhatu began to back off from the appearance of lax morals, and to take their cues from less outrageous Tibetan teachers. AIDS was a dash of cold water on the idea of dancing in the fields of great bliss through sexual freedom. Several American Zen centers have gone through a similar upheaval. The current climate of opinion in Buddhist America gives a lot more emphasis to the Hinayana precept against sexual misconduct.

At one Buddhist retreat, I fell in love, bonded with my lover, and wanted to move in with her and share a common life. Although our passion was reciprocal, she equated bonding with grasping. For her, the desirable Buddhist course of a love affair was to enjoy it completely and let it go. Parting and separation were opportunities to work with loneliness. Trying to stay together would be a denial of the truth of impermanence. In this Buddhist environment, direct intrusion between lovers was acceptable behavior; men would hit on her sometimes while she walked to dinner with me. Any jealousy I felt was my problem, not hers, and she advised me to handle it by practicing tonglen.

While I experienced unutterable emotional pain through all this, my Buddhist training really was valuable. Instead of interpreting the pain as personal injury, I clicked into the wide-angle lens mode, and cut the projection of my emotion onto her. The pain was happening in my mind, nowhere else, and I could unravel it there without blame. It turned into a philosophical woundedness that connected me to the vulnerability of all beings. The fundamental loneliness that Trungpa described in his lectures as the basis of practice was not just a Buddhist doctrine but a simple human fact for me, and his training taught me to make friends with it. Amazed to discover that I could indeed love and let go without expecting anything in return, I realized the Mahayana had to be something more than theory. Nor did I cling to any image of myself as an exploited victim. Never again would I have to control my world in order to avoid the emotional pain of jealousy, loneliness, or grief. Neither would I have to be controlled by anyone else. At the same time, I did not have to shut off love to achieve this; I could still feel.

On the other hand, I knew that I did not want a partner who found it so easy to let go of me, who would permit and expect me to permit direct intrusions between us, or who expected me to endure long separations from her with detached equanimity. And I knew better than to take seriously any friendship with people who thought it was some kind of Vajra dance to try and seduce your lover right off your arm on a date.

When I was teaching a class on meditation, one of my students quipped, "In the samsaric world, emotions are a problem; in Buddhism, you have them, but who cares?" I thought he had missed the point that caring is the essence of Mahayana, but his sarcasm echoed in my mind on so many occasions that it must have revealed a truth. I remembered it every time a fellow sangha member or teacher described painful or pleasurable emotions as "no big deal," an often used dharma slogan. Both phrases make a good ironic postscript to Buddhist declarations of love: "I love you, but who cares? It's no big deal."

Letting go is the favored Buddhist response to the need for friendship and love. Letting go is what we learn to do best; we let go of thoughts, we let go of territory, we let go of resentment, we let go of emotions and emotional needs, we let go of concepts, positions, and expectations, we let go of hopes and fears, we let go of friends, we let go of lovers and love affairs, we let go of marriages and commitments, we let go of health, wealth, and life, we even try to let go of loneliness and pain. Some Buddhists let go so well that they live apart from their spouses for several months out of each year. We are much more skilled at letting go, I think, than we are at getting close. Yet, as a long-term answer to the human conditions of basic anxiety and alienation, getting close has a lot more to offer. Of course getting close has to be preceded, and accompanied, by letting go so that you don't end up smothering your partner, and yourself. But many Buddhist meditators tend to regard letting go as path, and intimacy as a neurotic self-indulgence needing to be cured.

In the matter of domestic relations, I found that whether or not my partner was a Buddhist had nothing to do with how well we could get along. If two people are going to antagonize each other, they can use Buddhist reasons for their rejection as well as any. Conversely, if they are going to appreciate and cherish each other with generosity and patience, they don't need Buddhist terms for it, although Buddhist practice could be a definite help. They are probably better off avoiding the dharmic vocabulary entirely, lest they be tempted to substitute some type of orthodox Buddhist description for what they actually experience. I made a better choice of a mate when I dropped Buddhist criteria and acted straight from intuition.

Yet, though I did not regard Buddhism as a required asset in a partner, I did feel it was an asset in me. Perhaps only one member of a couple has to practice dharma in order to give dharmic qualities to the whole partnership. Shunryu Suzuki said: "Even though your spouse is in bed, he or she is also practicing zazen—when *you* practice zazen!... So if you yourself have true practice, then everything else is practicing our way at the same time."

A wonderful side effect of dharma practice is that it has the power to dissolve the gender war. In a reality system where the self is no more than a phantom, gender is too insubstantial to serve as a reference point for paranoia. I could as well have been born a woman as a man, and probably was, many times. But this time around, in the cosmic embrace of yin and yang, I play the male role. Or perhaps the male role plays me. Either way, there is no cause for shame, and every reason to dance.

10

THE PROTECTORS

BUDDHIST PRACTICE SESSIONS in Vajradhatu are opened with a supplication to the Kagyu lineage of Tibetan gurus, and include chants at various times of the day, especially at closing, addressed to a panoply of mythical beings called "dharma protectors." Additional supplications to deceased or still living teachers were added from time to time. While the teachers were alive, we supplicated for their longevity, and after they had died, for their rebirth.

The lineage in the opening chant begins with Vajradhara, a Buddha figure who did not even have a fleshly incarnation, but manifested and spoke to his disciples in dreams. He wears harem pants and jewels, crosses his arms and legs in Vajra meditation posture, and is colored blue. An embodiment of enlightened qualities rather than a person, he is perhaps an Indian Buddhist version of the Jungian archetype of the Self.

Ekajati, the queen of the three worlds and the chief protector, looks like a cosmic rock star: she was born with a turquoise lock of hair and an iron mole in the middle of her forehead, dwells in the castle of cosmic miracles, wears a white cloud, has one eye, one fang, and one breast, and is naked but for a tiger skin round her waist. A hundred iron wolves follow her around as helpers. She is invoked to banish doubt, sharpen practice, and eat the hearts of heretics.

Vajrasadhu rides a brown male goat, manifests as a mischievous child, has a retinue of warriors in armor and maidens casting dice, and eats doubters and heretics for breakfast. The four-armed Mahakala rises from a red charnel ground in a lake of blood like a cloud adorned with lightning, carries a hooked knife, sword, trident, and skull cup full of blood, and, like the other protectors, is invoked to eat perverters of the dharma as his food. Vetali has one face and four arms, rides on a white-blazed donkey, drinks the blood of ego, cleaves the heads from the destroyers of the teachings, and cuts their aortas.

This collection of uglies did not escape from the studio floor of *Who Framed Roger Rabbit;* they are tantric deities, though the imagery that we used to evoke them emanated mostly from the fertile brain of Chogyam Trungpa. Chants to such figures have been a part of Kagyu practice for several centuries. The protectors are persuaded to stick around and do their jobs by offerings of *torma* (barley cake) and blood, which makes their services considerably easier to obtain than your average contract hitman.

Besides the protectors, a host of real gurus, mostly deceased, is called upon to arise from space, approach from a blooming lotus flower, appear like the full moon, show oceans of displays of countless inconceivable miracles, dispel the degeneracy of the dark age, or grant their blessings so that confusion may dawn as wisdom. The gurus are not as nasty as the protectors, though the protectors are really the guru in wrathful garb. The gurus are endowed with the power to dispel obstacles, pervade all the vast worlds with limitless compassion, master the four karmas of pacifying, enriching, magnetizing, and destroying, bring peace, health, and prosperity, skillfully cleanse whoever sees, hears, or touches them, and send out a thousand rays of goodness and virtue. This is what they do for a warmup. Their main act is to display the great symbol of the universe for the liberation of all beings.

I began doing the chants with fellow meditators before I knew anything about their meaning in the total three-yana curriculum of Tibetan dharma. Trungpa's teaching style was to offer the experience first and give the interpretation later, if at all. As the long practice day dragged on and the sun crept slowly across the floor of the shrine hall, the level of inattention, boredom, and agony grew to the point where the struggle of a monitor trying to stop a tassel from flapping in the breeze would elicit gales of hysterical laughter from a hundred squirming meditators. About that time, the practice master, or *umdze,* and his or her assistants, would pull up the great drum in the corner, open the chant book, evoke a dharma protector, and start supplicating: "When the practitioner is tormented by sloth, be an arrow of awareness; when the practitioner has lost the way, be a torch of meditation; when the practitioner is confused by doubt, sound the great trumpet of confidence." The order and dignity of the ritual took over: everybody straightened up and joined in. Barley cakes and saké, the symbolic blood and torma fee, would be carried to a niche in the wall that held the shrine of the protector, or thrown outdoors as an offering to the lower beings, and the hysteria was expelled for the rest of the day. For serious obstacles, there was an exorcism chant to annihilate and pacify the *maras*—those evil demons who delight in making your nose itch, creating visions of cold beer on hot days, inciting rage, and parading hallucinations of genital organs in the woodgrain patterns of the floor. The practice of evoking protectors could thus draw a shield of nurturing comfort around the shrine hall, into which virtually any distractions could enter without destroying the stability of the environment.

As poetry, the chants were powerful and functional. They did what poetry used to do centuries ago: express the group mind, orally, in a ritual that held together the reality system of a culture. For years I had lamented the alienation of Western poetry from any important social role other than advertising commodities. Poetry had been reduced to a small, private act, enslaved by print, economically worthless for the most part, kept alive through small magazine grants and the compulsory assignments of English professors. The one place where poetry had preserved something like an oral tradition and a mass unifying role was in rock music, and even there it seemed to support a cult of self-destruction. The tantric chants restored poetic utterance to a place of social and spiritual importance.

But even though their phrasing and imagery are poetic, the chants are not quite poetry as we know it, in a Western cultural and literary sense. There is no individual voice in them, no uncertainty, and no internal tension of a mind struggling with itself. They are not supposed to explore the ambiguities of uncertainty; they are supposed to kill it, and improve practice. They are closer to Biblical prophecy than literature. While I experienced the chants aesthetically, they are not recited, nor were they written, for aesthetic reasons. These religious liturgies are also intended to produce loyalty in the people saying them, like the "Lord's Prayer" and secular pledges of allegiance to nation and flag. I kept wanting to beautify them by chanting them in fifths, but perhaps I was missing the point, or simply resisting their propaganda effect. The printed texts themselves are treated as objects of veneration: you don't casually read them like poems, nor should you place coffee cups on them, or leave them lying around on the floor.

The deities "are as real as you are," said one program coordinator. How could this be? Tibetan dharma divides the universe into three levels, or *kayas;* the *dharmakaya* is pure formlessness, like space; the *sambhogakaya* is vibrational, including the realms of light, sound, and thought; the *nirmanakaya* is material embodiment, such as the planet earth, or my flesh. Applying these levels to the computer in front of me, the dharmakaya would be the space it occupies, plus my awareness before it is shaped into words. The sambhogakaya would be the words, the light on the screen, and the thoughts communicated by that light. The nirmanakaya would be the hardware of monitor and keyboard, and my own typing hands. In the Buddhist system the three kayas are inseparable. It is possible, however, for a being to exist in the dharmakaya and the sambhogakaya without manifesting a body; such a being would be composed of thought, color, or vibrational energy. Whereas I exist in all three kayas, certain beings could appear entirely in the sambhogakaya, through dreams and visions, but would be no less real. At my death, I withdraw from the nirmanakaya temporarily, but in the sambhogakaya my presence would manifest to others through my work, their memories and dreams, my effect on their lives, and whatever vibrations I could muster.

The most appealing feature of this reality system is that it does away with the notion that the existence of an entity must be tied to a particular reference point. My existence is not restricted to my body even in life, but spreads out into the words in this book, for example, or into the memories of former acquaintances. As I grow in my path, becoming more and more liberated from the reference point of self, I may acquire the power of embodying myself in a number of forms—organizations, thoughts, systems—that will outlast my physical death. A buddha may thus manifest as Ekajati, Vajradhara, Chogyam Trungpa, any number of Karmapas, or as the mandala of a particular group. The mark of a buddha manifestation is that it does the work of Buddha: it teaches dharma and liberates sentient beings from samsara.

One of the protectors, Ekajati, is explicitly described as manifesting in all three kayas: in the dharmakaya, she is "self-liberated luminosity," a phrase used for complete enlightenment; in the sambhogakaya, she is "Vajrayogini," a deity who represents the enlightened form of passion; in the nirmanakaya, she is "the mother of all." So every mother, then, at some unconscious level, would be a physical appearance of Ekajati.

Here we are in the realm of myth, as described by Joseph Campbell and Carl Jung. Ekajati could also be said to have manifested as Cybele, Kali, Venus, Beatrice, and the Virgin Mary. We could call her an archetype from the collective unconscious. But Vajradhatu leaders always discouraged these kinds of analogies, perhaps because too much intellectual analysis robs the image of its power: you invoke Ekajati to safeguard your dharma practice and protect you from heresy, not to study her as an archetype. I believe the point is to surrender yourself to the image, to let it take you over and shepherd you into the heart of the mandala. Academic analysis forestalls this self-surrender by reducing the image to an object in the history of mythology. If I know that Ekajati is a cousin of Cybele, Kali, and Venus, then I know what is happening during the chant on a level that allows me to detach from its intended effect. It comes down to this: who runs the show, the guru or me? Everything in the whole Tibetan path comes down to this, one way or another.

When I first encountered the practice of invoking protectors, I objected to it on the ground that it amounted to a system of brainwashing. I was somewhat pacified by the knowledge that the deities are not supposed to be imagined as having any solid reality; they are called up from emptiness and dissolved back into it at the conclusion of practice. But this fact does not dissolve the basis of my objection. I am not supposed to be imagined as having any solid reality either; I am called up from emptiness at birth and dissolved back into it at death, moment to moment. So the deity and I are in the same boat, as far as emptiness is concerned. Either way, I still have to decide whether it is a good idea to allow my brain to go through this particular laundromat.

Both sides of the question of whether to accept myth as a ground for living can be argued cogently. Campbell, Robert Bly, and others have suggested that we need myth, because only mythic images can guide us out of the spiritual pit into which we have fallen. This line of argument goes back to *The Waste Land* by T. S. Eliot. But as Campbell himself points out, all mythologies are false. The alternative to a mythic reality is scientific rationalism. Myth is not open to question; it is handed down by higher authority, and interprets the physical universe to fit its own premises. A scientific reality can be revised; its premises are always subject to the test of evidence. Regardless of how high the authority of the scientists might be, their conclusions are at the mercy of phenomena. If the laboratory janitor can show by repeatable experiments that the Nobel Prize winner is wrong, then our reality must change accordingly.

Scientific rationalism is accused of bringing on the global crisis of the twentieth century, and many religious groups argue that problems like nuclear proliferation, famine, and environmental catastrophe have been caused by abandoning the mythic reality systems of religion. The great catastrophes of our age, however, have not been brought about by the scientific method itself, but because the power of technology has been placed in the service of political, social, economic, and religious myth systems that insulate themselves from scientific criticism, such as National Interest, Free Enterprise, the Great Leap Forward, the Master Race, and various brands of fundamentalism. Environmental polluters, for example, ignore scientific data on ecology; the mythical justification for their ignorance is usually drawn from some version of laissez-faire economics. If there is a way out of our crisis, it is far more likely to be discovered by the sciences than by any system of myth. Scientific rationalism was developed by a handful of people at great personal risk in the face of hostility from prevailing myth systems. It is by no means generally accepted, and still has a fragile status throughout much of the world. We do ourselves no service at all by discarding it completely in favor of myth.

Tibetan Buddhist dharma is somewhere in the middle of this issue at present. The Dalai Lama has stated that if scientific discoveries refute Buddhist doctrine, then the doctrine should change—an attitude far in advance of the evangelical Christians who insist that Biblical creationist theology should be taught in the schools as if it were a literally true account of the origin of species. Trungpa's students included eminent scientists like Francisco Varela, whose field is the nature of perception, and Jeremy Hayward, a Cambridge University doctor of nuclear physics who wrote *Shifting Worlds, Changing Minds: Where the Sciences and Buddhism Meet* (Shambhala, 1987). I saw psychiatrists and other mental health professionals do the protectors' chants without visible signs of revulsion, although their levels of personal resistance to the tantric myth system were no doubt in some cases a great deal higher than mine.

My objections and questions concerning the protectors were never answered, but the fluid softness induced by shamatha allowed me to do the chants anyway. Questions? Objections? Mythology versus scientific rationalism? That was just thinking. Let it go and say the chant. "Just do it," said Trungpa, and all the instructors trained by him. Since I had become so expert at letting everything go, it was no great problem to put my brain in the washing machine and let that go too. But there was always a voice telling me, "Remember, no matter what you say or do, I believe nothing." Sometimes I thought the voice was a dharma protector, conjured by the chant; and sometimes my refusal to believe, as an effect of shamatha, seemed like the very emptiness that prevented the deities from solidifying into gods and goddesses. I never knew for certain, therefore, whether my practice was orthodox or hypocritical. What seemed like ego in one session would slide into buddha-mind in the next. Many years passed and this contradiction never got resolved.

In hindsight, my first impressions were correct—all of them. The protectors are myths, handed down by a higher authority, which is not subject to question. They cannot be rationalized by interpreting them as creative visualizations that work with archetypes from the collective unconscious. Some psychotherapists make use of visualization techniques that may have a superficial resemblance to tantra, but in psychotherapeutic visualization, the imagery comes from the subject. The imagery of the chants came from Chogyam Trungpa. Its function in relation to me was not self-discovery or self-healing, but self-abnegation. Over and over, I evoked mythic beings of someone else's making, "as real as I am," and requested those beings to kill and eat perverters of the dharma, cleave their heads, and cut their aortas.

I could never be sure whether my doubt made me a perverter of the dharma, and whether I might not be praying for my own destruction. Later on I discovered that this was exactly what I was praying for; this is in fact the point of tantra, this is how it works. Trungpa had built its basic idea right into the form of the earliest group practice sessions, so that long before reaching the Vajrayana, you have already been stricken by it, like a deer hit with a poison arrow.

Destruction of heresy and ego, however, is only a small part of what the protectors are supplicated to do. They guard the meditator, banish nightmares, carry out Buddha activity, and dispel the calamities of plague, famine, and war. We ask them for freedom from disease, long life, glory, fame, good fortune, power, great and vast enjoyments, peace, abundant grain, and the accomplishment of whatever mind desires. The passion for attainment renounced in one section of text comes back multiplied in another.

I trusted that the killing, eating, cleaving, and cutting took place only in the sambhogakaya, and were not invitations to enjoy physical mass murders and cannibal banquets. What gets killed and eaten is the ego, the spiritual materialist urge to exploit dharma for personal advantage. But since ego does not really exist, then we must have been asking the protectors to kill and eat the illusion of ego, which my suspicious voice accepted as a reasonable request.

However we explain them, the basic purpose of the protector visualizations is to bind the student inescapably to the guru and his mandala. They should, and often do, set off all our internal alarm bells. Like any other group behavior, chant recitation pulls you into the system by exerting a pressure to conform. Most of the chants were done near the supper hour, and in the last half hour of a practice day, late at night, when my resistance was down and I was ready for sleep. The times chosen to say them were considered moments of maximum vulnerability to distraction by obstacles, like fatigue and doubt.

The paradox in the system is that shamatha at one and the same time protects you from brainwashing and prepares you for it. The mixed messages are enough to drive the questioning mind berserk even before entering Vajrayana, where the real risk of insanity is supposed to be incurred. The system is not called brainwashing, of course; Trungpa called it "taming the mind." The difference between the two is as thin as the edge of a flipped coin. Heads, and you're a cult zombie—a "vajradhatoid," as some of us called ourselves in moments of humor. Tails, and you throw away your lottery ticket without knowing if it had the winning number. The

Buddha said that the chances of encountering a genuine teacher and getting enlightened were about on a par with the likelihood that a turtle coming to the surface in the middle of the ocean would put his head through a single ring tossed on the waves. If the coin falls either heads or tails, you miss the ring. If it stands on edge, the ring starts to expand without limit, like the sound of a gong.

11

LIKE A BODY AND ITS SHADOW

I N THE CONTEXT of the mandala, you could usually spot sadhakas; they moved and talked like veteran Special Forces troops in the company of raw enlistees. Sadhakas were Vajrayana students who had finished all their preparatory practices and had taken abhiseka, the initiation into the higher tantras. They had secret hand gestures and rituals that ordinary meditators were not allowed to see. Some of them walked as if they were doing the Carlos Castaneda gait of power: balanced on the balls of their feet, hands curled, looking neither right nor left. They said cryptic things, like "You know, you can reach enlightenment in one lifetime." When you spoke with them, they might ask questions about you, but revealed almost nothing about themselves. They would scope out your neurosis, whatever it might be, smile knowingly as soon as they had found it, and dismiss you, or walk away. They were important people, imbued with "Vajra pride," as this coxcomb demeanor was termed; and until you reached their level, you were a virgin. At Seminary, they had police powers, and would report you to the *dekyong*, or floor chief, for violations of rules.

You walked past their closed practice rooms sometimes and heard their chanting punctuated by periodic waves of bells and drums, and the sounds made you want to do whatever was necessary to get inside and participate. In the kitchen you saw great platters of meats and cases of saké being prepared for their feasts. When the room was empty, you might be allowed in to clean up after them, and you saw fresh fruits and strange cult objects on the shrine, brilliant red wall hangings trimmed with rainbow colors, rows of long, low black tables, and a carpet of uncooked rice on the floor. The heavy incense that hung in the air made you think of an opium den.

The Seminary system culminated with a three-week intensive introduction to the Vajrayana; you were given permission, finally, to read the secret teachings from previous Seminaries. These transcripts had red covers, to distinguish them from the white-covered Hinayana and Mahayana transcripts, which were available to any member of the mandala. Receiving the red books was marked by a ceremony, which included passing the texts through purification smoke and taking a vow that you would not show them to outsiders. At the end of the Vajrayana intensive, Trungpa conducted a transmission of "Vajra energy" and empowered you to begin preparation for tantra.

Before hearing any Vajrayana teachings, we read the story of Rudra and received an admonitory lecture on the dangers of Vajra hell. What we were about to do, said Trungpa and staff members, was fasten our minds irrevocably to the guru with the golden nails of *samaya*, our commitment to the path. Between our samaya and the guru's mind, the ego was going to be squashed and eaten, like a piece of meat between two slices of bread. There was absolutely no way that we could make this commitment and still hang onto ourselves. "If we have any hidden neuroses or hot points in our experience," said Lodro Dorje, the Dean of Practice and Study in Vajradhatu, "they will be exposed. If we have buttons to push, those buttons will definitely be pushed."

Vajra hell is what happens to those who reject their teacher or try to leave the Vajrayana. Violating samaya, perverting the teachings, or using them to achieve the ambitions of ego were serious transgressions, but these could be atoned by confession and renewed commitment as long as we did not reject our bond with the guru. Trungpa described Vajra hell as a state of subtle, continuous emotional pain, much worse than divorce.

Rudra was a Vajra disciple of ancient India, perhaps real or quasi-legendary, perhaps an archetype of the shadow, who used tantra as justification for his criminal life. Since the Vajrayana teaches that there is no good and evil, and that passion, aggression, ignorance, envy, and pride are really buddha-mind in disguise, Rudra figured he could do anything he wanted. He opened brothels, organized gangs of robbers, and taught the tantras to his thugs in order to make them more efficient murderers. When his guru told him he was perverting the dharma, Rudra drew his sword in a rage and killed him. Up to that point his crimes had accumulated much bad karma, but still might have been atoned. By killing the guru, however, Rudra becomes a figure like Judas—there is no hope for him.

Transmission into Vajrayana was preceded by a personal interview with a high official, who would determine whether or not you were a suitable student. I know of very few people who were turned down, so passing this test must have been relatively easy. You did not have to demonstrate any behavioral mastery of the Mahayana paramitas. The best way to be accepted was to assert your "heart connection" to the vision of the "Vidyadhara," "the tamer of beings," as Trungpa called himself. This was a title he assumed in the early 1980s, and it implied more grandeur than his earlier titles of "Venerable," "Vajra Master," and "Jewel." In the interview, you should say that you long for a place in the Vidyadhara's mandala (and I'm sure many, perhaps most, really did); and it was helpful also to have mastered the terminology of the discussion groups. You ingratiated yourself by demonstrating loyalty to the group ethos, the same way you would in any church, corporation, or cult.

Overtly displayed skepticism might be a barrier to entering the Vajrayana. One Seminarian drank a toast to Vajra hell at a party, was reported to the staff, and found himself questioned very closely before they would allow him to proceed. Parties always included obligatory toasts to the Vidyadhara and the Regent, accompanied by patented devotional speeches that invited parody, but to parody them deliberately was a sure mark of a bad attitude. I told my interviewer that if I had cause to leave the organization I would do so, and I did not believe the furies of Vajra hell would offer me anything to compare with the pain of divorce. This display of independence made me a doubtful candidate, and I had to pass a second interview.

Of course, you ask yourself why you want to take transmission at all, but the momentum of the process pushes you further and further into it. Transmission was the gateway to the next phase. Why come all that distance only to chicken out on the threshold of the real stuff? Everything before Vajrayana was treated as a mere prelude to driving the supreme vehicle, the top-of-the-line magic carpet. The alternative to becoming a sadhaka was to remain a "lowly shamatha student," as one Hinayanist described herself. Would you elect to remain a peon forever when given a chance to join the aristocracy? Besides, I was desperate to know what went on in those little rooms with the drums and bells. I wanted to do the secret hand gestures, read the secret books, and be on the same level as the gait-of-power strutters, and if Vajrayana was a dangerous drug, I wanted a hit.

These motives are blatant spiritual materialism, precisely the sort of thing Trungpa ridiculed in his talks and writings. When the interviewer asks why you want to take transmission, it is unlikely that you would give such reasons, for they have little to do with dharma. But they arose inevitably from the system, and after all else is considered, they probably shaped many people's decision to go on. A sadhaka might say that spiritual materialism is the longing for enlightenment, expressed in the language of samsara. In this case, there is no such thing as entering Vajrayana for the wrong reasons, and we may soon find ourselves on the edge of Rudra's career.

Throughout the Hinayana and Mahayana levels, practice was considered to be "no big deal." You do it like brushing your teeth, you don't dwell on your progress or seek to gain anything by it, etc. But even at this level the message was mixed. The staff distributed little calendar booklets, in which you were supposed to keep track of how many hours and days per month you were practicing. At the end of the year these booklets were collected and sent to an office of Vajradhatu—a strange way of handling an activity that was supposedly no big deal.

Now, suddenly, everything changed, and practice became a Very Big Deal. We vowed to keep silent about what we learned, we had to prostrate to the master and supplicate him on our knees with palms joined in order to receive teachings, we sat up all night waiting for transmission, and finally, in a haunted, weird, colorful, comic-book atmosphere lit by the vague rose-gray of early dawn, we stood in line, exhausted, while Trungpa pressed his brass vajra on our foreheads and claimed us for the rest of this and all future lives.

I wanted to ask how practice could be simultaneously "no big deal" yet a big enough deal to merit all these incredible ceremonies, and a sentence in Vajra hell if you stopped. I wanted to ask why the whole mandala appeared to be organized around spiritual materialism, when one of Trungpa's most widely read books warned us against it; what brass vajras pressed on your head, secret gestures, bells, drums, and visualized dancing cartoon characters had to do with enlightenment; and whether the whole lecture on Vajra hell was really a massive indoctrination to prevent students from leaving or decreasing the value of the product by pirating the company logo. These were among the many questions I never raised publicly, and most of them were never answered. Within the Vajradhatu structure, there was no way anyone could press issues like this and get real answers. You would either be expelled as an obstruction, or at best would be met with a gentle and sympathetic silence that referred you back to practice. Such deep skepticism was defined as neurosis; and you began to wonder if that might not be exactly what it was after all.

In the major schools of Tibetan dharma, entry into the Vajrayana is preceded by a long series of preparations called *ngondros* (pronounced "nyindro" or "nindro"). Vajrayana has the reputation of speeding things up, of confronting and cutting through obstacles that might be put off indefinitely in the lower yanas. Ngondro is a quantum leap in the pace of confronting and cutting through. If shamatha is like taking items from your closet slowly and carefully one at a time, ngondro can be likened to pulling out all the shelves and drawers and tipping them upside down on the floor.

Most Buddhist schools have the idea that good practice, including prayer, accumulates *merit;* that is, it builds a tendency to stay with the dharma, seek out authentic teachers, and attract good fortune. In the Mahayana, merit must always be dedicated to others; keeping it to yourself is the same thing as destroying it. Ngondros are methods of accumulating merit rapidly, and then preserving it by giving it away. The liturgy that accompanies ngondros declares that you do them always for others, never for yourself.

Vajrayana students read the stories of the grueling mental and physical tortures that Marpa inflicted on his disciple Milarepa in the tenth century, to purify the bad karma Milarepa had incurred from murdering a whole village with black magic. We read how Marpa's own guru Naropa had kept squeezing Marpa for more and more gold to pay for the teachings, until finally, after Marpa had given up all his gold, Naropa picked up the gold dust and flung it to the wind, saying "I don't need your gold; the whole world is gold to me." We read how Marpa kept telling Milarepa to build stone towers for him as a price for receiving initiation, and when a tower was built, Marpa would say "No, tear it down, I didn't want it in that spot, I must have been drunk when I told you to build it there." Just at the point Milarepa was about to commit suicide, Marpa chose that moment to give him the teachings. The lesson in such lore is that you have to surrender whatever you are holding back, let it go, give in. Only after you have done this can you enter the Vajrayana.

Over the centuries, the purification hardships required of the initiate in Tibetan dharma became standardized and ritualized into the cumulative system of ngondro. The guru no longer meets with every student to individualize the means for driving you to the brink of madness. Instead, you are given a series of archetypal forms to visualize representing different aspects of the guru, and a sequence of practices to do in relation to those forms. The practices induce the same result: they call for a total involvement of body, speech, and mind aimed at eviscerating your old reality system. The guru is not physically present, but if you accept the tantric reality system, you and the guru are literally inseparable in the sambhogakaya; by night he sleeps with you, and by day he sits on your head.

In the Kagyu and Nyingma dharma traditions of Tibet, there are five ngondros, referred to in some texts as the "five hundred thousands"—100,000 prostrations, 100,000 Vajrasattva mantra recitations, 100,000 recitations each of the refuge and bodhisattva vows, and 100,000 mandala rituals. Completion of these practices is followed by Guru Yoga, a bridge into the Vajrayana mandala that includes one million repetitions of the Guru Yoga mantra. Ngondros are complex mental and verbal procedures that require a lot of counting, traditionally done on strings of beads called malas that can be worn around the wrist for easy access by the fingers. Our malas have 108 beads, a symbolic number in ancient Indian Vedic and Buddhist traditions. So 100,000 repetitions of a practice would actually be 108,000, or 1,000 rounds on the mala. Trungpa's students repeated the refuge and bodhisattva vows concurrently with prostrations, so that there were three main levels of ngondro followed by Guru Yoga. During this period you were also expected to complete your fifty half-hour sessions of tonglen.

Certain journalists, quoting teachers from other Buddhist sects, have implied that Trungpa did not teach real Buddhism but a watered-down version for American consumption, or that his teaching was corrupted by his his libertine outlook. After doing Vajrayana practices, reading texts on them by Tibetan authorities, and visiting Buddhist centers in the United States and Europe, I was satisfied that this allegation is untrue. The practices taught in Vajradhatu are as genuinely Buddhist as anything in the Buddhist world, and as far as I can tell without having been born into that culture, they offer the heart of Tibetan dharma. Trungpa translated the teachings so that Westerners could gain access to them, but without diluting or corrupting them in the process. Several of the greatest Tibetan masters have put their seal of approval on his work. The Sixteenth Karmapa wrote a proclamation to that effect, and Dilgo Khyentse Rinpoche, after the Tendzin scandal, insisted to Vajradhatu students that Trungpa had given them authentic dharma, and they should continue in it exactly as he had prescribed. This point cannot be emphasized too much in any critique of Vajrayana practice based on Trungpa's instruction.

The fundamental substance of Vajrayana—the ngondros, the sadhanas, the guru principle, the mandala, the ideal of devotion to one's teacher, the Rudra story, the warnings about Vajra hell, the deities, the protectors, and the underlying philosophy—was not Trungpa's invention, but comes from the traditional Kagyu and Nyingma Buddhist curriculum of Tibet that was itself handed down from northern Indian Buddhist tradition. Trungpa's students are sometimes startled by reminders of how respectful of tradition he was—as when they discovered, for example, that an ancient Tibetan description of a dharma court had been fulfilled in the organization of the court he had designed for them.

The single most important quality demanded of the Vajrayana student is devotion to the guru. You must long for the guru like a flower opening to receive the rain, flock to the guru for refuge like birds seeking shelter from a storm. You should pray to accompany the guru through all your lives like a body and its shadow, not separated for even an instant. Whatever you do should be done only to please the guru. Without the guru, enlightenment is impossible. The guru is the Buddha. Anything that happens to you, whether good or bad, is the guru's blessing and compassion. If it is good, be grateful to the guru; if it is bad, then it helps to wake you up, and so you should also be grateful to the guru. To regard the guru as an ordinary person is a perverted attitude. No matter what the guru does, you must accept it as a teaching. Before you take initiation, said Kalu Rinpoche, you should examine the teacher carefully and decide intelligently whether that person is authentic; but once you receive transmission and form the bond of samaya, you have committed yourself to the teacher as guru, and from then on, the guru can do no wrong, no matter what. It follows that if you obey the guru in all things, you can do no wrong either. This is the basis of Osel Tendzin's teaching that "if you keep your samaya, you cannot make a mistake." He was not deviating into his own megalomania when he said this, but repeating the most essential idea of mainstream Vajrayana.

Devotion is emphasized partly as a safeguard against sharing the fate of Rudra. He went wrong by disobeying the guru, who could have brought him back from his disastrous course of acting out the ego's darkest fantasies under the guise of transcending duality. Devotion would have liquefied the fixation on himself that led him to imagine he could benefit from his crimes. As a form of selfless love, devotion could have been a counterweight to his aggression, making him tractable, open to the guru's influence. When Rudra killed his guru, he entirely destroyed his connection to enlightenment, yet he had tasted enough of it to feel the unending pain of irretrievable loss.

The Vajrayana path is not theoretical, but propels the practitioner to actually enter the universe of no duality and no absolute reference point. The gateway to that universe is devotion. If there is no good and evil, no path, no wisdom, no attainment and no nonattainment, then pleasure and pain, yes and no, life and death, God and Satan, all amount to the same thing, and you really can do anything you want. All the energies of the universe are yours, for you are those energies. They are all sacred, none is forbidden. The kleshas are the powers of buddhahood. Such a vision of limitless freedom has burned many a rock star, poet, warlord, mercenary, and drug dealer to a crisp at an early age; and it may have burned up Trungpa and Tendzin as well, for they both died young from the fallout of their revelry.

Trungpa described the nondual vision as a return to fundamental sanity. He said that the Vajrayana transcendence of moral categories could lead to monstrous evil, but somehow it doesn't. It is "nontheistic energy." If there is no God to restrict the energy with commandments, there is also no Devil and no ego to be served by its corruption and misuse either. It is "self-existing" in the sense that it does not depend on or express any prior condition, nor, from its own point of view, does it lead anywhere. It is "basically good" because it precedes the division into good and evil. All human conceptual systems, including ethical rules, are projections of the ego, filters obscuring the direct apprehension of basic goodness. Our projections are made out of the same goodness—there is nothing else of which they could be made—but they distract us from buddha-mind just as waves mitigate the reflective power of a lake surface. Sanity is our original basic goodness, unimpeded by any conceptual system whatever.

The guru is the embodiment of this sanity. Devotion is supposed to bind the guru with the sanity inside of us, and eat the detritus of our projections for nourishment. Since the confusions of ego are products of sanity, in a sense, it is sound ecology to recycle them as fertilizer and fuel.

Devotion is really germinated in the lower yanas, but it is not yet called by that name. The freedom from dysfunction, the wide-angle lens mind, the power to work with pain and fear as resources, the panoramic awareness, appreciation for detail, softness and vulnerability, steadiness, patience, and all the other beneficial effects of shamatha cannot help but cause an upsurge of gratitude toward the teacher. A strong trust based on experience makes you open to learning more. The unconditional friendliness and warmth of bodhicitta is passion cleansed of grasping; the devotion of Vajrayana arises from the same passion. Devotion is a form of love. Virtually the same idea is taught by Christ in the Gospel of John: the master says his disciples must eat his flesh and drink his blood, he is the vine and they are the branches, if they remain in him they will bear fruit, he is the water of eternal life, the way, and the truth, and his new commandment is that they must love one another. The vine and communion images, in particular, could as well describe the unity of mind between guru and disciple that is supposed to be achieved by Vajrayana devotion.

Devotion could also corrupt and destroy both guru and disciple. What if Rudra's guru had said he was doing fine, understood the dharma, and should continue his career? Or what if the guru had asked for a percentage of his profits? What should Rudra's own students have done, if they wondered whether he was perverting the tantras and he ordered them to go on murdering as usual? If ethics are expressions of enlightened mind in the Hinayana and Mahayana, how can they be put aside in Vajrayana? How can any Buddhist vehicle disregard, for example, the five precepts against killing, stealing, lying, intoxication, and sexual misconduct, or the Mahayana rule against causing harm, and still claim to be Buddhist? Such questions occurred to me before I took transmission, but I went ahead and did it anyway.

"Why do you want transmission from Trungpa Rinpoche in particular?" my interviewer asked me. "He is known to be one of the most outrageous teachers around."

"I wouldn't want a teacher who was a goody two-shoes," I answered truthfully. "Such a person would not understand life well enough for me to have confidence in him."

Privately, I thought, if my guru turns into a Rudra, then I will detach from him and walk away. At that point my guide will have to be the guru within, and the betrayer of samaya who goes to Vajra hell will be Trungpa, not me. But maybe ngondro would destroy my ability to make that decision, or I would come to value my position in the mandala too much to give it up, or the guru would corrupt me by slow degrees.

Trungpa did not make this decision any easier by his own behavior; in fact, he seemed bent on stoking the agony by acting so bizarre that I wondered if he was capable of ordering us all to commit suicide. On the night of the Vajrayana transmission, he rambled from subject to subject in a series of blazing nonsequiturs, muttered about Polish tanks with nine forward gears, no reverse, no steering and no brakes, waited until we were dozing off and then shouted "Fat!" or "Fuck you!" into the microphone loud enough to burst our eardrums, pretended he was about to begin the transmission, and then free-associated his way into elocution word lists. In a previous talk, he had leaned forward, smiling, and said "Thank you for accepting me as your friend, teacher, DICTATOR!"

Had I wanted to base my decision on trust in his sanity, it would have been impossible. His prelude to transmission was a deliberate attack on that trust. I looked at his robed form on the throne and contemplated how he insulted us, played on our fears, kept us sitting all night until dawn, giving no hint of what he might do next, and it struck me that I really knew nothing about him, that he could do anything. I had already read in the Vajrayana transcripts where he described devotion to the guru as "unrequited love," which meant that we were supposed to love him, but he did not necessarily love us. "I love you all," he said, often enough. That is easily said, and is certainly no guarantee against betrayal. If I feared betrayal, however, I should not even have been there; from ego's point of view, the whole idea of Vajrayana is nothing but one huge betrayal after another.

At the time, I did not understand why I didn't just get up and leave. In the end the decision was not rational at all; it was scarcely even a decision, but a gut-level determination, combined with the momentum of all the practice I had already done. He could have said very little to dissuade me, as long as I remained convinced that he knew what I wanted to learn. It was like jumping from a cliff into a quarry pool—something I used to do as a boy. "You just do it," he said, "like having an orgasm"—an image that had uncomfortable associations with getting screwed. The person I had to trust was not him, but myself.

The effects that Trungpa produced were exactly the nature of Vajrayana consciousness generally: rational analysis, hesitation, the illusion of weighing contradictory factors and making an intelligent choice, the searching for a reason to trust another instead of yourself—these things were destroyed. You acted, finally, from simple desire. After the Hinayana and Mahayana foreplay, you wanted to see it through. You jumped because the cliff was there.

Trungpa's Vajrayana transmissions had the common element of

squeezing a heart response from the student, but they did not all have the same form. At another Seminary, after meeting with Osel Tendzin, Trungpa wept, then disappeared, leaving a tentful of Vajrayana candidates waiting for transmission. His attendants found him and asked him if he was going to give it. There could be no greater transmission, Trungpa replied, than his broken heart. A few months later he was dead.

12

I TAKE REFUGE: PROSTRATION

D EVOTION IS VALUED in Vajrayana as a means to destroy
doubt. Considered a refuge of ego, doubt is no longer cod-
dled—it has to be crushed. But if a choice must be made
between doubt and devotion, I think we are better off to prefer
doubt. It is essential to sanity, and therefore to enlightenment;
absolutely nothing in the path should be shielded from skeptical
scrutiny, especially not devotion. Doubt is the spy in the temple,
watching for signs of cultist corruption and hypocrisy.

On the other hand, unless we expel the spy, perhaps devotion
cannot do its work of fast-forwarding the mind into the Vajrayana
universe. This question calls for the most painstaking honesty in
any helpful critique of tantra. As a ground for further discussion,
I shall describe more specifically how devotion is built up during
ngondro.

Prostration is the first and most difficult ngondro. Like all the
other practices, it should be done for its own sake, not as a pre-
liminary task to get through so that you can hasten on to the next
step. Instructors say this about every level: get into the practice as
an end in itself, not as a means to abhiseka. Interestingly, the power
of abhiseka is made vastly greater this way. "You could become
enlightened by prostrating," they say, "it is a perfectly respectable
practice."

Prostration practice requires a shrine outfitted with the right

Buddhist paraphernalia, and surmounted by a picture of the guru who is credited with establishing your particular tradition of dharma. The source of the Kagyu lineage is Vajradhara. In the Nyingma lineage, the picture would be of Padmasambhava. Other Tibetan lines may have different gurus. Whether they actually lived or not is almost irrelevant to the effects of practice; all are depicted in archetypal form.

My first real encounter with Vajradhara was during a *lhasang,* or purification rite performed by Trungpa in a large shrine hall filled with 400 meditators. We followed a cart that was carrying an urn full of smoking juniper, chanting a Shambhala victory paean at high volume while he muttered mantras and waved the smoke toward us with a flag. Vajradhara was bright blue, his arms folded on his chest; the aura surrounding him pulsated with pink, lavender, rose, and sandstone red. He seemed to float on the juniper smoke while the chanting struck me like gongs and thrilled me like drums and bagpipes.

The practice icon of Vajradhara includes a whole fan of the gurus and bodhisattvas descended from him, plus the buddhas, the ordained sangha, the dharma texts, the protectors, the deities of sadhaka practice called *yidams,* and a choir of *dakas, dakinis,* and *dharmapalas*—little guardian spirits, genii, firefolk, faeries, whatever, who manifest the masculine and feminine creative energies of mind. All these are arranged in the pattern of a tree, suspended over a lake, whose mossy shores are crowded with humans and animals all prostrating. The humans and animals represent all sentient beings who have been my mothers in countless lives. Vajradhara is a smiling half-naked youth sitting on a lion throne, richly decorated in medieval Indian style. He has a topknot, a jeweled tiara, bracelets, earrings, and other finery. As you visualize and prostrate to the lineage tree, you are supposed to imagine that the features and mannerisms of your own teacher superimpose onto the portrait of the lineage guru.

A prostration session begins with fifteen minutes of sitting practice, followed by ten minutes of tonglen. Then you recite a lengthy liturgy of supplication to the guru, while on your knees with palms pressed together at heart level, in a posture called *anjali*. The liturgy is a confession of misdeeds, offering, renewed commitment, and summation of the principal stages of the path, concluding with a repetition of the bodhisattva vow, and an extended formula for taking refuge in the guru, the Buddha, the dharma, the sangha, and the protectors, bodhisattvas, yidams, dakas, dakinis, and dharmapalas of the mandala. In short, the whole religion is there, displayed in the icon and described in the liturgy, and you must orally declare your faith in it, accept it, supplicate it, and go to it for refuge.

Then you stand up and begin prostrating to it. You fold your hands in anjali, touch them to forehead, lips, and heart while repeating "I take refuge in the guru, I take refuge in the Buddha, I take refuge in the dharma, I take refuge in the sangha," and prostrate full length on a mat or board, with your arms and legs stretched out and your forehead touching the floor surface. All this time you are supposed to visualize the lineage tree in front, your father on your right, your mother on your left, and your worst enemy behind you. At the end of a prostration, you rise and count off one bead on the mala. Only 107,999 more to go. When a practice session is finished, you dedicate the merit and sit for fifteen minutes in shamatha. Sitting practice is the container for ngondro; you begin by establishing the wide-angle lens mind, and end by dissolving everything you have conjured into emptiness and giving the benefit away.

Every detail of this routine, as I performed it month after month, through winter, spring, summer, and fall, for three-and-a-half years, is pregnant with deep psychological wisdom, and there is not one thing in it that I would change.

Five hundred prostrations in one session was about the maximum I could ever do with my lung impairment. It took three hours—a half hour of sitting, ten to twenty minutes for tonglen, fifteen or twenty for the liturgies, and about two hours for the actual prostrations. One thing this practice requires is time, and another is a driving determination to get on with it, no matter how absurd,

compulsive, humiliating, enslaving, exhausting, unnecessary, useless, threatening, or suicidal it may seem—and it does seem all
those things at different stages. Without the driving determination, no one really has time to do this practice. No one would get
up and say "Well, I have nothing better to do with my life this
afternoon, so I guess I'll knock off a few hundred prostrations."
Like work, recreation, and love, you make time for it because you
need and want to. Perhaps during shamatha, perhaps through tonglen, or because of dharma classes, perhaps through riding my pale
horse, or through Trungpa's arduous and bizarre Vajrayana transmission, perhaps all of these together, a shift happened in me—I
had aroused the egoless passion for truth, and could not settle for
anything less. Duty, Eros, the Categorical Imperative, the inner
light, bodhicitta, whatever it was, had taken over my act. It was as
powerful and irresistible as the mystic's longing for God.

Ngondro instructors compare prostration to digging layers of
burned-on food out of a cooking pot that has probably never been
cleaned. What you want to do is recover the original nature of the
pot, but simple washing is not enough; too much crud is in there.
Before you can wash, you have to scrape. Prostration is also compared to cutting your own throat. It is the most direct attack on
pride that you could imagine, short of being commanded by the
guru to eat a handful of shit. Yet degrading the student is not the
point: the shrine, the icon, and the ritual of the practice all have
beauty and dignity. There is simply no role in this beauty and dignity for ego, other than to step onto the mat and commit ritual
suicide.

Prostrators report that they get angry and crazy during the practice, because it stirs up their neurosis. The angrier you get, the more
crud you are dislodging. A skeptic might wonder if the so-called
craziness is simply the healthy response of a sane, free mind to being
asked to commit suicide in the name of enlightenment. Regardless
of what emotional baggage we may be carrying around, the conflict between resistance, dishonored by the label "neurosis," and such
explicit surrender would be certain to stir up anger and rage.

Trungpa said to his ngondro students: "Why are you doing all these fucking prostrations? Do you think you're some kind of a slave?" He threw the ball right back to the student: decide for yourself what your anger means.

For the first 5,000 prostrations, I too, went crazy. I sang the liturgies like blues ballads, punctuating them with creative blasphemy, and parodied the whole enterprise by casting it as a cosmic prostate examination performed by tantric proctologists intent on rectifying my anomalies. One group of prostrators discussed, humorously I assume, hiring themselves out to perform proxy prostrations. You could sell surrender by the hour, or the number of rounds on the mala, and the economic activity would help the sangha support itself.

A sense of humor makes it possible to continue. After 15,000 or 20,000 prostrations, the first waves of craziness passed, and I settled into a routine. Always before practice I felt the familiar desire to put off an unpleasant chore. I lit the shrine, assembled my materials, and began sitting. Infinite space was there: the red cushions, the lavender carpet, the patches of sunlight, the blue sky, the hills in the distance, all floated without support from self; the self was the scene, or the scene was the self, it made no difference. Whether I looked for one or the other, I found the same things. A field of profound peace ensued, in which thoughts would appear, run their sequences, and die.

The guru who shows my mind as dharmakaya continually showers me with blessings. I cannot receive them unless I practice. It is difficult for any sentient being to find a free and well-favored practice situation. I have that. And I won't have it for long: the life of beings is like a bubble; death comes without warning, and this body will be a corpse. At that time the dharma will be my only help. I must practice now, while I have the chance. Because I continually create karma, I must abandon evil deeds and devote my time to virtuous actions. I must cut desire and attachment. The homes, friends, comforts, and wealth of samsara are like a feast before the executioner leads you to the block.

I and all sentient beings, limitless as space, take refuge in the very embodiment of the ten directions and the three times, who is the source of the 84,000 collections of dharmas and the king of all the noble sangha.... I take refuge in the glorious guru, the kind root guru, the yidams and devas of the mandala.... I take refuge in the Buddha, I take refuge in the holy dharma, I take refuge in the noble sangha, I take refuge in the assembly of dakas, dakinis, dharmapalas, and protectors who possess the eye of wisdom....

Flop. I'm being hoodwinked and buggered by a Tibetan cult leader. Flop. I take refuge in the guru, I take refuge in the Buddha, I take refuge in the dharma, I take refuge ... flop. I'm full of confusion and clinging, but what the hell, flop it down on the mat. Flop. I take refuge in the guru, I take refuge ... flop. So this is humiliating, but at least I've got enough sense to recognize genuine virtue and prostrate to it. Flop. Oh really? Thank you, gurus, that I'm not a sinner like everybody else, is that what this game is called? Flop. I take refuge in the guru, I take refuge in the Buddha, I take ... flop. I want my father's house. Flop. The guru is only the best in myself, so why not prostrate. Flop. So are you really prostrating to yourself then? Hail Rudra, Prince of Darkness. Flop. I take refuge in the ... flop. Let's see, 108,000 prostrations is the equivalent of crawling 1,000 yards if each bead on the mala gave you one-third of an inch of forward motion. I take refuge in the guru, etc. flop. What about those monks who do their ngondro ten times over, making a total of one million prostrations. Just flop it down, whatever it is, unwind this knotted skein. Flop. I could prostrate to anyone, even the worst ego-infected scourges of the earth, buddha-nature is present even in tyrants. I could honor it there as well as anywhere else. Flop. I take refuge. Am I doing this right? I can't see the image anymore. There it is. The lotus under Vajradhara is a calyx of rose and lavender flame.

His face was supposed to remind me of Trungpa, but it had a shifty tendency to slide into the faces of long forgotten acquaintances, relatives living and dead, or the Monty Python comedians. My father on my right, my mother on my left, my enemy behind, who for one year's worth of prostrations was an IRS tax auditor, all prostrating with me. The scene trails off into complete vagueness, and I have to settle for its main features. The tax auditor counts off mala beads as if figuring out my bill. My father prostrates grimly, as if following the instructions of a bad boss. My mother prostrates with the same combination of sardonic humor, curiosity, and willingness to try anything that she had when she was alive. She smiles at me from the side: "Is this how it's done, dear?" Then she farts and holds her hand over her mouth: "Oop! Gee, I hope that was just gas."

It is a very crowded landscape. Emotionally it is so crowded that there is nowhere left for me to hide, I have no privacy, nothing of my own. Here are my parents, here is my enemy, here are all my mothers from all the lifetimes I have ever lived, and there is the lineage, the buddhas, the dharma texts, the sangha, and the guru — and there, too, are the archetypes and projections of my mind. I am surrounded on all sides. And what am I doing? Why, giving in. Letting go. Giving birth, in a way, humble, naked, earth-bound, giving up the ghost of me. And setting an example for my family and my enemy to do the same, and wishing they would. Ignore them I cannot. I can love them, hate them, accuse them, defend myself against them, and my responses are there as yidams, *devas,* dakinis, and all the rest. Sometimes I felt crowded out of existence, I had no defenses anymore, I was just a big carpet of moss by the lake.

This was so crude and colorful, it was like wallowing in liquid candy canes. Everything glowed with unearthly light: the icons, the pewter glass covers, the pictures of Trungpa, the Sixteenth Karmapa, Khyentse Rinpoche, Kalachakra, Shakyamuni Buddha, the red and gold shrine cloths, the lavender walls, the clouds with their variegated shades, the mountain, the distant scenes mirroring one another in the windows, the red cushions deepening to rose, the brass gong catching the sun on its burnished sphere. And the plants in the room, silent green companions to this persistent and repetitious dismemberment of pride, as if they were waiting to be fed with the scraps. And always a few flies, buzzing the sky-light glass.

When I looked inside for myself, I found only this field of images. When I looked outside for the images, they had no names or divisions; their colors and forms were all creations of the mind's perceptual apparatus. Looking in, I saw the reflection of the world; looking out, I saw the reflection of mind. So it was all mirror. There was nothing being mirrored. The in and the out were the same thing.

Glimpses of *thamal gye shepa,* ordinary mind.

One taste. It was true.

"Prostrator's high," said Doubt.

I found it acceptable to prostrate to Vajradhara, who was an image of my innate clarity and wisdom, to the dharma, which is truth, to the ordained sangha, whom I scarcely ever saw, and to the lamas of the Kagyu lineage, most of whom were safely dead. But prostrating to Trungpa was quite another matter. He was a living person, and flattening myself before his throne 108,000 times gave him tremendous power over my life, more power than any Western culture has imagined since the days of Pope Innocent III. Prostration brought him right into my mind; it was putting my heart in his hand, taking off my clothes and saying "Here I am, do with me what you will."

You do the same thing every time you take a flight somewhere, Trungpa once said; you put your life into the hands of the pilot, and you have never even met that person. What you are trusting is not so much the pilot, as the system.

After his cremation, which happened around the time I had completed 55,000 prostrations, Trungpa was safely dead, too. But my perception had been altered to the point where I perceived his death as having been for my sake. He lived to teach dharma, and died when his work was done. In his great compassion for me, he had removed the obstacle of his physical existence.

Then I was sorry he was gone. Around eighty and ninety thousand prostrations, my gratitude toward him was truly overwhelming, and I lost my resistance to visualizing him on the guru's throne. He was everywhere else; why not there? I suffered a lot of agony during prostrations because I could never get enough air. I was angry at my chest for refusing to support my activity. One night I dreamed that Trungpa and I were in bed together. There was nothing sexual about it. The bed mat was the place where I prostrated, so it was like being on my practice site. He was naked, vulnerable, physically frail, crippled, paralyzed on one side of his body, and scarcely able to walk without help, much less prostrate. His chest was exposed. He smiled at me. My anger disappeared and I wept.

The night he died, a great storm swept over the whole northeast, and my electricity went out, stopping all my clocks at the moment of his death. The phenomenon of the stopped clock happened to other students. As far away as Oregon, a student had just finished moving out of an apartment, and went back in for a final look around. He noticed an electric clock on the floor, and unplugged it. Adjusted for the different time zones between Oregon and Nova Scotia, the clock was unplugged at the moment Trungpa's vital signs had ceased.

Carl Jung called these kinds of juxtapositions "synchronicities." They are too filled with meaning, too accurate a reflection of our minds, to be dismissed as coincidences. During my ngondro practice, such occurrences were commonplace. Perhaps they happen when we begin to live in a reality where the mind and its perceptual field are the same thing. The assumption of the individual observer looking out at a separate world has been torn down, making room for experiences that are not filtered through that assumption.

Everyone who stayed long enough at Trungpa's cremation saw the rainbows. The rainbow is a Buddhist symbol for emptiness, and the appearance of a rainbow at cremation is supposed to be the sign and seal of a great teacher. In the Buddhist view, all of reality is like a rainbow: insubstantial, nothing in itself apart from perception, yet "objective" in the sense that we can agree it is there, radiating and swallowing forms the way light splits into individual colors and recombines. And like a rainbow, all of reality is an emanation of the guru's mind.

The sky over Karme-Choling, Trungpa's first practice center in the United States, was thickly overcast on the morning of the cremation ceremony, but then turned bright blue around our hill when the lamas torched his body and conducted their rituals. Strangely, it continued to be overcast elsewhere. Many people had already left before the rainbows began, a little after lunch. I looked up and saw brilliant colored rings around the sun. I looked to the side and saw arches of color in the distance. Several conventional rainbows appeared one after the other. Then a cirrus cloud grew long bony fingers and went through a brilliant sequence of colors: gold, rose, turquoise, and pink. It was nowhere near sunset, and there were no polluting industries in the area. Reporters who saw this display implied that it was caused by chemicals thrown into the flames, but the rainbows were happening thousands of feet above the cremation site. Any chemicals from the relatively small fire that consumed Trungpa would have had to possess remarkable qualities indeed to cause such effects, no less marvelous than the nonmaterialist explanation that a dead, or transmogrified, guru, the tantric rituals, and the total dharmic environment could arrange the weather into a living symbol.

The Vajrayana students were not done yet with weather synchronicities. Those who attended the teachings, empowerments, and abhisekas given by Khyentse Rinpoche during that period will remember how the weather seemed to reinforce his rituals with dramatic symbolism. When he gave blessings, the rain would begin to pour down violently around the tent, and when he gave teachings, it would subside. Rain is a traditional image for the guru's blessing. "The guru continually rains down *amrita* of blessings," said my prostration liturgy, amrita being a holy drink that intoxicates ego.

I had very little doubt left when I finished my prostrations, on Guy Fawkes Day, almost six months later. The jester Doubt had prostrated along with all the other sentient beings, and it made him so weak he could hardly laugh. My resistance was almost destroyed; I had turned my bowl right side up, so the lamas say, and now further teachings could be poured into it. I was a flower open to the rain. Every good thing that had happened for me in the last five years I attributed directly to the compassion and generosity of the guru, who had given me this precious path. Rain dripped from the eaves of my house, and the full moon was obscured by clouds. I still knew hardly more about Trungpa or Tendzin personally than I had known when I started prostrating. My loyalty and trust for them was not based on any knowledge of their characters, it was inculcated by practice. The mantra that Khyentse had taught to bind us closer to the guru was reverberating all the time in my head. Devotion, up to that point, had won.

13

ORDINARY MIND: PURIFICATION

FTER PROSTRATIONS HAVE scraped and loosened the crud
from the inside of your cooking pot, mantra practice,
the second of the "hundred thousands," flushes it out.
Like the first ngondro, mantra is sandwiched within shamatha
and tonglen, but the envelope now includes prostrations. The mandala ngondro, similarly, will be contained in shamatha, tonglen,
prostrations, and mantra; Guru Yoga will be contained in shamatha,
tonglen, prostrations, mantra, and mandala; and finally, the Vajrayana tantras will include all the practices leading up to them, layer
upon layer. This telescoping structure reminded me of the "Twelve
Days of Christmas" song. Ngondro is a form of programmed instruction in a highly complicated system of mental, verbal, and
physical rituals, invented hundreds of years before any Westerner
came up with the concept of programmed learning.

Kalu Rinpoche wrote a clear exposition and rationale for the
different ngondros in *The Gem Ornament of Manifold Oral Instructions* (KDK Publications, 1986). His work explains that the purpose of mantra is to purify bad karma—*digpa* and *dripa,* in
Tibetan—what we would call the accumulated baggage of our
past, the leftover resentments, fears, hesitations, and hangups, the
habit of believing our projections. Vajrasattva mantra, I was told,
would break up and purify any tendency to solidify our kleshas into
concepts.

Where irritation might normally result in a thought such as "this person is a jerk," mantra practice works to interrupt that movement from emotion to concept, leaving the irritation as a direct, pure experience. If it does not solidify, it cannot leave a stain—that is, a *samskara,* an obscurity in the mind, a projection, a propensity to cause harm. Irritation without concept is wisdom and sensitivity: wisdom because it reflects suffering accurately, sensitivity because we can feel. Judgments attempt to close off the wound; they point the irritation outward toward an object, so that we can protect ourselves. But every action has an equal and opposite reaction. The judgments we send out come back to us, amplified. The usual ways of trying to get rid of irritation only fasten us more firmly into the painful routines of samsara. If no attempt is made to close it off, emotional woundedness becomes the basis of our compassion for the suffering of others. The mantra ngondro is a fast method for kicking the habit of projection.

Vajrasattva mantra practice begins with twenty minutes of shamatha, five minutes of tonglen, the prostration liturgy and imagery, a token number of prostrations, and homage to the lineage of gurus. Vajrasattva himself is the guru in the form of a peaceful deity who symbolizes the originally pure nature of mind. In form he is a boy about nine years old, seated in meditation posture directly over your head. Although his gender is male, his prepubescent age downplays masculinity; he also has feminine qualities. Kalu describes the details of the visualization in his *Gem Ornament.*

Vajrasattva is pinkish-white; he sits on a moon disc in a ring of lotus petals, wearing lapis lazuli earrings, rainbow-colored harem pants, a vest and a scarf; in his right hand he holds a *vajra*—a small brass object, symbolically decorated, each end bearing four curved

prongs evenly spaced around a central axis, so that one end mirrors the other. The vajra is the embodiment, not merely the symbol, of pure buddha-mind: its symmetry recalls the satori of looking within to see the mirror of the outer world, looking out to see the mirror of the inner world, and realizing that both vistas are reflections of each other, deriving from nothing that exists in between. The four curved prongs and the central axis are the enlightened forms of the five kleshas, which in their purified state are the five wisdoms. In his left hand, Vajrasattva holds the bell used in tantra to proclaim enlightened mind. Light rays brighten and radiate from his heart center, inviting all the wisdom buddhas of the three times and the ten directions to come and participate in the practice. They approach with the steady speed of a snowfall, until he is filled with light.

In his heart center is another moon disc, like a platter; around the edges, standing upright, are the Tibetan syllabary characters for the mantra "OM VAJRASATTVA." In the center is the letter "HUM," which in Tibetan is shaped like the number "3" with an extra ring, a teapot-spout on the bottom facing left, and a line and circle for a crown. As you repeat the invocation to Vajrasattva and recite the sacred hundred-syllable mantra, the letter HUM, which in the visualization is a living organism resembling a white fish standing on its tail, begins to exude drops of cleansing amrita, a thin white liquid very much like human mother's milk. It drips down, slowly fills the HUM, pours from the spout, fills Vajra-sattva, overflows his seat, and dribbles into your head through the crown. From the head it permeates your whole body, percolating down through chest, arms, legs, and abdomen, slowly turning brown and black from all the accumulated excreta and rotten blood of your sins and diseases. Then the amrita, like a cosmic enema, flushes out through your palms, anus, and the soles of your feet, sinking deep into the ground. Septic pumping trucks are not necessary—the ground is sunyata, emptiness.

Kalu's exposition in *The Gem Ornament of Manifold Oral Instructions* includes the text of the hundred-syllable mantra. It supplicates Vajrasattva to enter you completely and purify all your blockages, and it rejoices at the same time, like singing in the shower: "*hum ha ha ha ha ho.*" The mantra would not have the same effect in English unless it were rendered into poetry and perfumed by centuries of devotion. In Sanskrit, it is a thrilling, rhythmic, peace-giving incantation; "every syllable is completely blessed," said Khyentse, and has power to purify negative actions even if we don't understand it. As you recite the syllables, you have the sensation of tuning in to the radiant psychic field of all the monks, nuns, and bodhisattvas who have done this practice before you.

When practice is done, you repeat the short form of the mantra, "Om Vajrasattva Hum," 108 times, visualizing that you are completely filled with clean amrita and that it shines outward from your pores in every direction. During the concluding liturgy, Vajrasattva forgives you and everyone for all our misdeeds; then all outer phenomena melt into Vajrasattva, who melts into the mantra, and then dissolves into yourself. The session is finished off with tonglen, shamatha, and a dedication of the merit to the benefit of all beings.

A Tibetan letter, in this reality system, is not just a mark that stands for a human sound. It is a transcendent form of life, the very heart of pure, benevolent wisdom, the gift of universal compassion and generosity, a skillful method of bringing us into the experience of lost innocence and moving us toward buddhahood. It is like the source of the elixir given to Psyche by the god Mercury, but the source is, and always has been, inseparable from ourselves. Our own mind is the Big Mind, the dharmakaya of infinite space, our speech and letters are the Big Letter, the Logos, the sambhogakaya of communicative energy, and our bodies are the physical Buddha, the nirmanakaya of form, all merged, not into one, but into zero. The fact that we can visualize the letter in this way makes it true. There is no other truth to contradict it.

Could the same argument be made for the truth of a hallucination? Would it be valid, for example, to say that if you visualize
me as the snake in the Garden of Eden, your image is true, and if
you kill me, you are slaying a genuine embodiment of evil? The
Vajrayana visualizations are different in several important respects.
They are given by the guru, not invented and projected by me.
While they have no power unless I personally evoke them, my role
is to follow exactly the instructions of my master. Any craziness or
individuality I bring to the process is assigned a definite role, sub-
ordinated to the form that I did not devise. This fact in itself distinguishes my personal craziness from genuine tantra. Without the
guru, it is difficult to see how the two could be distinguished, and
so in this spiritual tradition devotion may be vital after all.

Another distinction between hallucination and tantric visualization is in how we relate to the images. A tantric image is understood to be the meeting place of the guru's mind and my mind,
emerging from emptiness and returning to emptiness at the end
of a practice session. I know from beginning to end that it has no
more objective reality than a rainbow. My tendency to believe in
anything has been unhinged and cut loose throughout; I am therefore somewhat protected from believing that a tantric deity is a
messenger from God who could order me to slay infidels. This is
the basic difference between theism and nontheism. Still, psy-
chotics doing tantra are at risk of precisely this sort of confusion,
and Buddhist masters usually tell them to stay away from it.

Since my lung impairment has been so much a center of awareness, and so important as a determiner of my actions, I could not
help but focus mantra practice on my lungs, hoping that the visualization would clean out my sarcoidosis and restore my ability to
breathe freely. In the long run, however, that hope is part of what
has to be flushed. There is nothing wrong with wanting good health,
but our desire for perfection signals also an unwillingness to learn
from negativity and the old struggle to reject death. I ended up
visualizing that I flushed the disease, the hope, the fear, and the
conflict, all at the same time. Perhaps this was the right course.

Whatever is happening, you bring it into the shower with you, bring it on in and get it clean.

After a few months, my whole attitude about being impaired relaxed, and there was physical improvement as well. The disease went into remission and stayed on a plateau, neither improving nor degenerating. My next chest X-ray four years later showed that it was clearing up. I will never regain the use of the scarred membranes, but I could still do a great deal with what I had left. No one could say with scientific certainty that the improvement was caused by the mantra; I also took prednisone and stayed away from smoke. But just as the ignorant grasping at pleasure creates a psychic environment that fosters illness, the mantra creates an environment that fosters health, whether or not it can magically banish a particular disease. It is significant that my need for prednisone was and remains minimal, and I have been able thus far to escape some of its worst side effects.

Always during the visualization, the amrita refused to enter the hard dark spot in the middle of my chest, but flowed around it instead, cleansing the edges and isolating it from the rest of my body. I concluded at last that perhaps the spot was meant to be there, and I should just leave it alone. As Mount Meru, it would be an anchor for future practices.

Many times while reciting the mantra I wept, and the fluids spilled out of my eyes and nose like an amrita overflow. The whole ngondro process is a constant affirmation that we really are fundamentally pure. That discovery in itself is enough to elicit tears. We are so caught up in the haunted specter of human evil, in our wars, mass murders, and machinations, and our power to obliterate ourselves with weapons and pollutants, that we forget our basic purity, we lose touch with it because we no longer have faith in it. So much of Christian puritanism teaches us instead that we are depraved from birth, that everything we have to enjoy was won by violent struggle and moral corruption, or that our destiny is eternal damnation unless saving grace can be injected into us by an external Supreme Power.

The cadences and the words to the song "Amazing Grace" are utterly tender and soft, revealing the weeping of the heart that longs for contact with the purity we have lost. Yet the first line ends with "a wretch like me," as if we are still condemned from the start, as if we could not both surrender to the open softness of recovery, and yet be courageous enough to drop our wretchedness and assert our beauty and strength. The visualization of Vajrasattva acknowledges the innate brilliance and clarity that we never lost. Buddha-mind is just our own original nature, shining through a nightmare.

I went on having feelings of aggression, jealousy, and greed; I fantasized about carrying a dagger in my shirt so I could plunge it into the heart of a polluting industrialist, I wanted to smother my father, I wanted to shout obscenities out my car window at drivers who violated my space, I wanted to rant and rage and rave. "How's my driving?" said the jester to Vajrasattva inside my head; "you see any problem, call 1-800-Eat Shit." Such impulsive, wild, irrational feelings of hostility and passion are extremely common symptoms of ngondro. You are dredging the bottom of a lake and you might find anything down there—broken bottles, tires, old fire extinguishers, rusty weapons, dead bodies wearing concrete shoes.

The practice is a regularly repeated counterforce to the dramas and confusions of discursive mind. The amrita breaks and sweeps away the timeline we create in order to maintain ourselves as a character acting out a plot. The commitment required to sustain this effort over months and years literally reshapes your life, just as surely as a flowing stream reshapes the landscape. The act of sitting in one place over and over reciting the mantra, no matter what else is going on—domestic conflict, job demands, wandering attention span, successes and failures—draws all other activities into the practice and then subordinates them to its influence. Habit is turned into ritual; the blind flow of internal dialogue is interrupted and flushed before it can freeze into opinion, and then turned into mantra; thought is turned into color.

Childhood memories emerge like beggars rescued from the gutter, newly bathed and combed and standing before the conscious mind in their youthful naked glory. You see the world sometimes as William Blake saw it, with children twining the white wool of lambs, and angels playing in the trees. Maybe this is why Vajrasattva is visualized as a child.

A practice session of 500 mantras took me about three hours. At the end of the second hour I would get extremely restless, but the energy of my restlessness increased the speed of the mantra and the force behind the expulsion of the amrita. The discomfort of resistance now added depth and power to the whole experience. At the end, I noticed more and more fully the constant rollover of consciousness and phenomena, as if my entire existence were a mass of mud revolving in a mixer, with conduits leading to and from the similarly churning world. Not only did the mud constantly change from top to bottom, but the content itself never stayed the same. There is absolutely nothing that is not rolling over like this, even my fascination with the liquid qualities of mind. My surrender to it, my letting go, was part of the shift. I knew that it must be like this to die. My life was like the burning fragments of a fireworks explosion falling away from the center in the pattern of a star, until they burn out and the star disappears. But the rollover itself never stops; containing the star of the fireworks explosion is a celestial star, doing the same thing on a different time scale. And containing that is a galaxy, and containing that....

Somehow consciousness is liberated in the rollover process, just as heat and light are released from an explosion, and my body is a momentary form for that consciousness within the larger pattern sequence of karma. The question of obstacles to enlightenment became almost irrelevant, because the obstacles themselves are fragments in the heat, they are in there rolling over with everything else. Yet they are experientially real enough—we really do get stuck on ourselves, and develop lines of habit that are limiting, painful, and unnecessary. Nevertheless "I" am nowhere, turning in the cosmic sandmixer, and what is this intelligence riding and shining as the sand turns over and over, what are the little facets of light?

"You will feel good if you share the big mind and vast space and brilliantness of it," said Trungpa, "you'll have a great time, you'll have a fantastic time ... high class and good, good quality." My little mind was busy trying to understand the whole thing, and instead I was exploding. I was sitting in the middle of a fireball trying to take notes.

Late in November of 1987, I met Osel Tendzin at a Vajrayana dharma program, a year before the fireball of his disgrace landed on the Buddhist world. I positioned myself in front of his throne so that he would see me when I put up my hand.

"You, *arhat*, great bearded one," he addressed me; "isn't your hair grayer since the last time I saw you?"

"Indeed, Sir, it is."

"What is your question?"

"You said that pleasure and pain are one."

"I said that, yes."

"But surely you could not have meant that there is no difference between an orgasm and a headache. Were you referring to the experience of the difference?"

"Go further."

"Every time you speak I hear echoes of that difference."

"Am I giving you a headache?"

"It might be the other. . . ."

"Well I didn't want to ask!"

". . . but I'm not sure."

"That's it, right there: they are the same thing."

I told him about the rollover, the burning, the exploding star. "What is that?"

"Ordinary mind," he said, *"thamal gye shepa."*

"Sometimes the intensity is so bright I want to put up my hands to shield my face; and then I see myself from all directions at once, putting up my hands."

"Ahhh, getting into the Vajra world, are you?"

"What is that seeing from all directions?"

"*Mahasukha*. Great joy. The next time you put up your hands, dance. Whirl. Chant. But keep your samaya."

"This is samaya, right now."

"It couldn't be anything else. It's thick, like pea soup."

"For me there is more color in it."

"What would you say?"

"Cosmic marmalade."

"What color?" he asked.

"All colors."

"Oh yes. Cosmic. But thick."

Someone asked a question about how to work on their practice. He said "That is a Mahayana concept. We're not playing games here, this is Vajrayana. If you want to work on your practice, you had best do garbage duty in the streets of Calcutta. That is how you work on your practice; let's be real." Tendzin said that in the Mahayana, we have seats on the plane, called paramitas, but in the Vajrayana we discover that we are the pilot. If we chicken out, the plane will crash, and that is Vajra hell.

The condescending ruthlessness of his remark about garbage duty was a warning signal, among many others, but this time I was not the butt of his condescension, and it did not bother me. Tendzin had accepted me as a member of his world. The devotion built up by my ngondro flowed uncritically toward him. A vision of cosmic marmalade, apparently, had greater value in that world than all of Mother Teresa's work on behalf of the poor.

After his talk was over, I started walking toward my car and met him on the way, our second accidental encounter. He was surrounded by his retinue of attendants, who moved into position to shield him from me. I hung back so as not to intrude on his exit procession. He saw me and opened his arms. I came toward him and he put his arms around me, and we hugged for a long minute, weeping, squeezing and patting each other like brothers who had been separated for hundreds of years.

"Goodbye for now," he said, squeezing my hands. "We will meet again." He smelled of alcohol.

As he left, I kept shivering for several minutes. I was flattered, inflated, overjoyed that the wall surrounding him had given way for me twice, and I was charged with electricity. It was love, too. It was like being in love all the time, not with him especially, but with everything. A door had opened. Without knowing why, I began remembering in detail our conversation about AIDS in the airport bar, and I knew there is no love without death. Love and death are the two mirrors, reflecting each other to infinity.

At Seminary, Trungpa said "Loneliness is like playing your guitar beside a waterfall." I was astounded at the literal accuracy of his image. I used to hide in my room alone at Seminary sometimes, playing my guitar for company, and in the background was the sound of water from the bathroom faucet, left open so the pipes would not freeze. The music was my dharma practice, and the water was the level of my devotion at that point, trickling just enough to keep from freezing in the pipes. Over the years of ngondro practice, the faucet opened more and more, letting flow an unstoppable deluge with rainbows and white foam, obstacles emanating from it like mist. The deluge was the continuous motion of all experience.

14

BLESSINGS: THE SACRED MANDALA

A SINGLE SESSION of the mandala ngondro takes over an hour to prepare. When I was ready to begin, I pulled a wide straw basket in front of me that contained about ten cups of uncooked saffron-colored rice, a few herkimer diamonds, precious coins, and a brass plate about seven inches in diameter. After purifying the plate with a ritual hand gesture accompanied by recitation of the Vajrasattva mantra, I slowly and dreamily recited a page and a half of mandala liturgy while arranging handfuls of rice on the plate to symbolize what the text described. The ritual draws the universe as a sacred mandala, including myself and all I possess or ever will possess, imagined as a buddha realm of wealth and delight. The pure ground is the golden earth, evoked by pouring out a carpet of rice onto the plate. The circumference is bounded by a Vajra wall, created by dribbling rice around the edge, like the jasper of the New Jerusalem.

In the center is Mount Meru, the support of the universe. Around the sides are four mountains and continents representing the physical and mental cosmos in ancient Indian mythology. The enlightened kingdom they contain includes a mountain of precious jewels, a grove of wish-fulfilling trees, the wish-fulfilling cows, the grain that needs no toil, the universal monarch with the precious wheel, the wish-fulfilling gem, the precious consort, the precious minister, the precious horse, the precious elephant, the great vase filled with treasures, the goddess of gaiety and laughter, the goddess of flower garlands, the goddess of song, the goddess of dance, the goddess of incense, the goddess of lamps, the goddess of perfumed water, the sun and the moon, the white umbrella, the victory banner unfurled, all the plentiful wealth of gods and men, millions upon millions of countless treasures in as many universes as there are atoms, all this I offer to the gurus, buddhas, bodhisattvas, yidams, dakas, dakinis, and dharmapalas, please accept my offering with kindness for the benefit of all beings, having accepted it please grant your blessings. The poem went on for several stanzas. Reciting it was like sweeping the strings of a celestial harp.

The assembly of gurus, buddhas, and the rest are all visualized in the clouds adorned by rainbows. The brilliance of the shrine almost hurt my eyes. The lineage holders whose pictures decorate the wall, Trungpa, the Sixteenth Karmapa, Khyentse, Kalu, Tendzin, and the icon of Vajradhara, seemed actually present as receivers of this gift.

Then, having done the long form of the offering once, I swept the rice into the basket and began the short form used to rack up the 100,000 repetitions: "The earth is perfumed with scented water and strewn with flowers, adorned with Mount Meru, the four continents, the sun and the moon; imagining this as the buddha realm I offer it so that all beings may enjoy that pure realm." Trying to maintain the visualization of the lineage tree in the clouds, I took a handful of rice in my right hand, laid out Mount Meru in the center and four piles in each of the four directions, the sun and moon in the upper left and lower right corners respectively, swept the mandala into the basket and counted off a bead on the mala held in my left hand.

Eventually I could do this quite fast, 108 mandalas in five minutes. The hand motion falls into a certain rhythm: ding, ding, ding, ding, ding, ding, ding, swish. The rice rattles softly on the plate; now and then one of the herkimer diamonds, or a coin, makes a loud clank. I did most of this ngondro during a three-week retreat, going from 9:30 in the morning to 6:30 in the evening every day, with a break for lunch. Hour after hour, the liturgy repeated itself in my head and the rice splashed across the plate and was swept back into the basket. By 6:30 I had reached about sixty rounds. My back ached, my right forearm ached, my left hand was tired, my mind was screaming with boredom, my brain was dizzy and drunk. But my senses were sharp and my heart was happy and free.

Sometimes the motion was like factory work. Years ago, when my job consisted of inserting 5,000 sheets of metal into a press machine, one piece at a time, stamping each with a set of holes, and placing them on a skid, I would fall into a rhythm: lift, push, stamp, click, slap; lift, push, stamp, click, slap. Hour after hour, checking my watch to measure how long before the next coffee break. I would pause to wipe the sweat off my forehead, and move around to ease the ache in my shoulder.

Before and after my retreat, I was going through the difficult, heart-ravaging process of getting my father into a nursing home. He was incontinent every day. He got up in the middle of the night and went for walks in the nude. He collected sticks and piled them on his porch. He attempted to cut down the neighborhood trees with a handsaw. He gathered other people's shoes and hid them in a suitcase. He left the stove on. He ate catfood occasionally, when he would eat anything; usually he had to be fed. I was trying to finesse the situation so that my brothers and I would get to keep his house as our inheritance, in a country that has no government system of care for the elderly, and nursing home care costs exceed $2,500 a month, when you can even find a placement in one. While I plotted and schemed to hang onto my share of his house, in my practice I was giving it all away for the benefit of sentient beings. The two ideas coexisted comfortably in my purified brain.

The mandala ngondro sends a message to the unconscious over and over: "Let it go. Let it go. Give it away. Let it go." The practice builds a pattern of opening the hand and giving at the level of preschool child's mind—the level reached by handling a physical substance like rice, pretending it is mountains, gold, jewels, sun, moon, and stars, in a setup very much like a sandbox. I giggled often, remembering when I was two or three years old, unloading sand from a toy truck.

The differences between mandala practice and childhood play are even more important, for these differences reach another level of mind. This level requires the freshness of a young child combined with the splendor of an angel—a clean and colorful shrine, plants and flowers, sunlight and open air, sparkling glasses of fresh water, incense, and mirrors; the limitless imagination of giving, the patience and discipline to bring momentary impulses under the direction of dharmic form. The assumptions of the mandala ngondro are magnificent: that myriads of universes *can* be given away presupposes infinite regality and wealth. That I myself am the gift is conveyed by the structure of the mandala itself: Mount Meru is my spine, my axis, my material nature, that which connects heaven and earth; the four continents of the four directions are my four limbs, the sun and moon are my yin and yang, my masculine and feminine energies, the perfumed water and flowers are my inherent purity, fragility, and beauty, the goddesses are my creative powers, the white umbrella and the victory banner are my wakefulness, the king, consort, and minister are my powers of intelligence. Turned inward and held, it is egocentric megalomania; turned outward and given away to the buddha-mind of infinite rainbows, it is a microcosm of all sacredness, Dante's rings of paradise multiplied exponentially by Buddhist cosmology and modern astrophysics. I had prepared for this moment since the beginning of my first few minutes in shamatha, when I rode outward on my breath and dissolved.

Like a child, sitting in an imaginary land of gold and jewels tossed before the feet of elven kings and queens and all the heavenly host. In the morning the sun shone through the east dormer windows. By noon a patch of light from the sky window appeared on the wall and crept across the rug behind me, toward my seat. After lunch, the light patch had moved directly in front of me, shining on the rice basket, turning the brass mandala plate to bright gold. It was summer. Near 4:30 I started humming softly while throwing the rice. I heard the soft undertone of the hum, the rice splashing rhythmically on the plate, the birds outdoors, a dog barking in the distance, a truck passing up the hill. Then all was silent, except for the window fan, the rice, the soft hum.

By six o'clock I stopped for the closing stages of tonglen and shamatha. The mighty rainbow panoply of elven kings and queens vanished slowly into the blue sky. The patch of light had reached the shrine. It crept up the front wall. Just as I was dedicating the merit to the liberation of all beings, the light moved onto the Karmapa's face. I stared into his shining eyes and broke out in gooseflesh, opening even further, infused with color and joy. It felt like entering a vast cathedral with high stained-glass windows and whispered voices, a sense of complete, wonderful, inexplicable awe; but the cathedral was my own room, my heart, my mind, my world, and the ceiling was the sky. The noise of the fan was like distant rolling thunder, echoing down ten dimensions and returning on itself.

The yard is a heaven of flowers and shrubs.

I have given away the yard.

My practice continued on into the fall. In late September, a Tibetan Gelugpa lama stayed in my home for two days as my guest. He was newly arrived from Nepal to assume directorship of a Buddhist center in the United States and did not speak English very well. My conversations with him took place mostly through his Nepalese interpreter, a young monk.

The interpreter had dark eyes, a shaved head, and a bright smile, with very white teeth. The lama was a cockeyed man in his fifties, wearing a maroon robe over a yellow sleeveless vest that exposed one bare arm, in Tibetan monastic style. He laughed a lot and could only look at you with one eye at a time. He shook my hand and grinned.

I showed him the dharma room where he would stay, the best room I had. Everything was vacuumed, dusted, washed. The plants on the slate terrace surrounded by windows, a woven green and purple filigree of broad leaf and spear leaf, the mirrors on the back walls reflecting the shrine, the roof window letting in the sky, the side windows overlooking the fall-colored, forested hill, the rose lavender carpet, all were as ready as I could make them. If I had been able to offer him a mansion like the one I helped clean for Trungpa and Tendzin, I would have been overjoyed to do so. I would have called on the members of my local meditation group to help me prepare it for him.

He asked me in Tibetan if I practice a lot. The interpreter translated. I said fifteen hours a week, but I had just finished a three-week retreat of eight hours a day. The lama said "Ohhhh, ohhhhh," nodding and laughing warmly. He said my dharma room was a good place for practice. I said yes, and that I had built it myself: I had cut open the roof, installed the sky window, constructed the dormer and paneled the sides with glass, laid the slate floor, put in the mirrors and the carpet, everything. I said in the morning the hills are reflected in the mirrors, and when I practiced, the blessings of the Karmapa poured into the room through the sky window like rays from the sun.

"Ohhhh," he said, "ohhhh, blessings," and laughed that same rich laugh, grinning widely.

He asked what teachings I had learned. I said my teacher, Trungpa Rinpoche, taught that teaching and practice go together: practice without teaching had no direction, and teaching without practice was too intellectual. He said "Ohhhh," again, "ohhhh," chuckling, and squeezed my hand from across the table. He said I was very fortunate: I was rich and had attained favorable circumstances for practicing the dharma, and I had met a great teacher in this lifetime. Trungpa was a great teacher, he said, and I was lucky, very lucky, that I had encountered him.

The lama asked about the local meditation group that I taught, which he had come to address. I told him who the members were and what we had studied. He said I was using my time to benefit others and therefore had not wasted my precious human birth. I said I was grateful to him, to Trungpa, and to the other Tibetan lamas for bringing the dharma to my country. I thanked him for his willingness to teach us.

When we ate dinner, I was embarrassed because I did not know whether to say my Buddhist meal chants in English or let him say his chants in Tibetan. He was embarrassed too. I felt awkward and shy, conscious that I was not enlightened and that he must know my secret. Finally I deferred to him as the master and he said his Tibetan chants. Then I realized that he felt awkward and shy because he was not sure whether to eat the fruit I had given him with his hands or with a knife and fork. He was waiting for me to begin so that he would know what to do, and I was waiting for him to begin because he was the lama. I picked up the fruit with my fingers, and we all laughed.

When he addressed the local dharma group in Tibetan, he wore a yellow cape. His words were translated by the interpreter. Half the crowd of forty left before he finished, and I felt that it was my fault. The other half basked in his warmth. We discussed emptiness and compassion. I confessed to him that I kill noxious insects in my house, but I always pray before squashing them that they will be reborn as humans in a land where dharma is taught, meet a great teacher, and become enlightened; so was I harming or benefiting them? He shook his head vigorously and wagged his finger at me, even before my English words had been rendered into Tibetan for him, and the group laughed. He said I was benefiting and harming them at the same time. He added that I must not kill the insects, but must find another way. He continued to smile at me.

At the end of the evening, my fellow dharma group coordinator took his picture. When the film was developed, the photo showed a rainbow in the middle of his body, with his smiling face surmounting the colors. In the picture he looked as if he were slowly turning into a rainbow. Nobody knew yet that he had cancer of the stomach, and would soon die.

The next day I took him and the interpreter out to the Buddha circle in my yard.

Before I knew anything about mandala practice, I had constructed a circular rock garden, flanked by four shrubs and five flower beds, with miscellaneous stones, flowers, and patches of moss rising from the gravel, and a huge boulder of schist in the center, surrounded by ferns and green elephant-ear leaves with white blossoms. Later, when I studied the mandala ngondro, I saw with amazement and shock that my garden was a detailed replica of that mandala: the gravel was the powerful Vajra ground, the flower beds were the Vajra wall, the rock in the center was Mount Meru, the shrubs were the four surrounding mountains with their continents, the elephant-ear plant was the precious elephant, the white blossoms were the white umbrella, the ferns and violets were the goddesses, the standing stones were the various inhabitants. I had done all this unconsciously, as if following the map from my practice instruction sheet, a full year before receiving it.

I asked the lama to pose on the center rock for a picture. He did, grinning like a boy. Then he gave the camera to his interpreter and drew me toward him for another shot, clasping my hands so that I would be included with him in the center.

Before leaving, he gave me a white scarf, a picture of the Dalai Lama, and two packets of pills for my health that had been specially blessed. I gave him a teaching gift of a hundred dollars for his center and felt vaguely ashamed. "Blessings," he chuckled, imitating with his hand the motion of sunlight pouring through my sky window onto the shrine. "Blessings."

The lama could not have known that when my drug-addicted younger brother Brian would borrow my long-suffering mother's last ten dollars, he would always say to her, "Blessings, Ma, blessings," imitating his born-again Christian minister. Brian was killed at the age of twenty-eight in a drunk-driving auto accident. My mother kept a picture of him in army uniform on the mantle. He was a smiling rogue. Every year on the anniversary of his death, she sent a check to the drug rehabilitation center that had helped him, writing one word on the memo line: "Blessings."

When the lama had left, I went back into my dharma room.

The whole atmosphere was awake and crisp. Walking into it brought on a pleasant shiver, like entering an air-conditioned temple from a humid street. He must have blessed it.

The day after his visit was Sunday, the day of the full moon. I made 5,000 mandalas on my gold plate, giving away everything, even my underpants. I finished the 100,000 mandalas that day.

I went outside and contemplated my rock garden mandala. On the day before I finished my ngondro, a lama had sat on my rock, pulling me in with him, and blessed my practice room. The sun went down behind the ridge. A rainbow appeared in the clouds. A hand of cloud formed overhead, like the beckoning cloud hand at my guru's cremation. Another cloud took the shape of a winged garuda, flying fast before the wind. White bones appeared in the wrist of the skeletal cloud hand. I looked for the Shambhala snow lion and saw that too, the paws, the swirling mane. The dragon hid behind the rainbow, showing only the fire of his breath.

The woman who shared my house came home and walked toward me slowly, grinning like a little girl making an offering of peace. We had been fighting a lot and would split up within a year. Her hair was the color of autumn leaves. She said she was Mother Nature. I said "How do you do, Mother Nature, I'm Father Time." She smiled, lifting her eyebrows, and presented me with the huge ripe yellow face of a sunflower, embedded with seeds, like grains of rice. It was another perfect replica of a mandala plate. It was like the eye of a honeybee. She knew nothing about mandalas, and less about my practice, and did not know I had finished ngondro that day. When I saw the sunflower, I knew that the dakinis had returned my gift to them, like the student and the lama ritually exchanging a white scarf. My eyes filled with tears and I laughed. Tendzin's words flashed briefly: "They are the same thing."

She spun around like a clown and pulled a pink balloon out of her pocket, blew it up, and tied off the end.

"The life of sentient beings is like a bubble," said my liturgy. "Death comes without warning; this body will be a corpse."

We hit the balloon back and forth across the deck. It was a bubble. It was our life, and the life of sentient beings. Over the planet Mars, the full moon rose in the east.

15

THE GURU IS THE BUDDHA

THE GURU WAS a skeleton seated in flames. Pale blue light surrounded his arms. The skull wore a bonnet of orange and purple fire, adorned with the sun and moon. White bodhicitta rose up the spine like smoke. The eye of wisdom stared from his forehead like a jewel. The power of speech was a blue jewel in the bones of his throat. The orange flames that surrounded him faded infinitely away to darkness, lit by strange bright writhings over a forest of dark tongues.

When I raised my eyes to the hills of October, I was burning in the miles of orange, yellow, red, and purple trees. I walked slowly to the secret garden by the stone wall. A gray-haired aging man, I sat and chanted my offering in the richly colored ivy, in the brilliant saxifrage, in the long marsh grass, in the cattails, in the reeds spangled by blue stars and white lace, in the dried withering greens and browns of autumn. All this as countless as the atoms in oceans of galaxies, I set out before you and offer you, assemblies of gurus, buddhas, geniis, invisible spirits of the rocks and trees, the mountains and the mist, you who display your colors like wind in a peacock's tail; and you, you torrents of cloud pouring steadily across the sky. You oceans of flower petals, you countless millions of pentangles, stars of David, arches, pillars, snowflakes and colored dots. You spider webs and spider fascia, you insect eyes, you fly wings, you hairs on the body of a bee.

Om, O sovereign, you are the nature of all. Nondwelling, free from coming and going, like space, you are beyond any mark of arriving and departing, yet like the moon in water you manifest wherever thought of. Shri Heruka, subjugator of the hordes of mara, gurus, yidams, dakinis with your retinues, I supplicate you now with faith. Grant your blessings so that I may realize this illusory body as nirmanakaya. Grant your blessings so that I may realize the life force as sambhogakaya. Grant your blessings so that I may realize my mind as dharmakaya. Grant your blessings so that I may realize the indivisibility of the three kayas.

The Guru Yoga liturgy I chanted was six pages long, single spaced. Most of it was a succession of four-line stanzas, invocations to every lineage guru from Vajradhara to Trungpa: Nagarjuna, who saw the meaning of *dharmata*, glorious Savari who attained *mahamudra*, glorious Karmapa who tamed the untamable ... after each name there was a "who" clause specifying in verse the accomplishment of that figure, and the fourth line of each stanza ended with "I supplicate you, grant me coemergent wisdom." The names and the rhythms of the clauses piled up like clouds, sounding always the same refrain: "I supplicate you, grant me coemergent wisdom." It is all done with hands in anjali. There are twenty-seven repetitions of "I supplicate you, grant me coemergent wisdom." I memorized the entire liturgy. I could sit in the garden and say it without paper in my hand. The text is a full course of instruction as well as a poem, preceded by over an hour of all the practices I had learned up to that point.

After the liturgy comes the mantra, a simple Tibetan phrase meaning "Karmapa enter me." This is said one million times. The repetitions are counted on a mala with side beads to keep track of whole rounds.

Never in my life had I known what it was like to merge so single-mindedly into a powerful mental river that flowed always and irresistably in the same direction. My small thoughts bobbed along on the current like twigs. The presence of Trungpa became so palpable that he turned into furious wind and rain beating on the dormers, spread through the clouds in sunset colors, gleamed softly down on the lawn at night, and gathered in the valley with the early morning fog. He was in the faces of the shoppers I saw at the supermarket, in the child's whining and the mother's irritated scold.

Kalu explains in *Gem Ornament* that in Guru Yoga, the guru is the embodiment of the three kayas. His body is the sangha, his speech is the utterance of the dakas, dakinis, and dharmapalas, his mind is intelligent infinity. He is also the fourth kaya of supreme bliss, the union of the first three. The entire phenomenal world is the display of the guru's compassion, emanating from the emptiness of mind.

Khyentse taught that each of us is composed of four mandalas, corresponding to the three kayas, plus a fourth, which is the unity of the three: the outer mandala, the inner, the secret, and the most secret. The guru appears in each mandala in different forms. In the outer mandala, the guru is the lama, the visible human being wearing robes who sits before you on the throne and gives teachings. In the inner mandala, he is the yidam, the personified form of enlightened energy depicted as a deity and evoked in the Vajrayana practices. In the secret mandala, he is the dakini, the feminine creative powers of mind who are always depicted in Tibetan iconography as companions and consorts of the guru. In the most secret mandala, the guru is the intelligence and compassion of your inherently enlightened nature. Guru Yoga is performed to open ourselves completely to the experience of *adisthana,* the blessing of the guru pouring into us from every direction at once.

Carl Jung commented that he did not think Westerners should practice Tibetan dharma because it would undermine their identity as Westerners. He was entirely correct, if we substitute the word "ego" for Western identity. Guru Yoga highlights in bright red the cultural barriers that a Westerner might face in making a complete transfer of consciousness to a tantric Buddhist reality. The guru is the mythic embodiment of community life, like the old Pharoahs of Egypt, or the Emperors of ancient China and Japan. He is the source of all morality, and is therefore not limited by moral law. The view of emptiness, perhaps, distinguishes the figure of the Buddhist guru from the god-emperors of the ancient world, but the practical consequence of who obeys whom results in a similar political relationship.

If we transpose Buddhist terms into the language of Catholic theology, the guru is nothing less than the Holy Trinity. His body is the Christ, which is also the church. His speech is the Holy Spirit, which is mystically the communicative and healing energies of God. His mind is the nondwelling, immanent and transcendent, everlasting Father—like a sphere, said the medieval Christian philosophers, whose center is everywhere and whose circumference is nowhere.

In the orthodox Christian system, however, the Holy Trinity is, and must forever remain, absolutely transcendent of the human being: in heaven we may enjoy the presence of God, but we are not, and can never be, God. In the Vajrayana Buddhist system, the guru is the three kayas, my teacher, the entire lineage of my teacher's teachers, the Buddha, my experience, and myself. Through Guru Yoga, my body, speech, and mind become the three vajras, or indestructible magic wands, of the guru. My mind is the guru's mind, and my body and speech do the guru's will.

Unlike the Christian concept of God, the guru does not create the universe; the guru *is* the universe, and the emptiness from which it emanates. The guru is Godhead, perhaps, God without the concept of God. To us, God is God, if we have been brought up to use such an idea; but to Itself, God is nothing, or nothing we can imagine. The primal nothing, the dharmakaya, is the guru's mind.

Guru Yoga equips the Buddhist to understand Christian and Platonic mysticism—and to perceive whether a mystic is speaking from personal knowledge. Meister Eckhart, the fourteenth-century Dominican monk from Germany who was accused of heresy by the Roman Church, now made perfect sense to me. One could transpose his Christian terms into a dharmic vocabulary and find in his sermons descriptions of Ordinary Mind, Sacred World, the idea of mandala, mahasukha, the unity of the kayas and their inseparability from experience, and the dakini principle—the manifestation of deity as a living creative presence in the playful joy of the here and now.

I understood Dante Alighieri in a new way as well. His Beatrice is the dakini, the feminine spirit of dharma; his Virgil is the lama. The Inferno is the world of ego, and the Purgatory is ngondro, which, in Dante as well as in the Vajrayana, begins with prostration to overcome pride and ends with the recovery of lost innocence. Dante's entire universe is a structure of interlocking mandalas. At the end of his Purgatory, Virgil, his lama, performs an abhiseka ceremony for him, and Beatrice, the dakini, takes over as his guide.

Near the end of his Paradise, Dante is allowed a great contemplative vision by the intercessary prayers of Saint Bernard to the Virgin. Saint Bernard's sincere and powerful devotion is what makes the vision possible. The whole universe is drawn out as a vast mandala in the shape of a rose, in which all the saints and saved souls are ranked in hierarchies and have equal sight of the glory of God. Masculine and feminine principles are balanced carefully on opposite sides of the circle. In a similar way, before starting a session of Vajrayana practice, the mandala must be drawn, and prayers uttered to invoke the presence of the yidam. The tantric Buddhist universe is a sacred mandala of buddhas and bodhisattvas, who in this analogy would correspond to the saints in the Christian paradise. Dante's devotion is a highway to the experience of "the love that moves the stars," and devotion has exactly this importance in Guru Yoga.

To a Buddhist, however, Dante's universe feels much too small to contain the vastness of Big Mind, limited as he was to the Ptolemaic scheme of the cosmos and the Biblical timeframe of creation. His God is placed outside the revolving spheres of the planets and stars, an Aristotelian Prime Mover contained somehow within a three-ring love circus.

Long before I had finished Guru Yoga, everything came alive; the whole of existence was a collective mind, giving rise to beings and events the way individual minds give rise to thoughts. Trees had spirits; I could feel and speak with them. I met a counterpart of my prostration tree by the edge of a lake, a venerable oak standing like a druid magician at the height of his powers, wearing his green cape of spells, arms raised, waiting to greet the bolt of lightning that would release him from his body and turn him into a god. I saw the aura of the tree shimmering around its branches, and the roots drawing water from the lake. When the leaves were seething in the wind, it was like hearing a creature from Tolkien. I prostrated to the tree and was answered by the voice of a loon.

When I read Homer again after many years, I realized with amazement that my awareness, my way of seeing, were now very similar to his: everything in the world was alive—clouds, streams, waves, mountains, rocks, islands, trees, were living presences that speak and interact with us. Just as the forest behind my home was quite literally an extension of our collective unconscious, and could be read like the lines in my hand for clues to the patterns of meaning in my life, so the heroes in the Homeric poems could read the flights of birds, the movements of seals and the patterns of weather. Intelligence and awareness were everywhere, generalized throughout the environment and localized in specific places and beings.

The three yanas of Tibetan dharma now appeared to me as a single unity. They are a map of how to enter the mind of the guru—or how to recover a sacred ground which has been raped by some polluting industry, where concepts flock, settle, and strut about like seagulls picking over a dump. The first yana boycotts the products of the ego mining and construction company; the second reduces them to their original materials, or refunds them to the manufacturer. The ngondros go right onto the plant site and break up the process by which the precious wealth of the earth is converted into avalanches of cheap trash. Blind habit is turned into conscious ritual; discursive mental gossip is turned into mantra; ignorance is turned into wakeful stillness. Guru Yoga returns the site to the owner. The Vajrayana sadhanas are the sacred ceremonies conducted on the purified ground.

It was clear to me why the guru is essential to Vajrayana. Suppose in order to dispense with the danger of surrendering to the guru, I had learned these practices from books, or from renegade students, and proceeded to do them on my own, without connection to the guru's mandala. Inevitably, I would pervert the rituals into some sort of obscurantist fantasy or personal magic. Surrender of self is the gateway. It is what makes the rest of the practices effective. They cannot work unless the guru gives his authorization, empowerment, and blessing, because otherwise I could never get beyond the limited perspective of myself doing the practice.

I was halfway through Guru Yoga when the news broke about Osel Tendzin infecting an unknowing student with AIDS. Tendzin offered to explain his behavior at a meeting which I attended. Like all of his talks, this was considered a teaching of dharma, and donations were solicited and expected. So I paid him $35.00 to hear his explanation. In response to close questioning by students, he first swore us to secrecy (family secrets again), and then said that Trungpa had requested him to be tested for HIV in the early 1980s and told him to keep quiet about the positive result. Tendzin had asked Trungpa what he should do if students wanted to have sex with him, and Trungpa's reply was that as long as he did his Vajrayana purification practices, it did not matter, because they would not get the disease. Tendzin's answer, in short, was that he had obeyed the instructions of his guru. He said we must not get trapped in the dualism of good and evil, there has never been any stain, our anger is the compassion of the guru, and we must purify all obstacles that prevent us from seeing the world as a sacred mandala of buddhas and bodhisattvas.

I felt no antipathy toward him, perhaps because ngondro had hollowed out and collapsed my resistance from the inside. This is the logical continuance of the suspension of judgment in shamatha and the inability to set limits on the teacher. For years we had been conditioned to obey the whims of both Trungpa and Tendzin, taking them all as instruction. We would willingly dress up in semiformal attire and wait until two in the morning for a talk by the master which never came; and when it was announced that he had cancelled the talk, we would laugh at his deliberate toying with our expectations, assuming that he meant to loosen us up and connect us more thoroughly with the present moment. Only the previous month, I had seen new students who were waiting for Tendzin to give them refuge vows put off hour by hour, shepherded from place to place by staff members, and kept up half the night only to be told that the vows had been postponed until the next day. A student doing ngondro may accept whatever the teacher does with equanimity, detachment, and humor for virtually the same reasons that someone who is drunk or stoned all the time stops caring about pain. When everything is a show anyway, no more real than a rainbow, there is no cause for alarm.

Tendzin's account of his conversations with Trungpa was challenged by other senior disciples, who claimed that Trungpa would never have said such things, and would never have led anyone to believe that the laws of nature could be suspended by practice. It was a difficult dilemma: if you chose to believe Tendzin, then Trungpa had been simply wrong in telling him he could not transmit the disease, and the consequence of his error would be the loss of human life. But what then became of the axiom that the guru cannot make a mistake? Understandably, Trungpa's closest students found it easier to conclude that Tendzin was lying. But if you chose to disbelieve Tendzin, then Trungpa may have been wrong in allowing him to remain as Regent, or perhaps in choosing him at all. If you wanted to retain your belief in Trungpa's infallibility, then the whole event had to be interpreted as the guru's attempt to wake us up. But to what? The reality of betrayal?

To me, the whole episode had the mark of a trickster. I was not so sure that Trungpa would have been incapable of giving the advice Tendzin attributed to him, even while knowing full well that it was wrong. I had heard Trungpa say, and read in the transcripts of his secret talks, that in Vajrayana, you just do what you are good at without any implications of ego or enlightenment, whether laying around or being a hitman. Trickery, disruption, masquerade, and outrage were things that Trungpa was good at, and he immensely enjoyed them. None of his earlier tricks that I knew about had caused permanent harm or taken life, but unless ngondro and Guru Yoga had destroyed your power to question, you would surely wonder whether his last few years of drinking might not have pickled his brain.

I also found it credible that he would have said in sincerity what Tendzin claimed he said, actually believing that practice would interrupt the karma of the disease. Hagiographies of the Karmapas and Milarepa say that they could control the weather, levitate, fly, vanish, make multiple copies of themselves, cure plagues, and leave footprints in solid rock. In one story I heard about, a Tibetan lama had ordered his Vajrayana disciple to step down into a cesspool ditch, pick up a handful of raw sewage, and eat it. When the disciple obeyed, so the story went, the sewage turned into heavenly ambrosia, and he entered the enlightened realm where shit is gold.

Belief that ritual purification can prevent the transmission of HIV is definitely not out of line with the Vajrayana reality system. After experiencing that reality system, I was ready to believe it myself. It really is possible to reach a point where you think you could munch up a handful of raw sewage and be immune to the microbes it contains because you are acting on command of the guru, who is the Buddha and would never cause harm to you. The diseases are probably emanations of thought anyway, products of an impure outlook, solidifications of egoistic attitudes or crystalizations of karma, and you believe that if you smash those attitudes with devotion you will be safe.

On the other hand, personal safety is not the point. Vajrayana is supposed to pull the rug out from under you. "If we have buttons to push, those buttons will definitely be pushed." Same old mixed message.

When Vajra masters get sick, their students say that their sickness is the karma of *others* which the masters have taken on voluntarily out of their great compassion. So when the masters die of their sickness, they must be dying for us. The guru is not a person like us—to think so is a perverted view, according to Kalu—therefore it cannot be thought that he would have no power over death.

In response to our supplications, the guru is reborn in another body in order to remain with us until we are liberated. I heard Tendzin's illness explained by his servants in this way: it was not a consequence of any folly or self-indulgence on his part, but the karma of his infected partners, that he had deliberately imbibed for them. In what way they benefited was never made clear to me, although one could safely assume the benefits did not include physical cure.

On the night of Tendzin's explanation I was unable to sleep. My thoughts were like tangled springs in an obstacle course of barbed wire, and I walked around them carefully. I could not give up that moment of having recognized the brother I had lost for hundreds of years. I felt like a boy in a Catholic melodrama, living and longing for the approval of his sainted priest brother, who turns out to have been molesting and giving AIDS to the altar boys. As his heart is breaking, the younger brother secretly gloats: "I always knew he was no better than I am; now that he is out of the way, I don't have to live in his shadow anymore, I can be myself." I wept because I loved him, and I laughed because Doubt, the jester in cap and bells, had been right. This weeping and laughing—was it not orgasm and headache? "They are the same thing."

I practiced Guru Yoga, and then my sleep was just limitless awareness in pure space, lit by passing cars and passing dreams. In the morning I drove home and walked into the woods, still doing Guru Yoga. It was the middle of winter. Everything was dancing and whirling in a strong wind. The sound was moaning all through the forest, modulated by distance, variegated by branches clashing and rubbing together.

I stared at the leaning, bobbing trees, the confusion of stumps and fallen logs, the crooked pathways, the patches of snow, the white boulders, the solitary fence posts, the tall withered stalks of weeds, the stripped bushes, the distant hills, the sun shining and darkening behind the clouds. Repeating the Guru Yoga mantra over and over, I remembered that all form is the guru's body, all sound is the guru's voice, all thought is the guru's mind. I remembered that mind, experience, and phenomena are one, and that every last detail of the forest is a symbol in the mandala of the unconscious. I knew that the next thing I saw would be a form of the guru, and it would say something about the crisis I had just witnessed.

A few seconds after having that certainty, I saw a lean animal with a heavy reddish coat, a brown, bushy tail, a thin face, and high pointed ears—a fox. He was walking nose down in the meadow and batting something with his front paw. Seeing me, he disappeared in the weeds.

I knelt with my forehead against a tree, listening to the wind. It never stopped for even an instant. My cat crept up close to me and nuzzled inside my coat. He huddled away from the cold against my chest, nursing on my buttons. I folded my arms around him and recited the mantra while he purred.

The omens came thick and fast toward the end of winter. It would have been comic except for the pain. Just before the sudden death of a family child, a strange black cat showed up from the woods, yowling and prowling around the house, and the largest plant in the dharma room came crashing unaccountably to the floor. My father lived on and on. I went to his insurance company to inquire about the details of his policy, and the salesman tried to sell me one for myself.

I finished Guru Yoga in the early spring. I wondered if there would be anything like the signs that had thus far marked the end of each of my ngondros. Precisely in the moment of formless devotion at the conclusion of the one million mantras, there was a knock on my door. It was the insurance salesman I had consulted about my father's policy. He was not looking for me; he had not even known where I lived. He explained that he was lost, and had stopped randomly at my house to ask for directions. We recognized each other and shook hands. I didn't know the client he was looking for. He bid me good day and left.

16

DANCING BETWEEN THIS AND THAT

THERE WAS NO abhiseka that year. Tendzin went into retreat and Khyentse gave us another practice to do. He said there were serious obstacles to the rebirth of Trungpa, which we could overcome by collectively reciting three hundred million Vajrakilaya mantras. For Vajrayana students, the mantras were accompanied by a visualization of the guru as Vajrakilaya, a wrathful yidam with three faces, surrounded by flames, holding a *kila*, a three-sided dagger, in two of his six hands. As you imagined the figure and recited the mantras, this dagger representing nondual egoless compassionate insight pierced your whole being, killing ego on the spot.

The point of the practice was to purify our attitude toward anger and conflict. Normally we are unable to see conflict as a manifestation of enlightenment; we cover up negativity, turn away from it, or treat it as a problem to get rid of. The real obstacle, however, is our exclusion of negativity from the sacred outlook of Big Mind. Vajrakilaya would slay this obstacle. He is the enlightened form of wrath.

To motivate mantra recitations, practice centers displayed large drawings of "kila thermometers," modeled on United Way charity drive posters: a hollow kila, calibrated in millions from the bottom up, was gradually colored in from bottom to top as the quantity of mantras accumulated.

Khyentse was nicknamed "Mister Universe" by Vajradhatu students. When he was teaching at Karme-Choling after Trungpa's cremation, a fellow student had said to me, "I get the feeling that he is as far above us as I am above my dog." I laughed in momentary agreement, but then I reflected on the means by which that feeling is created: the throne, the ceremonies, the master's esoteric knowledge, the elaborate rituals that he knew and we wanted to learn, the forms of obeisance we accorded him, the luxuriant accommodations we always made every effort to provide him as a sign of our respect and devotion, his special robes and colors, his luxury automobile and chauffeur, his procession of attendants, the wall of secrecy that kept us from observing him too closely. It was all good theater—it created a willing suspension of disbelief, and projected us into a sacred atmosphere. You became the rainbow. As the master of rainbows, Khyentse was the mystical mirror image of ourselves.

In practical terms, however, your submission is inculcated just as thoroughly as a dog's obedience, perhaps more so. Like brainwashing and propaganda, all the ngondros work by constant repetition, by programming the mind to devalue and give up any reality, any cultural attachment, any questioning process that could act either as a counterforce or an alternative to the guru's universe. The devotion opened by ngondro has nothing to do with personal knowledge of the guru. All you really know about him is the practice and its effects on yourself. It occurs to you that he must have known about those effects from the beginning, and they become the empirical basis for loving him. From one side of the double mirror, the guru's universe is complete enlightenment, and there could be nothing outside of it, no counterforce or alternative whose reality is not somehow made from enlightenment and parasitical to it at the same time. From the other side, once you understand the full magnitude of what is involved, it is curtains for the self and its choosing and questioning of reality systems. Yet one feels an inexplicable urge to get on with it, perhaps the same sort of urge that motivated the kamikaze pilots.

To believe that Khyentse was as high above me as I am above my dog, I had to believe that we were of different species. Perhaps

Khyentse only looked human because he had taken a human birth to help liberate me from samsara, but really, he could, and did, take any form: the form of Vajrasattva, Padmasambhava, or Vajrakilaya, of a medicine Buddha, Vajrayogini, an electrical storm, or my mother. This is what all the protectors' chants and all the prostrations, mantras, and mandalas had prepared me to believe. Khyentse emanated from the dharmakaya like a superior being from outer space—or inner space (essentially the same thing)—as an act of compassion, to strike me with his rays and kilas, to show me who I am, to free me from the chrysalis of ego and wake me up. But if such a being could wake me up, and I could become like him, then I must be the same species after all.

When I saw him on his throne, he appeared human enough. His long gray hair was tied back, and his breasts and fat rings shook as he climbed into position and seated himself with a thump. He scratched his testicles, snuffed, coughed up gobs of phlegm, and spit them into gold-colored cloths held by his monks. He wore necklaces, perhaps malas or amulets, which I could not identify from my position in the audience. He looked like a Tahitian king who had finally subdued the British Empire.

If we fulfilled the destiny that he imagined is possible for us, every man and woman would be a king and queen. No wonder the Chinese try so hard to extirpate Buddhism from Tibet. What could Communism, technology, and the industrial system possibly offer to a people who are already kings and queens?

After Khyentse's teachings I retired to the Karme-Choling living room and stared at the big rock in the corner.

"What do you think of devotion?" said the elderly woman next to me. I said I didn't know. She said "How convenient it must have been for the lamas in old Tibet to have their servants believing in it. Everything to please the guru. How it must have motivated those women to toil up the steps of the Potala Palace with their jugs of water for the lama's household. Those steps are no joke, believe me, I saw them."

I looked at her, and recognized again the face of Doubt. She had echoed my own thoughts, adding the image of the stairs. She was like one of the three faces on the yidam of Vajrakilaya. I remembered her years later, when I received abhiseka; her comment struck me like a dagger. What it killed in me was denial, and disrespect of myself.

When Tendzin died, the leadership changed in Vajradhatu. Trungpa's Tibetan son, the Sawang, became the supreme figure. There was no organized discussion or debate about this selection among the general members; it was made from the top. The Sawang was presented to the Vajrayana students at abhiseka, sitting on a throne, dressed in Shambhala regalia, with an array of pins and medals that his father had designed. The students were instructed to come onto the stage one by one and do obeisance to him, bowing and touching his ring. I did not know the Sawang and had no reason to object to his leadership, but the ceremony of his confirmation seemed an odious display of everything I disliked about the system. I secretly rejoiced that I did not live in a theocracy, and could still walk away with all the political rights given to me by the Western democratic republic my ancestors had fought to establish and protect.

The young Jamgon Kongtrul, a Tibetan student of the sixteenth Karmapa and a Kagyu lineage holder, swept quietly back and forth in dignified procession between his apartment suite and the tent where the abhiseka was conducted. He smiled at everyone, and lacked for nothing that could be given to him by his entourage of devoted personal servants. In a dialogue reported to me second hand, he was asked whether he would choose to be reborn. If his next life could be as pleasant and comfortable as this one, he replied, he would certainly wish to come back. When he left in his chauffeured black luxury automobile, we lined both sides of the road to wave goodbye and throw flowers. That was a good, honest answer, I thought. It did not deny Kongtrul's privileged status, or seek to explain it away as a form of "skillful means" to help us. If my next life could be as pleasant and comfortable as his, I might wish to come back too.

In 1992, Jamgon Kongtrul died in his chauffeured luxury automobile, however, under circumstances that made me wonder if his life had been so pleasant and comfortable after all.

The Vajrayogini sadhana is the first post-abhiseka practice of the Vajrayana that Trungpa taught to his students. It is one of the higher tantras from the Tibetan dharma menu, part of a practice group called Anuttara Yoga, whose place in the total scheme of tantra is outlined in Trungpa's book *Journey Without Goal* (Prajna Press, 1981). Vajrayogini is a feminine yidam, the guru imagined as the enlightened form of passion, who dances on one leg between samsara and nirvana. She personifies the wisdom of the mixed message—neither this nor that, and possibly both at once—which in Vajrayana Buddhist philosophy goes under the names of "coemergence" and "one taste."

According to this philosophy, ego and egolessness emerge together in the mind, moment by moment, in everything we say, do, and think. A desire for a glass of water, in the moment of its arising, is an example of egoless passion: inherently pure, basically good, a response that precedes any notion of self. As it flashes through the conceptualization of how to obtain water, the notion "*I* am thirsty, *I* need water," coemerges with the desire; so the two experiences, passion without self and passion as the desire of a self needing an object of gratification, occur more or less mixed. Passion without self is enlightenment, and passion as the desire of a self is tinged with the anxiety of hope and fear. Normally we are not aware of the egolessness of passion because we habitually ignore it; the experience of passion as the desire of a self diverges from its egoless root, and we must then live it through in the realm of ego, or samsara. On the other hand, it would not be correct to think that desire must be extinguished as the cause of our imprisonment in samsara; this approach is called "dwelling in nirvana," and amounts to throwing the baby out with the bathwater. We would be trying to get rid of the egoless root as well as the egoistic byproduct. The answer is to let ego emerge, detach from it, and experience fully the egolessness which coemerges with it at the same time. The "letting go" of the lower yanas trains us to do this.

Coemergence applies equally to all the kleshas, to neurosis, to the path, and to the whole of life. The egoless form of anger, for example, is pure wrathful energy, like fire, neither moral nor immoral in itself, but potentially dangerous. It is an especially vivid and immediate form of wisdom, like a mirror reflecting bright sunlight in your face. Woven into this experience is the notion "*I* am angry," and following that, all the conceptualizations that go with aggression: "*I* have a right to be angry, this person is a jerk, my cause is just," and the like. Egoless anger is like a scepter, sword, whip, or dagger that slays obstacles to wisdom, while aggression is like suffocating smoke. Both forms emerge from the same root— enlightenment. If we attach to aggression and believe in the thoughts generated by it, we land in the suffering of samsara. If we try to get rid of aggression by uprooting anger, we dwell in nirvana, which is a more subtle form of ego and would therefore lead us back again sooner or later into the realms of samsara.

The "one taste" of coemergent wisdom is the balance between samsara and nirvana, yes and no, the single cosmic marmalade that contains all sense perceptions. One taste means saying neither yes nor no to any experience, but living thoroughly whatever happens, with full awareness of its texture, qualities, trajectory, echoes, and aftereffects.

All the mixed messages of the path lead toward coemergence with greater and greater insistence. The spiritual materialism in the system that teaches you to cut through spiritual materialism is an example of ego and egolessness arising in the same mandala. If you reject the system outright, you have preferred samsara; if you accept it uncritically, you have preferred nirvana. The double effects of detachment in shamatha show the same coemergence: getting free from dysfunctional cycles is liberating, but shielding yourself from emotional risk is dwelling in nirvana. Meditation protects you from ideology while making you vulnerable to exploitation by the teacher, and this is the same coemergence of ego and egolessness, requiring the same balancing act between yes and no, doubt and faith. Transmission, ngondro, and Guru Yoga move the act closer and closer by continually raising the ante, and with it, the poignancy of the coemergence. That poignancy is "broken heart," an unmitigated, unconditional tenderness without shield.

The role, and the gender, of Doubt kept shifting through the various phases of this journey. During one phase, the jester was ego, during another she was coemergent egoless wisdom. Often it was impossible for me to tell them apart, but one thing I knew for certain: if the jester was killed, the wisdom would die with him or her, and so would the authenticity of the path. In that direction lay the nirvana of the cult zombie.

"It is absurd," she said, "to claim that an orgasm and a headache are the same thing, or that you should say neither yes nor no to the experience of sitting on a hot stove. Your own body, fortunately, has more sense, and will make the choice without consulting your philosophy."

Mother, you are absolutely right, but must I always let my body tell me what to do?

Vajrayogini wears a necklace of severed heads which stand for thoughts, cut off before they can turn into samskaras, or subconscious opinions. She offers a skull cup of amrita, a liquor that intoxicates ego. The idea is that when ego is intoxicated, egoless wisdom will coemerge. She is the coemergence of passion. The tantra that evokes her lasts for five to six hours, ending in a group feast of meats, cheeses, grapes, barley cakes, and alcohol, which represent the blood and flesh of ego. Strict vegetarians and recovering alcoholics who cannot touch alcohol are allowed to substitute symbolic meat and drink for their symbolic flesh and blood.

All the practices of shamatha, tonglen, the ngondros and Guru Yoga are woven in and out of the tantric ceremonies, building toward a climax in which the practitioners mythically assume the identity of the yidam. I use the word "mythically," which preserves the bias of Western scientific rationalism, but the identity is quite literal. Once all your concepts of self have been uprooted and given away, there is no reason you cannot be whatever identity you decide to assume. The yidam is the guru, who is the Buddha, who is empti-

Vajrayogini

ness, who is the kayas, who is one taste. The roles we play in the world are just intelligent rainbows displaying themselves in space. From the beginning the whole point of practice has been to prepare the way for this consciousness, and the tantra brings it on through a dazzling sequence of poetic, musical, and theatrical effects that appeal to all the senses of touch, smell, taste, sound, and sight. You are not just watching the show—you *are* the show. But it is a great deal more than a show; every detail in it, every word and line, every object, every symbol, and every gesture, have been selected, not merely to represent, but actually to embody and proclaim the experience of egoless mind.

Readers who are not Vajrayana students may have had the opportunity to attend a tantra that Tibetan masters offer to the general public. This is the Kalachakra Tantra, which has been given in the West several times by Kalu Rinpoche, Jamgon Kongtrul, and the

Kalu Rinpoche giving the Kalachakra Tantra in France, July 1987.

Dalai Lama. The power and method of all tantra can be felt vividly in this example. The Kalachakra Tantra continues over several days. Inevitably, part of the experience, especially for an untrained Westerner, is bewilderment and boredom, perhaps exasperation at not understanding all the gestures, chants, rituals, and musical interludes. These responses make no difference; they are comprehended in the tantra and do nothing to obviate its effects. Kalachakra is a yidam who transcends time, and has a special relationship to the kingdom of Shambhala. As in other tantras, the incantatory levels keep building cumulatively toward the mythic/literal identification with the yidam, which includes a fusion between our own original enlightened nature and the wisdom principles of the universe. I remember especially well the moment in the Kalachakra Tantra given by Kalu when the Tibetan horns blew, and thousands upon thousands of images of Kalachakra poured into my brain from all directions at once. No explanation can account for such

The Kalachakra mandala

effects; the mental faculty which attempts to explain things is super-seded by them and overwhelmed.

You realize after a few experiences like this that a political analy-sis of Tibetan dharma as a theocratic support for the power of the lamas is far too simplistic, entirely excluding from consideration what happens when the tantra is actually practiced. The philoso-phy behind tantra is as profound as anything in human thought, and its psychic technology, the system for altering perception, might have come to us from another world.

For the Western scientist, there is no science without an observer who stands outside the phenomena being observed, who is thought to be free of values that would predetermine evidence or hypotheses and who, it is believed, can objectively study and model the subject. This distance between the observer and the phenomena is essential to scientific method. We could not actually believe the reality system of a psychotic, for example, and still function effectively as a scientist of it. We cannot study induced changes of consciousness and participate in them at the same time, for participation compromises our objectivity. By the same logic, we could not be a Buddhist and remain a good Buddhologist. Tantric psychology is religion, not science; the observer identifies with the value system instead of studying its effect on consciousness.

For the tantric practitioner, however, the notion of an objective observer is a myth. Mind and phenomena, observer and object, ego and egolessness, coemerge in the same space. There can be no objective knowledge or truth apart from experience, which is what it essentially is, anterior to any separation of subject and object. The "independent" observer is what tantra slays with daggers, abnegates with prostrations, atomizes and purifies with mantras, gives away with mandalas, overwhelms with music, and converts with mythic identification into yidams dancing joyously on its corpse. This is done to liberate experience as pure field, neither out far nor in deep, real nor illusion, self nor other—pure mirror image with no reference point of that which is mirrored.

In the deepest sense of the word, the guru is the field itself. Once the observer has been completely given up to the field, then all of its wealth, all of its perceptions, all of its thought, come back to you in the form of enlightened energy—enlightened passion, action, attraction, repulsion, work, bliss. What was pride in samsara turns out to be cosmic generosity; what was aggression turns out to be the sword of intelligence; what was greed turns out to be beauty; what was envy turns out to be order; what was ignorance turns out to be vast accommodating spaciousness. Further training consists of ritual exercises in performing what are called *the four karmas:* pacifying, magnetizing, enriching, and destroying. These are four means by which a buddha or bodhisattva can prepare the ground for the teaching of dharma.

At times, the experience of tantra was everything I have described here and more, and at other times it was boring and silly. The yidams were like unemployed crazies from a Tibetan comic strip; the bells, drums, cups, and vajras were like toys a month after Christmas; the gurus of the lineage were like names from a surrealist directory of physicians; the chants and mantras were like bad poetry endlessly repeated, or what is just as tedious, good poetry endlessly repeated; the objects on the shrine were like the fantasies of a manic obsessive/compulsive, and the entire ceremony was like building a Ferrari to drive across the street to the mailbox.

The venerable doubting jester did not dissolve. He stepped forward now wearing denim jeans, a greasy T-shirt, and a John Deere cap, chewing on a stem of grass. "How much did those thingies there cost ya? Wow, I guess you gotta have money to be a Buddhist, huh? Somebody must be makin' some bucks off it. You mean you have to sit there and say all that stuff for six hours straight before you can eat a meal, and you can't get up to go to the bathroom or nothing? And what does that do for ya? Can it fix my tractor? Can it pay the doctor bills for my sick kid? Can it get me a job? Here, have a beer."

I turned to him and began to chant: "Om, O sovereign, you are the nature of all. You are beyond any mark of arriving and departing. Yet, like the moon in water, you manifest wherever thought of. Shri Heruka, subjugator of the hordes of mara, I supplicate you now with faith."

"You're weird," he replied.

"Thank you," I said.

17

A PACK OF CARDS

T RUNGPA WARNED THAT all the benefits of ngondro could be lost by indulging too much in skepticism, failing to practice, and wallowing in bad attitudes. When I read this warning in the transcripts of his Seminary teachings, he was long dead, and I had already become a sadhaka. His admonition had an opposite value for me than what he had intended—it assured me that I could drop the whole indoctrination. All the repetitions, all the self-programming, all the obeisance rituals, all the cult loyalty, everything, I could burst the dreaded bamboo tube like a snake-skin and walk. The entire process could fail. This was heartening news.

John Marks, in *The Search for the Manchurian Candidate: The CIA and Mind Control* (McGraw-Hill, 1980), describes the secret campaign the CIA conducted during the 1950s to find out whether or not a human being could be completely programmed as the instrument of another's will. CIA experiments along these lines required human guinea pigs, most of whom were found outside the borders of the United States. A prominent psychiatrist at McGill University in Montreal, Dr. Ewen Cameron, conducted research with CIA funding on unwitting mental patients which involved "de-patterning" or wiping out their memories with heavy doses of drugs and powerful electroshock treatments. He manipulated fifty-three patients and their families into believing that these measures were necessary cures for mental illness, when in fact he was acting on a secret agenda that had nothing to do with their welfare. After he had produced a blank mind in his subjects, he accepted more CIA funding to discover whether he could program in new patterns of behavior. He locked up patients in total sensory deprivation for over a month and administered drugs, one of which was LSD, that altered their perceptions and paralyzed their internal body functions. All this happened with the tacit approval and support of the psychiatric profession.

The CIA also conducted research into many other methods of brainwashing, and demonstrated an interest in the psychic technology of Vajrayana Buddhism. Generally, Marks concludes, their efforts to produce a "Manchurian candidate" were fruitless. Something in the human subjects always resisted total control. Partial and temporary manipulation could be achieved, but it proved impossible to completely program the mind of another person. As a crowning irony of the CIA's efforts, the most famous of the drugs they used to alter personality, LSD, was ingested by their own experimenters, leaked randomly through the population, and turned into the basis of a counterculture which challenged the authority of the government that supported the CIA.

The sleep and sensory deprivation inherent in some Vajrayana practices resemble the political "re-education" techniques used by totalitarian states against dissident prisoners. In one practice, the student goes alone into a sealed cave for three weeks and imagines death stage by stage; in another, students visualize cutting strips of flesh from their bodies with which to feed all sentient beings; in another, they tie themselves into vertical boxes so they can sit all night in meditation. Like the self-criticism sessions documented in Communist regimes, every practice is accompanied by ritual confession, repentance, and supplication to the guru for renewed acceptance and forgiveness.

Unlike the various political indoctrinations, however, including the experiments described by Marks, the Vajrayana practices are not forced on the student but are voluntarily assumed for a purpose in which both the student and the master concur. Forced indoctrination is a form of aggression, directed against the very sanity that Vajrayana is supposed to liberate. The Buddhist path sets out to tame aggression by gentleness, detachment, accommodation, and surrender. Only after the student has transferred loyalty from ego to bodhicitta do the methods of the path intensify their force. Ngondro compounds the intensity, and sadhanas depict the yidams aggressively trampling and stabbing the remnants of resistance. It is always the student who sets the pace for this, however; the student chooses when to take the vows of entry into the different yanas, when to do retreats, and when to prepare for the next step. Practice is a subject of mutual consultation between student and teacher. If the student is too aggressive, or has a confused understanding of the view behind a particular level, a good teacher will advise additional classes, or recommend a gentler practice.

The fact that the CIA search for a Manchurian candidate failed is a strong vindication of the Buddhist view that human beings possess inextinguishable brilliant sanity from the beginning. Indeed, due to the phenomenon of coemergence, even very aggressive techniques of behavioral control are bound to include enlightened energy. At Seminary, I met a disciple who had served in the Marine Corps. "Boot camp was enlightening," he said, "but the men didn't know it; all they related to was the aggression." It is not beyond imagining that some of the same techniques could be used to elicit sanity.

Vaccination works by injecting elements of the deadly organism into the bloodstream, while the remedies of homeopathic medicine resemble the disease, thus stimulating the body's own natural responses. The ancient king Mithridates protected himself against poison by ingesting small quantities of it over a long period. Vajrayana has a similar logic.

Still, when the vaccination and the disease are the same thing, I did not trust the vaccinator. A path of liberation should not merely replace one conceptual system with another. The relationships among Buddhist ideas in the three-yana journey suggest that they are an ideology, not a science of mind; and as ideology, they would in the long run obstruct more than facilitate enlightenment, if we include in that term freedom from our own concepts. The Vajrayana student is persuaded to accept these ideas primarily by repeating behavioral forms that instill compliance and devotion, not because of any self-evident truth in the ideas themselves.

A Vajrayana work by Lama Shabkar, *The Flight of the Garuda* (Kathmandu: Rangjung Yeshe Publications, 1986), urges us to examine our mind, which does not arise anywhere, dwell anywhere, or go anywhere; its qualities "are like those of a stainless sphere of crystal"; its essence is "empty" and its nature is "luminous." This realization is supposed to comprise enlightenment. If so, then enlightenment is nothing; for the term "mind" has no meaning in this passage apart from totality itself. "Exactly," the teacher might say. "Empty" means without definition; "luminous" means giving light. So mind is nothing and everything at the same time. After we have said this, we are no wiser than before. Language without meaning is gibberish, until its key terms become the basis of a religion. Then it is something more serious: it is doctrine.

Most Buddhists I know did not claim to understand these terms, but accepted the premise that they must mean something to the teacher. So the absence of meaning is actually a help in maintaining the infrastructure of religion; you discount your own intelligence, deferring to what you imagine is superior wisdom, and hanging in there waiting for the light to dawn.

Ego in Buddhism is composed of five skandhas, or heaps of impressions: form, feeling, perception, formation, and consciousness. Form is the physical body, the primary distinction between self and other; feeling is the appearance of klesha around the seed of form: grasping what is pleasant to self, rejecting what is inimical, and ignoring the rest. Perception is the sensual tagging of phenomena in terms of the kleshas, as either attractive, threatening, or neutral. Formation is the sorting of phenomena into conceptual categories so that they can be manipulated by intellect; consciousness is the entire world of the six realms of samsara, managed by the central headquarters of the self.

A mind interested in truth, however, must ask why these divisions should be so convenient to Buddhist teaching, and whether they represent any genuine processes in the psyche or are merely, or mostly, conceptual categories. It must be acknowledged at the outset that they have quite as much provocative subtlety as the schemes of Freud and Jung, but this fact does not make them true. Where, for instance, does feeling leave off and perception begin? Does form cause perception, or does perception cause form? Is form a subspecies of perception? Why are there only six realms in consciousness, why not ten, or a hundred? The distinction between the animal and the human realms is particularly crude. The animal realm in Buddhism represents a state of mind characterized by dullness and ignorance; but anyone who works and lives closely with animals realizes that they are not dull, do not ignore what is important to them, and for that matter are not even "animals," except to a human point of view that insists on lumping diverse and complex beings together in metaphors to confirm its own value system.

Trungpa's lectures on the *Abhidharma,* the ancient Buddhist text on the skandhas, attempted to explain how they are affected by meditation. He said that practice unwinds the connections between the skandhas so that they cannot integrate as ego. I could never find anything in meditation experience to correspond with this explanation. My thought and feeling just ran by themselves; I saw no connections to unwind, other than the deconditioning process I have already described. I wondered how the integration, disconnection, or very existence of the skandhas could ever be subjected to a test of scientific truth.

The Buddhist scientist Jeremy Hayward, in *Shifting Worlds, Changing Minds,* provides an intriguing and valuable discussion of the relationship between the skandhas and modern Western cognitive science, but does not directly take up the question of whether the skandha system amounts to a mythological doctrine, especially in its relationship to the categories of the Vajrayana. Hayward's dismissal of behavioral psychology is less than satisfactory: he does not do justice to the full complexity of its discoveries, and he tends to oversimplify behaviorism as "stimulus-response" theory, obscuring the differences between reflex and operant conditioning. Nor does he acknowledge the profound understanding of purely behavioral conditioning demonstrated by shamatha and ngondro.

In Hinayana one learns that there are five basic kleshas: passion, aggression, ignorance, envy, and pride, although some texts add jealousy for a total of six. If we go with five, they line up with the five skandhas, but if we go with six, they can be made to match the six realms.

In the Vajrayana there is a premium on five, for here they turn into the five buddha families. Aggression, passion, pride, envy, and ignorance are really the enlightened energies of vajra, padma, ratna, karma, and buddha, respectively, but corrupted by the illusion of self into the skandhas. Trungpa's *Journey Without Goal* explains the buddha families convincingly as five types of psychological energy, which we can authenticate from experience. But in the Vajrayana they are more than psychology, they are universal principles. Even as a psychological paradigm, they are not self-evidently more authentic than, say, the twelve personality types of the zodiac. The buddha families correspond to the five directions: north, south, east, west, and center; and the five ancient elements: earth, water, air, fire, and ether. They are even assigned colors that change according to whether the buddha family energy appears in its inherent purity or filtered through ego as a klesha.

Altogether it is a fascinating system, but truth requires that we question its assumptions. Is a klesha something that resides "in the mind," or is it a form of relational behavior that requires the existence of society? Is the judgment that identifies some behavior or thought as "klesha" itself free from societal values? If the buddha families are universal principles, are they present from the beginning of the cosmos? Could they be used to classify astronomical data? Would it be possible to come up with more or less than five buddha families? Why would it be any less "true" to base the kleshas on the Western scheme of the seven deadly sins, and the buddha families on the seven virtues—prudence, temperance, justice, fortitude, faith, hope, and love? What, exactly, makes the Buddhist system any more valid than the Christian?

At Naropa Institute, Trungpa devised a space awareness exercise to give students the direct experience of the buddha families: the Maitri program involves going alone into a succession of five unfurnished, carpeted rooms, each with a color and lighting scheme that expresses a particular form of buddha energy. The ratna room is yellow, the karma room green, the vajra room blue, the padma room red, the buddha room gray. You assume a different meditation posture for each room.

When I spent time in these rooms, my perception of color kept changing in interesting ways, but I did not notice any distinct energy structures in my mind. The rooms themselves do evoke five kinds of energy, but this may be little more than the interplay between perception and environment, and proves nothing about inherent psychic structure. If there had been ten different rooms and postures, I think they would have evoked ten energies. When I came out, there was heightened sensitivity to light and color and dissociation from analytical activity, but similar effects occur after emerging from natural caves. Designed on the assumption that the five buddha families exist, the Maitri program means nothing as a confirmation of them. It may be creating what it purports to reflect.

Whenever we find neat numerical correspondences in a system of thought, it is a sign that we have encountered not rational knowledge, but myth. The twelve Greek gods and goddesses match the twelve stops that Odysseus makes on the way home from Troy, which are echoed in the twelve signs of the zodiac and the twelve axes that his arrow penetrates after he strings the great bow. The twelve disciples of Christ symbolize the twelve tribes of Israel, the five wounds of the Crucifixion parallel the five wits of a Christian knight, etc.

Ideology and myth are closed systems handed down by higher authority; they are internally harmonious and consistent, but do not accurately model anything outside themselves. They are mental schematics that attempt to connect the individual to the larger patterns of history, astral motion, or divine purpose. The social function of myth is to establish a shared consensus of belief that holds a particular community together and defines its reason for existence.

The way Tibetan dharma has been handed down through the centuries fits the pattern of transmission typical of closed myth systems. The recognized authority for all truth is the guru, who is a physical human being, a high lama or abbot, but must not be conceived as a person. Since the guru is not a person, then the student cannot contradict or revise his teachings. You are invited into the guru's mandala to develop the skills of question and debate, but only on the premise that your own autonomy is given up. He sits on a throne; you prostrate three times before him, kneel, fold your hands in anjali, and supplicate him to teach. Within that form, it would be a courageous student who could speak up and say, "Maybe your whole idea system is false." While masters have added extensive commentaries to Buddhist doctrine over the years, they are in the main elucidating footnotes, not fundamental challenges. A challenge to the doctrine is heresy, potentially leading to the creation of a schism in the sangha—one of the inexpiable faults that send the student to Vajra hell. The primary value is not truth, but community cohesion, which is exactly what myth systems are intended to preserve.

It may be objected that the scheme of the five kleshas and the five buddha families was never intended as a science of mind, but is simply a tool to help us liberate ourselves from pain. We cannot define or confirm the existence of a klesha with anything like scientific accuracy, but on a pragmatic level we know what it means to experience jealousy, envy, pride, aggression, and stupidity; we suffer from these things every day of our lives. The Buddhist idea system is there to help us turn our experience into a positive, expanding wakefulness, and of course, when the system itself becomes an obstacle to further expansion, we are as free to give it up as we were to take it on.

There is one key escape clause in Buddhist dharma that negates the mythic/ideological status of its doctrine: the teaching of emptiness. The entire intellectual system of Hinayana is denied by the *Heart Sutra*, the basic document of the Mahayana path: "there is no form, no feeling, no perception, no formation," says Avalokitesvara, running through the whole gamut of the skandhas, the four noble truths, the dhatus, and the eight kinds of consciousness. All the idea systems and mythic embodiments of the Vajrayana are conjured from emptiness, and returned to it at the end of the practice session. It is recognized that none of them have any objective status of "truth" as opposed to fiction, but are evoked purely as a means to the end of experiencing Big Mind. The duality of truth and falsehood itself is transcended. We can use any Buddhist concept the same way we pick up and use the practice materials of tantra. There is no need to subject a double-ended, five-pronged brass object to experimental tests to determine whether it is a vajra before handling it in a ritual sadhana. The meditator, the vajra, and the sadhana all arise from nonduality, and have no final existence or nonexistence, one way or the other.

I am not sure whether this escape clause is sufficient to protect the mind against the orthodoxy that tantra invites. Again it is a delicate balance between extremes. In Vajrayana, you do not just use the mythology, you are led to become one with it, until the distinction between mythology and truth has been quashed. At that point you arise again like a fish leaping from water, as the embodiment of the myth.

Hayward, Fritjof Capra, and others have noted that the doctrine of emptiness is thoroughly compatible with the discoveries of quantum physics, and this observation has given some scientific legitimacy to the Buddhist system. Stephen Hawking and Niels Bohr, however, both warned against trying to press quantum mechanics into the service of confirming Eastern mysticism. The attempt is "absolute rubbish," said Hawking, and amounts to abandoning physics.

In the fictionalized history of Buddhism given by its own sacred texts, the teachings of tantra were first devised by the Buddha at the request of the king of Shambhala, who needed enlightened practical instructions to help him work with emotions and the world of politics. The doctrine of emptiness alone was insufficient as a guide for how to conduct oneself like a king. In a sense each of us, as king or queen of our own realm, has the same need: how to apply the consciousness of enlightenment in ordinary situations.

Plato raises this question in the allegory of the cave, when Socrates asks whether a person who had grown accustomed to sunlight would be able to function well if he returned to the world of darkness. The listeners agree that he would cut a sorry figure at first, and do as poorly in the cave as the philosopher might do in courts and marketplaces. Some medium is necessary to bring the insights of Big Mind back into the village of discursive thought. The array of the five buddha families, the four karmas, and the idea of mandala might provide a good working metaphor for the conduct of daily life.

The usefulness of a metaphor stems partly from our ability to think outside of it. The metaphor clarifies reality as long as it is not confused with reality. At some point, Socrates must drop the image of the perfect Republic and return to the original idea it was devised to convey, which is the meaning of justice and its application in the political world. If his image is elevated to the status of a utopian model, then little of practical value has been gained.

Vajrayana practice inculcates the mythology of tantra so thoroughly into the mind of the student that there is no possibility of maintaining the distance between terms implied by metaphor. There is no distance: reality and image are the same. As an unfortunate practical consequence, thought and personal relationships tend to become dominated by Buddhist platitudes, cliches, and organizational slogans. All cults turn their members into company mouthpieces, and every one of them runs the same risk, Vajrayana no less than others. Originality is unwelcome; it is regarded as an impulse of the ego which must be processed out of the mind before enlightenment can occur. "If you find something in my talk that is not in Trungpa's writings," said a program coordinator, "then it's just my ego."

The dilemma is an old one: through innovation and originality, the pioneering master finds a way to enlightenment, but when the way is consolidated into a system of ideas, it leads onto the sidetrack of orthodoxy and obstructs the students. Yet if there is no consolidation, no one else can benefit from the master's discoveries. Robert M. Pirsig's attempt to develop a "metaphysics of quality" in *Lila* (Bantam, 1991) is one of the better contemporary discussions of this dilemma. Pirsig takes the "both . . . and" view which I have suggested is necessary for the Vajrayana student. He does not reject consolidation, but compares it to a ratchet which keeps the previous gain until a new master comes along to make the next.

The Buddhist path is supposed to be a system for producing masters, not merely for preserving their gains. In the multiple-yana curriculum, the orthodoxy established at one level is smashed in the next: Mahayana negates the skandhas and the four noble truths with emptiness, Vajrayana negates emptiness with tantra, and Maha Ati, I presume, though I have never been trained in it, negates tantra with crazy wisdom. Still, there is something fishy about the notion that a master can emerge at the end of it all, like a fine quality car from the assembly line. The heart says that it cannot be so, that masters are not made by conformity to systems, that true masters have the power to condense the whole curriculum at any point and make it dance in the facets of a jeweled thumbring, and that if students would be masters, they must take this power for themselves.

"You're nothing but a pack of cards," said Alice in Wonderland to the Red Queen and her cohorts, announcing that she was stepping beyond the premises of their reality system. The student of tantra might do well to take up her cry and hurl it at the deities, gurus, and ideas of the Vajrayana. But we could be more precise; we could acknowledge the sacredness of the Red Queen's energy, rather than merely dismissing her with contempt: we could say,

"you're nothing but a wrathful form of Ekajati"; and to her heads-
man, "you're nothing but Vajrakilaya." What is actually acknowledged in the tantra is "You (and I) are nothing *and* Vajrakilaya,"
which is both dismissal and appreciation, the philosophical ground
of tantra. With that premise, you cannot step out.

The only reality test that an ordinary meditator can apply to
the Buddhist system is whether it expands consciousness: whether
it helps us in daily life to transcend suffering, love one another,
notice and cherish our world, and move past our limits. In the end,
this may be the only test that matters.

To make such a test requires doubting, autonomous adults, who
are both in the Buddhist process and outside of it at the same time,
who surrender without surrendering, trust without trusting, examine and discuss without believing, who are willing to go to the
guru's party and do the deed, but bring their own condoms, insurance policies, and white umbrellas.

18

ART AND DHARMA: BEAUTY IS TRUTH

A GOOD WAY TO assess whether Tibetan dharma expands or restricts consciousness might be to examine its effect on creativity. Theocracies are notorious for repressing artists, and turning their works into conduits of "correct" ideas. In general the Buddhist system is far too pacifistic and tolerant of diversity to repress, but doubt takes nothing for granted. It seems probable that the sect most likely to wither the creative arts would be founded on a body of doctrines protected by the guru principle and handed down through a strong authoritarian tradition. An honest look at the relationship between the path and the arts does not turn up any definite conclusions. The record is mixed, and the issue remains arguable both ways.

Tibetan culture produced sophisticated and colorful schools of *thangka* painting. These are religious icons, usually done on cloth, depicting the various mandalas and their manifestations of the buddha as guru, yidam, and dakini. The subject matter is monotonously similar. Many Westerners take these thangkas out of context and use them as art objects to decorate walls, but this is really a perversion of their intended function. Their purpose was to focus visualization and orient the mind for specific dharma practices. They were not created as art in the Western sense, but as supports for the practice which in turn shores up a myth system and its accompanying priest-controlled political state. The same point can be made of Tibetan sculpture, statuary, and other physical artifacts, as well as of Tibetan music and poetry. The statues are buddhas, bodhisattvas, and yidams, the artifacts are practice materials. The musical instruments open and close practice sessions, accentuate liturgies, and sound at intervals during tantras as part of their cumulative effect.

Tibetan literature is mostly a vehicle of dharma. The great yogi Milarepa, who is in some sense the national poet, spontaneously produced tens of thousands of devotional poems and songs, creating a celebratory genre that is never far removed from the didactic end of inspiring Buddhist practice. Another strong role for Tibetan and Indian Buddhist poetry is revelation, delivered from the sambhogakaya. There is no secular Tibetan fiction to speak of, other than folk tales and allegories.

The whole of Tibetan creative art is a magnificent aesthetic achievement. The very script invites meditation, and the system of writing, which presumes a "seed" vowel present in all the other vowels, builds the idea of coemergence right into the syllabary characters. But I find there is something disturbing about the cohesion and totality of it all, as there is about a medieval monastic environment whose assumptions control every activity, and make deviation from them unthinkable.

Dante's *Divine Comedy*, masterpiece though it is, disturbs in the same way. Every detail is chosen to reflect a worldview outside of which nothing else can exist. Each book has thirty-three cantos, with a prologue at the beginning for a total of one hundred; each canto has a three-line rhyme scheme, *terza rima;* each level of being has nine circles that match and counterpoint one another from book to book; the miserable couples of hell are paralleled by hopeful couples in purgatory and joyous couples in paradise; the direction and meaning of all existence are explained, our place in it assured, the path to salvation mapped out, the dangers and obstacles defined. Dante's vision might seem like peace, the peace that passes all understanding, but it is madness too. It attempts to reduce the whole universe to order and perfection, and to shut uncertainty and chaos into a little hole in the earth. If it did no more than this, it would be cowardice in the guise of love.

Perhaps Trungpa felt that the integrity and cohesion of Tibetan dharma were restrictive as well as liberating, for he certainly introduced into it both chaos and space. His abandonment of monastic vows and his playboy lifestyle among the English were perceived as betrayals by some of the other Tibetans who had escaped with him into India. The meditation centers that he established in America did not preserve a pure Tibetan decorative style, but mingled it with elements of Zen, Shinto, Eagle Scout camp, and British Victorian.

From the beginning of his career in America, Trungpa attracted artists and poets to his circle, and did his utmost to inspire them to produce work with sacred outlook. To this end, he seemed willing to forego the religious approach entirely and present meditation in a completely secular and psychological framework. He drew together a galaxy of brilliant minds at the launching of his college, Naropa Institute, whose instructors and guests have included at various times such intellectual and creative luminaries as R. D. Laing, Gregory Bateson, Allen Ginsberg, Ann Waldman, Ram Dass, William Burroughs, Diane di Prima, Philip Whalen, Gregory Corso, Rabbi Zalman Schachter, and many others of comparable stature and fame.

Most of these figures were not tantric practitioners; they were drawn to Trungpa because of his own creativity, brilliance, and playfulness, because of their respect for the Tibetan tradition he represented, because of Allen Ginsberg's prestige and active support, or because Naropa quickly acquired a reputation as a place where all forms of creativity could meet in an atmosphere of mutual respect and exchange. The presence of creative stars in and around Trungpa's mandalas does not necessarily say anything one way or the other about the effect of Vajrayana on creativity. Some poets resisted his system intensely; W. S. Merwin was humiliated and driven away in an incident that turned into a scandal known as "the great Naropa poetry wars." Trungpa commented to his Seminary students occasionally that poets and writers were self-centered, difficult to work with, and unwilling to accept discipline. All strongly centralized political and religious organizations tend to make similar criticisms of writers and artists.

In the way he presented Buddhist dharma, Trungpa did whatever he could to stimulate creativity through the direct experience of egoless mind. The Shambhala program brought in various arts, from court dancing and tea ceremony to flower arrangement. Trungpa's lectures on art, transcribed in a compendium titled *Dharma Art Sourcebooks,* are not yet available to the general public, but they contain some of the most fruitful teachings on aesthetics since Aristotle. They do not comprise a school or conceptual system; their effect is basically to erode the boundary between aesthetic and ordinary perception, and to free up our creative inspiration.

Dharma practice relaxes the critical faculty and dissolves the blocks that hold us back as artists. The axiom that "if you keep your samaya, you cannot make a mistake" might be an invitation to hubris in the world of personal relationships, but in the arts it is unquestionably healthy. It exorcises the specter of having to produce "significant work," and encourages us to manifest without fear.

For a dharma practitioner, most of Western aesthetics arises from vipashyana, the first stage of awakened mind. Beauty is the experience of the self-existent beingness and brilliance of an object, logic, or process—self-existent in the sense that it has no meaning or explanation other than itself, nor does it require one; brilliance because no concepts impede our direct sensual or mental apprehension of being. Like all phenomena, beauty is impermanent and unconditional. In beauty, we see the *it* or *is* outside the limits of habit. The tangle of leaves and grass is there in all its detailed shades of green, but eludes definition. It is the precision of its own laws, entirely beyond the meanings and concepts we might attach to it. Yet it is also ourselves, for we are both perceiving and creating it with our perceptual organs. Beauty is the wide-angle lens mode, the experience of the double mirror, the image, process, or logos reflecting itself without support from an absolute reality.

"Beauty is truth, truth is beauty," said Keats. The Buddhist recognizes in this line a Western version of the *Heart Sutra:* "Form is emptiness, emptiness also is form." Both refer to the same experience: Truth, or form, is the undefined beingness of the scene. Beauty, or emptiness, is its unsupported perceptual brilliance. The equivalents could also work the other way around: beauty is form, truth is emptiness. They are coemergent and inseparable. Keats recognized the experience as enlightenment when he added: "That is all ye know on earth, and all ye need to know." In "Ode to a Nightingale" he included the realization of compassion, suffering, impermanence, and one taste: "Fled is that music; do I wake or sleep?"

Like the hallucinogenic effects of mescaline or psylocibin, a work of art is a shock treatment of sorts, paralyzing habitual mind so that unconditional, self-existent beingness and brilliance can be perceived. But shock treatment is only made necessary by the fact that we do not normally perceive in this way; we do not truly *see.* Instead of paralyzing it from the outside, meditation unravels the ignorance of habitual mind from within. When the stage of vipashyana is reached, all our surroundings have self-existent beingness and brilliance. Even if they are unendurably ugly, the ugliness is perceived as utterly, unconditionally true, and there is always a certain beauty, sometimes poignant and painful, in the recognition of truth.

On one level, art is necessary because we do not meditate; if we did, beauty and truth would coemerge everywhere as conditions of daily life. The swearing of stalled drivers on a backed-up freeway is both choreography and music, which tells nothing but truth about the interplay between human consciousness and freeway traffic. As art it requires no interpretation, it is just there. A mind steeped in meditation sees it that way; a mind trapped in thought must first get out of the traffic jam, and then watch a film that choreographs sound and stalled drivers, and maybe the traffic jam of thought will be interrupted long enough for the beingness, brilliance, truth, and poignancy of the highway traffic jam to come through.

The tension between habitual mind and beauty is at bottom the intertwining of ego and egolessness. Perception of self-existent, unconditional beingness and brilliance is the egoless experience. The ego of an object or process is its meaning, its conditions, its explanation, interpretation, and commentary, which are supplied by human thought. The object or process in itself has no meaning, though it emerges wrapped in a package of ego. Art succeeds in evoking beauty when it takes off the package and connects the mind directly with being—though the package, too, is being, and can be experienced that way.

To a meditator, all ordinary perception is made aesthetic by the practice of leaning into every experience with an attitude of awareness, curiosity, and detachment from the temptation to interpret. They are all emersions of beingness and brilliance. Truly horrible events may shock our ignorance so severely that we are unable to relate with them at all, but a master can dance even with these. The fact of suffering in the texture of experience evokes not only beauty, but the compassion that is inseparable from it. Beauty also contains karma—the record of consequences, the matted, bloody place in the grass where the dog lay down with his mouth full of porcupine quills.

Great artists, like Homer, Tolstoy, Thoreau, Flannery O'Connor, or Isabel Allende, have the power to induce that feeling of direct perception, the discovery of egolessness in the package of ego, the brilliance, suffering, and compassion that emerge inseparably from any experience authentically lived. The dharma practitioner, however, aims to deepen and steady this perception into a constant state of mind by transcending the reference point of self. A dharma practitioner does not need art as a separate technique for evoking beauty; art becomes the same thing as living. The function of art in a culture of dharma practitioners is to reflect, induce, and celebrate the state of mind in which beauty and ordinary living have become the same thing. Good art is a form of dharma.

Something like this function must have shaped the arts in Buddhist Tibet, for practitioners there had uninterrupted centuries in which to create a dharmic culture. The Tibetans may not have produced a Tolstoy because they had no need of one. To an outsider, Tibetan art may look like religious propaganda, though the brilliant sacredness of it convinces all but the most opinionated cynic to withhold judgement.

Has American Vajrayana Buddhism fostered good poetry?

Meditation heightens creativity by welcoming whatever the mind sends along. Vipashyana is a perpetual brainstorming session, where thoughts flow unimpeded by censorship. Good poetry, however, is not quite plain thought. Art shapes language toward a result, and this requires exclusion and control. The American Buddhist aesthetic does not favor such terms; it favors the spontaneous release of raw perceptions. At best, its poems are like butterfly wings glimpsed in the morning fog; at worst, they degenerate into unmemorable, prosy, conversational trivia mingled with dharma platitudes.

Trungpa's poetry, like his comically inept singing, was often casually and unapologetically bad. It was insulated from criticism during his lifetime because everything he wrote, said, painted, or sketched had the status of Holy Scripture. But no good purpose is served by denying the truth. Trungpa danced from the profound to the trivial and silly with twinkling leaps. Many of his poems are little more than slogans:

> Let us celebrate in the name of sanity,
> Let us proclaim the true discipline,
> Let us rejoice:
> The eternally rising sun is everpresent.
> In the name of the lineage, I rejoice.

—*First Thought, Best Thought* (Shambhala, 1983), p. 67

Let us also, one is tempted to add, march to the fields singing the Shambhala anthem, and be happy in our work.

"As the thunder gathers rain," Trungpa wrote, "flowers drink water;/Arrogant greenery has no hesitation,/Summer provides festivity, and life is worth living." The image of summer turns into the stock sentiment expected of a Shambhala warrior, suitable for printing on program advertisement brochures.

A text of poetry introduced by Trungpa to his students as "Egoless Revelation" illustrates how sloppy his judgement could be, even when he intended otherwise:

> That mind of fearfulness
> Should be put in the cradle of loving-kindness
> And suckled with the profound and brilliant milk
> of eternal doubtlessness,
> In the cool shade of fearlessness. . . .

The adjectives "profound" and "brilliant" are Shambhala buzzwords, meaningful in the context of those teachings, but like most adjectives, they do not render authentic experience; they confirm a shared orthodoxy. The ending "-ness" is repeated four times in four lines, and like all accidental or purposeless homonyms and rhymes, it distracts attention from the meaning of the passage. The only image is banal—and condescending to the student as well, if it implies that a person with ego fears is a baby who needs to be breastfed.

Insofar as it helps to destroy the anal-retentive tyranny of excessive criticism, bad writing on the part of the master can have a liberating effect on the creativity of the student. But much depends on the reasons why the writing is bad. The life in the passages I have quoted above has been suffocated by the burden of their orthodoxy. The point was not to produce beautiful verse; it was to provide a shared doctrine for a particular social group. But even as doctrine it is lifeless, especially when compared to the Christian Apocalypse or the King James translation of the Twenty-third Psalm.

Similar faults afflict much of the material that passes for poetry in the *Shambhala Sun,* or in most official publications that treat the arts as appendages to the political needs of an organization.

There is too much reliance on dharma jargon, insufficient attention to craft, and excessive loyalty to didactic purpose. The works of Trungpa and Tendzin, while they lived, were enshrined, not by their literary merit, but by the guru principle, which assured that everything they uttered would be studied reverently as a guide to art and life. Masters and elders thus become artistic models for reasons that have nothing to do with art. The higher levels of the Shambhala program are dominated by Trungpa's calligraphy, Trungpa's anthem, Trungpa's ideas and vision, and Trungpa's poetry, decked out with good measures of music by the Shambhala Director, based on Trungpa's epic of Gesar, a Shambhala Rigden king. This is a stultifying level of saturation, even when the ideas, music and poetry manifest brilliance, which they often do. For a dharma system to inspire good poetry, as opposed to political correctness, deep criticism must be invited and engaged, especially if it is heretical. Trungpa himself appeared to invite such criticism; the structural forms that he bequeathed to Vajradhatu invite it and shut it off at the same time.

Buddhist-inspired poetry, according to Allen Ginsberg in "Meditation and Poetics" (*Ordinary Magic,* ed. John Welwood, Shambhala, 1992), is a "process or experiment," a "probe into the nature of reality and the nature of the mind." It requires complete openness to the next thought or the next image, for you can never predict what you will think.

Ginsberg quotes John Keats on "negative capability," but his aesthetic preference is for the spontaneity of Whitman, Williams, and Olson. Ginsberg favors "letting go of thoughts and allowing fresh thoughts to arise and be registered, rather than hanging onto one exclusive image and forcing Reason to branch it out and extend it into a hung-up metaphor."

The role of Reason, which might also be called craft, in poetry, is devalued by this statement. Letting go of thoughts is an excellent technique for encouraging the raw material of a poem to emerge; but to turn raw material into a masterpiece worth memorizing, as Yeats, Milton, Shakespeare, Donne, Pope, Keats, and Byron well knew, requires months and years of sustained effort and discriminating judgement. It is doubtful that Keats' exacting, carefully worked formal odes and Spenserian stanzas, with their sonorous iambic pentameter lines, could have been written as "probes" or "experiments." They required finding and counting rhymes, calculating the rhythms of metrical feet, testing alternative phrases, hanging onto images, and branching them out into "hung-up metaphors:" "His soul shall taste the sadness of her might,/And be among her cloudy trophies hung."

Of course, there is nothing wrong with presenting raw material, or exploring the authentic movement of consciousness in the poem. This practice has its own kind of appeal. Ginsberg's work is established in American literature and deservedly praised for its honesty, courage, autobiographical nakedness, and tough broken heart. What I am questioning is whether the Buddhist aesthetic in practice is really as open and welcoming of diversity and good art as it purports to be. The probing spontaneity of American Buddhist poetry, indeed, American poetry generally, is at constant risk of solidifying into an unhealthy bias against the craftsmanship of well-wrought metaphors and exactitude of phrasing, expressed in rhymed and metered verse.

A good poem is worth committing to memory. Here is a simple test for quality in a poem: would you take the trouble to sit down and memorize it, so you could say it to your friends? There are remarkably few Buddhist poems in English that pass this test. They are as casual and spontaneous as the effort required to write them, consciously intended to be like seeds on the wind, blowing from nothing into nowhere.

The tradition of the English language masters—Shakespeare, Milton, Yeats—is filled with carefully composed poems which are a genuine pleasure to learn and recite, not because they let go of thoughts and get on to the next perception, but because they stay with a perception, by means of sustained, disciplined form, to the fullness of its inherent beauty. All good poetry has in common the dharmic goal of inducing beauty, as I have defined it here. Coemergent beauty and truth are no different from *thamal gye shepa,* Ordinary Mind. Ironically, Milton and Homer come closer to evoking it than American Buddhists, not because the classic poets had "right view," but because they were faithful to their original inspiration, and disciplined in their craft.

Consider Milton's description of an angel:

> ... six wings he wore, to shade
> His lineaments Divine; the pair that clad
> Each shoulder broad, came mantling o'er his breast
> With regal Ornament; the middle pair
> Girt like a Starry Zone his waist, and round
> Skirted his loins and thighs with downy Gold
> And colors dipt in Heav'n; the third his feet
> Shadow'd from either heel with feather'd mail
> Sky-tinctur'd grain. Like Maia's son he stood,
> And shook his Plumes, that Heav'nly fragrance fill'd
> The circuit wide.... [*PL* V. 277ff.]

The picture is sustained and carefully, lovingly wrought. The pentameter verse, the sensual images, the diction, and the melding of Biblical and Greco-Roman frames of reference all combine to visualize an enlightened, superior being of sacred beauty and power. This is a being with no ego problem, a bodhisattva from the sambhogakaya such as those imagined in tantra, sent on a holy errand to give mankind the chance for heaven without suffering. Milton's doctrinal preconceptions are irrelevant; the description inspires faith in human possibilities because it is good poetry, and for no other reason.

The Sanskrit mantras of the Vajrayana evoke Ordinary Mind by absorbing the energy of discursive thought into disciplined form. Their images and music, their assonance, consonance, and alliteration, their measured repetitions and syllabary rhythms, are powerful in themselves, and are made still more powerful by meditation in a proper practice environment. The masterpieces of English poetry are mantra in this general sense. They take the thought and experience of ordinary life and cast it in language that shimmers with Ordinary Mind, like shining from shook foil. They induce beauty because someone took the trouble to work and shape language to that end, in obedience to nothing but the requirements of the poem itself.

Homer knew that good poetry has the power to send the mind into the wide-angle mode of awareness through mantric form: *"Menin, aieda, thea,"* says the first line of *The Iliad;* "Of the wrath, sing, goddess, of Achilles the son of Peleus...." The Greek word *"aeida"* meant not only to sing, but to chant, to praise, to wail, which in epic poetry was best done in hexameter verse. After 3,000 years, his lines are memorable because they evoke the pathos, panorama, and broken heart of egolessness erupting from the ferocity of aggressive emotion:

> *Mei se, geron, koilaisin ego para nausi kicheio*
> *e neun daytheunont e heusteron autis ionta,*
> *mei neu toi ou chraisme skeptron kai stemma theoio.*

> Let me not find you, old man, by the hollow ships,
> either loitering now or coming back later,
> or your staff and fillet of the god will not protect you.

So warned Agamemnon, in a burst of shocking arrogance against a priest of Apollo. These words are a rejection of the priest's appeal for his daughter's freedom, a contemptuous attack on bodhicitta that brings on the tragic slaughter of thousands. In that one Greek text is the seed of every war in history, from the fall of Troy down to the massacres of Bosnia and Los Angeles. There is ego in the content (literally: *"ego para nausi"*) and Big Mind in the poetry. The Big Mind, induced by the mantric hexameters, is the mode of vast and compassionate perception, the insight into the rhythmic beauty of inevitable fate, or karma, working through the tragic stupidity of human acts. The truth one finds here is the same truth conjured by the Vajrayana, not because it represents a Buddhist outlook or idea system, but because it is faithful to experience.

Buddhist dharma has the power to revitalize Western literary and religious traditions, by bringing us back into contact with their original inspiration. This can only happen if dharma itself does not decay into doctrine. In practice, since we always have to do with real people, doctrine and dharma come in the same package, like ego and egolessness. The role of Doubt is to tell them apart.

19

NOTHING HAPPENED

W HEN I STOPPED practicing the Vajrayana, it was partly in order to test whether my practice had become a way of ignoring the issue of cultural relativity in Buddhist teaching. The risk was the loss of all its wonderful benefits, and a sentence in Vajra hell. But how genuine is any form of enlightenment that has to be chased all the time by constant visualizing, devotional prostrating, counting of mantras, chanting of liturgies, attendance at sangha events, donations, dues, and fee payments? Was all this not a sidetrack? If I could be enlightened "on the spot," "right now," as Trungpa had assured in my very first encounter with him, then why not just declare that I had done it already and move on? Or was I still waiting for the cosmic harmonies of conjured choruses?

Always there was another level of commitment looming ahead on the Vajrayana conveyor belt: Gampo Abbey, the Kagyu monastic center on Cape Breton, Nova Scotia, had started hosting traditional three-year retreats. The prospect of a three-year retreat humbled the practice I had already done and irritated my drive to make progress. The everlasting desire to advance had grown wearisome beyond telling, and for me the only remedy was to give it up. That meant giving up any pretense of attainment. Goodbye to Ordinary Mind, One Taste, Great Joy, and the rest of the cosmic marmalade.

My first post-practice sensation was enormous relief. I was still my own master in all things subject to my choice — especially in what I did with my time on this planet. That did not have to include racking up millions of mantras on a kila thermometer to purify my so-called obstacles, bring back Trungpa, or save the world. Nothing required me to saddle myself compulsively with an activity I did not enjoy.

Then my mind began to de-program itself again. It was once more possible to think outside the concepts of the three-yana curriculum. Leaving unanswered for a while longer the question of whether one could think outside the nonconceptual truth of dharma, I made an effort to expedite the de-programming stage by avoiding dharma jargon. I searched for language that had nothing Buddhist about it, and that would express truthfully the nuances of what I actually perceived.

At the same time, I gave up trying to base personal relationships on dharma consciousness, or the bodhisattva ideal, neither of which led to my establishing an enduring bond with another human being. Instead I looked for what I could do at any given moment to respect and care about myself and others, communicate honestly, and live my needs and experiences as they actually arose, with no thought that I was on a spiritual journey or had to bring everything to an all-consuming path. This was as difficult as it had always been, but it was a joy to attempt; inconsistency in the result does not matter, as long as the effort is more or less continuous.

I accepted anger and jealousy as the normal, inevitable psychic equipment of mammals, instead of regarding these emotions as obstacles to expanded consciousness. In the buzzwords of dharma, emotions are "confused" but "workable"; "confusion" can be transformed into "wisdom." I wondered if I had ever "worked" with emotions at all, beyond living them fully and noticing their textures in my body and mind. But it is unnecessary to characterize them as either confused or wise, and I was not sure that doing so had taught me anything.

In Vajrayana, since pleasure and pain are supposed to be the same, there is no need to avoid negative emotions, and it is all right to do things that provoke jealousy in someone else. I threw this idea out the window. A person who does not distinguish between an orgasm and a headache would probably register a flat line on a brainscan. There had never been any doubt in my mind which experience called for the aspirin tablets. I stopped imagining that giving myself or someone else a headache was a good practice opportunity. "If we have buttons to push, those buttons will definitely be pushed." Everyone has such buttons. It is quite legitimate, even admirable, to avoid causing ourselves and others the pain of pushing them.

In particular, I gave up detachment—either teaching that it was a good idea, or trying to maintain it myself. It does not seem possible that we can love all sentient beings in a general compassionate way, without deeply attached caring, to the point of grief and anxiety, for the happiness of concrete specific beloved beings. Generalized warmth is not love to me. Love is appreciation of detail. My mother loved the length of my bones and the skewed disproportion of my gaze, which reminded her of a great uncle she enjoyed telling me about. My obtuseness toward the practical demands of life drove her nearly berserk with irritation, and my refusal to take her side against my father was a lasting grief that she never forgot. Genuine love cannot be separated from the pain of attachment, not as long as we are alive. I loved her sense of humor, her penetrating sarcasm, her endless family stories, her refusal to give up her Anglo-Canadian identity. Losing her left a wound in me that will never heal, and I do not even want it to heal. The idea that I could "let go" of her in some pseudo-evolved transcendence of personal pain dishonors her and dishonors love.

Buddhist teachers talk about "emptying out" knowledge, as if knowing anything were an obstacle to wisdom. Shunryu Suzuki said you must clear your mind, and Trungpa often used the expression, "Back to square one." The Western romantics had the same idea: Thoreau regretted that he was not as wise as the day he was born, and Wordsworth assured his readers that one impulse from the "vernal wood" had more wisdom in it than all the sages. In the deconditioning stage of practice, emptying out is necessary and good. Taken too seriously, "beginner's mind" or the "unknowing" of mysticism becomes a convenient excuse for intellectual laziness. So I threw that concept out too, and henceforth decided to learn and memorize whatever appealed to me. My head turned into a library of quotations in different languages, a delightful boarding house of dead authors and sages that spoke to each other around the breakfast table.

An interest in classical languages that I had long put off in order to follow the path came back to the surface; I taught myself Latin grammar within a year and started reading Vergil. But this learning was the same thing as a dharma practice: it involved discipline, patience, meditation, exertion, sensitivity to wisdom, and generosity toward myself. My study of Latin was expanded by the vast perspective of Big Mind. In fact I could never have taken genuine pleasure in it until now. In *The Aeneid* I saw coemergent egolessness and karma in the divinities, bodhicitta in the hero; in her all-consuming passion, Dido was both yidam and hungry ghost, and her suicide was a leap into Ordinary Mind as well as an act of revenge. The Latin language is a gateway to half the languages of modern Europe; French and English are to Latin what the construction trades are to architecture. I doubt that I would have responded so fully to this difference without the appreciation of speech conferred by dharma.

However much we might seek to avoid having our buttons pushed, life will push them in any case. The most dramatic intrusion into my console panel happened the summer my house was robbed. I had feared for a long time that enterprising burglars might one day scope out my rural situation and make off with the musical recording equipment with which I spent so many hours in creative solitude. The week before they came, I was obsessed with robbers. I read the Latin stories of Apuleius about gangs of thieves breaking into houses in the disintegrating Roman empire, and every item in the newspaper that caught my eye had to do with breaking and entering. The sense of dread that often precedes impending disaster weighed on me like a drop in barometric pressure. I saw omens again: attacks by strange yellowjacket wasps, and a sick raccoon that came out of the woods, sat in my front window, and then tried to pull open the screen door.

One evening I took the picture of Trungpa off my shrine, intending to use it as a model for a pencil sketch. It was like removing a protective spell: burglars broke in the next day while I was gone for only a half hour on an errand, and made off with five thousand dollars' worth of electronic hardware. They took nothing from the computer room. Maybe they didn't have time. On the other hand, my pictures of Khyentse and the Dalai Lama decorated that room, both on the door and above the computers. It was an interesting coincidence.

This was hardly my first or worst experience of invasion. Most people who reach the age of fifty have had to suffer loss many times, not as a spiritual exercise, but simply as a consequence of living. I have been chased by an insane drunk wielding a two-by-four, rammed accidentally on the highway, had my life threatened with a gun, lost numerous loved ones to the fell thief Death, and been a party to domestic upheaval since boyhood. But it was the first time I had been deliberately marked in my own home by a cunning hidden predator. The violation was not merely a property loss. Someone had gone to great trouble: checking my location, spying on my movements, biding their time, and striking when my back was turned. Given the number of burglar-committed murders in my area, I could not be sure they would stop at theft, or were finished with me. I had spent years building my little house, my dormers, my porch, my garden mandala, my flower beds, my academic livelihood, and now thugs had kicked their way in and knocked it over in thirty minutes.

The spiritual path gives you certain preconceptions about how one should behave in such circumstances. They run like this: turn the other cheek, have compassion for the thieves, if they take your coat give them your cloak, pray for those who cause harm to you, let go of the injury, suffer the intrusion for what it teaches you, love your enemies, cling to nothing, and so forth. I had learned enough of this kind of advice from both Buddhist and Christian authors to write my own bible.

Instead of modeling my behavior on spiritual concepts, I decided to make a response that was true to my instincts, even if that meant dispensing entirely with religion. All my instincts told me to fight back. I installed a security alarm system, put in gateposts, turned my woods into an obstacle course for vehicles, joined a Neighborhood Watch, posted my property to give myself some legal protection in the courts, and bought Mace, Pepperguard, and a 9 m.m. semi-automatic pistol, just in case the predators wanted to stage an encore while I was home. Taking each of these steps gave me a healing strength. I had found and crossed a clearly-marked bridge, from what I thought I should be to what I really am. When I blasted targets in the back yard, that bridge collapsed, and I knew I would not return.

My spacious tolerance for criminal behavior vanished. It was never more than a wishy-washy, sentimental reluctance to set limits, born of the romantic illusion that robbers and murderers are really persecuted Robin Hoods. They get away with their selfish malice because, as a state, we lack the will to crush them; and the image of the criminal as an American rebel hero has rotted away our collective respect for law so long that now we may lack not only the will, but the power.

Vajrayana folklore is equivocal enough so that I was not at all certain my choices were really heresy. The Buddhist tradition is full of stories about saints who were unconditionally nonviolent, and gave their very flesh in compassion to feed predators. The same tradition has other stories about bodhisattvas who beat thieves within an inch of their lives, and lamas who wiped out whole gangs of robbers in order to bring food to starving villages. Zen has always had a comfortable relationship with the martial arts and the samurai warrior disciplines, which do not exactly advocate turning the other cheek under attack. No Buddhist sect has ever been able to gain enough prestige to deliver a final doctrine on the use of force which is binding on all Buddhists. In Tibetan dharma, force that prevents harm to others is really compassion, and is not only acceptable, but mandated. Harmful or deadly force is not acceptable as a defense for yourself. It is a deviation from the bodhisattva ideal. I let the ideal go hang, and did what my heart told me to do.

The path as a set of prescriptive rules had been destroyed, melted down in the furnace of my anger. But dharma kept radiating from the glowing coals. What my heart told me to do was rather more complex than it seemed. In Neighborhood Watch I had to take on responsibility for my neighbors; if I wanted them to care about me, I had to care about them. The loss of my electronic things, my musical cocoon, had brought me out of my isolated house and onto their doorsteps with empty hands and a sad story, and if I had no community spirit to offer from the experience, I would be just another victim crying foul.

The German Shepherd I bought for a guard dog had hip dysplasia and needed surgery. My love for her grew like fields of flowers, nourished by the ashes of my anger, and I became the nurse, guardian, and protector of my guard, spending almost as much money for her benefit as I had lost in the robbery. Through her I discovered dogs; I discovered how they speak with their bodies, how a dog might touch your jacket with her nose if she wants you to go out with her, how she tells time by what comes next in your routine, and reads your state of mind in your hands, face, and gait. I loved the smell of dogs, their wet noses and tongues, their wild excitement and pleasure when they realize that you cherish them, their endless curiosity and devotion. In a nearby town, a black Labrador went back into a burning house to try and wake up his drunken master, and died with him in the smoke. No bodhisattva ever demonstrated a greater commitment to the welfare of others.

As for the robbers, I cursed them; I prepared a rhymed, mantric incantation to poison the things they had stolen, calling on the protectors of the ten directions to sow discord between them, turn their profits into sources of mutual betrayal, and make their contempt for the human image open in their guts like a bone spring trap in the stomach of a polar bear. But my heart intervened; I could not press this curse home without also praying that its fulfillment would slay their stupidity and wake them up to their own buddha-nature. Destroying them would be no victory at all. Others would replace them, perhaps myself. In order to curse them properly, I had to pray for their benefit. Framing my curse as a blessing, too, would protect me from its boomerang effect. They were no doubt used to being merely cursed, and probably gloried in it. The only thing that would really make them fry was to send them dharma.

Then I saw the wisdom of the protectors' chants I had been reciting for ten years: "Eat them as your food, O black protector, cut the aortas of the perverters of the teachings, kill them and bring them to dharmadhatu."

And so all my negative emotions might as well have been positive. They destroyed my concept of the path only to liberate the path itself, which is nothing other than authentic response, fully experienced. I did not have to live up to some spiritual ideal by turning my anger into compassion; anger *is* compassion, this is its essential nature. We cannot experience it that way if we ignore its total context. In order to shape anger into an effective self-defense, for example, we must give love, labor, and commitment to ourselves and others. So our anger becomes an inspiration to love. In order to hurt those who have hurt us, we cannot merely rave and kill, we must send them some truth they would prefer to ignore. So our anger becomes an inspiration to tell the truth. We think to get revenge is merely to hurt our enemies, without realizing that the revenge motive can be satisfied even more completely by being a mirror for them, which is the same thing as stripping off the cover of their lies. Of course our lies are going to be stripped in the same process; every action has an equal and opposite reaction. And when criminals play that stripping role, they are not just criminals; they are wrathful buddha *herukas,* like Vajrakilaya. So vengeance becomes an inspiration to dance on the corpse of falsehood.

The loss of my things was an irritation. Some were covered by insurance, which I spent on my dog. When I framed the monetary compensation as a gift to her, it was not difficult to give.

The guru principle now began to appear in a more positive light. I was not about to check back with any Buddhist text or teacher to determine whether my choices had been right or wrong; that would have been silly. It was past time to make my own decisions, and all of our decisions are inescapably our own anyway, even if we flip coins, cast the *I Ching,* or ask for a guru's judgment. We still have to decide what to do with the judgment, prophecy or coin toss. But I was listening all the time to the results that flowed from a given choice. I did not need to will myself to listen, it had become an ingrained habit, cultivated first by dharma practice, and eventually running on its own power, like breath. This habit is the inward guru.

The robbers and the dog were the mental forms of the guru: the yidams. The first yidam struck with a kila, the second healed with a friendly tongue. The first said "What would you do if your comfortable, secure situation were violated? Can you let it go?" The second said "If you cannot let it go, then hang onto it for my sake, and watch how you melt." The whole episode had been a tantra. It had come in through the gap left by my removal of Trungpa's picture, tore open my cocoon, revealed who I really am, destroyed my theories about spirituality, blew off my romantic ignorance about crime, and stoked my anger and love into a glowing coalbed of Ordinary Mind. Everything considered, I had to admit that the Vajrayana was pretty good stuff.

The guru principle in Tibetan dharma seems as if it would rob you of autonomy—that was always my fear—but it may work as a channel for giving you autonomy, all ripened with colors, claws, feathers, and flames. The guru is like the philosopher king in Plato. The Republic is a metaphor for the well-ordered mind directed by prudence, temperance, justice, and fortitude. The philosopher king is the individual's commitment to truth. The king assumes state power as a public service, not for personal gratification. That is, the king has no self-interest. He gets nothing out of it. He understands clearly that the passions of greed and ambition, which corrupt rulers in the political world, lead to personal suffering and disharmony unless they are disciplined by the four virtues. His role is to establish an environment where the virtues can be cultivated and preserved. His objective and expertise is the attainment of happiness. If the citizens do not obey the philosopher king, then happiness will be wrecked, like a ship in a storm that is controlled by mutineers who know nothing about navigation and hold the captain hostage to their whims.

Like the dharma, Plato's four virtues are passionless. Prudence is *prajna*, wisdom without self. Temperance is *shila*, the Mahayana paramita of discipline, the power to subordinate impulse and appetite to the desire for wisdom. It could also be the paramita of patience. Fortitude implies the paramitas of patience and exertion; and justice in Plato is an overall balance of mind which is essentially meditation. The paramita that has no counterpart in Plato's four virtues is generosity. The Christians noticed this lack and sought to complete the list by adding their three theological virtues, one of which is love. Christian love and Buddhist generosity are parallel.

The guardians of the Republic are specially educated to protect the order of the system and the rule of the king. They are parallel to the emotions in the individual. Plato compares them to dogs, disruptive when ignored and ill-treated, valuable when properly trained. In a Buddhist mandala, the guardians would be the dharma protectors who are charged with maintaining the integrity of the practice environment. My guardians were the outraged folks in my head who urged me to put up the gate, install the burglar alarm, and acquire the weapons, and they were very like thoroughly aroused barking dogs. Just as Plato's guardians cannot be allowed to run the Republic, these folks have to be brought under the rule of reason; otherwise they take over your act and turn you into a vigilante. The consequence would wreck happiness for them as well as you.

The guru principle is really no different from Plato's overall picture of Justice. The end is pretty much the same in both teachings: the Buddha wanted to cure suffering, Socrates wanted to find the source of happiness. The guru's mandala repels and attracts for the same reasons the Republic does, and can be defended with the same arguments. It is an elitist vision that comes from the top down, but is nonetheless the opposite of a totalitarian political state: both the mandala and the Republic are symbols of enlightened mind. Samaya is the Buddhist word for the rule of the philosopher king. The virtues and the paramitas are a condition of balance, with the discursive thoughts and appetites directed toward their own business by Reason, Wisdom, Bodhicitta, the inner Guru, the commitment to sanity. Socrates compares a man governed by ambition and greed to someone mauled and dragged about by wild beasts. In the same way, a person whose actions are controlled by the impulses of discursive thought is like a city in the grip of mob rule. Osel Tendzin called this mental state of affairs "the democracy of the mind."

The Vajrayana mandala is probably the closest thing I will ever experience to Plato's true intention in the Republic. Plato does not go beyond the level of presenting an idea, and for that reason, in comparison to the Vajrayana mandala, the Republic feels rigid, abstract, and theoretical. "It would never work" has been the typical reaction of its readers for 2,300 years. Jacob Needleman, in his brilliant discussion of Plato, points out that philosophy *cannot* go beyond the level of ideas, it can only lead us to the threshold where spiritual discipline takes over. The discipline, he implies, is the system that takes the idea beyond intellect into the heart, the center of the psyche, where it has the power to transform what we do.

The three-yana curriculum is such a discipline. The ideal of Justice in Plato is the idea of guru in the aspect of self-rule: autonomy instead of autocracy. In Vajrayana the point is not to obey the guru, but to *become* the guru—a completely responsible, sane, balanced, regal human, in full possession of your best and worst faculties. This type is honored in many traditions by titles like rabbi, master, roshi, lord. If the energies of mind are barking dogs, you train and direct them; if they are tempestuous waves, you ride them; if they are frivolous intruders, you crush and eat them; if they are starving children, you feed them; if they are mating and playing couples, you throw rice on them. The dogs ask only that you do your job, which is to devote yourself to their benefit. A mind where the guru is enthroned is like the inside of a shrine room.

I decided to keep the gun. I knew that if I ever used it on a human being, morally and psychologically it would fire in both directions at once, like the sting of a bee, which kills the owner as well as poisoning the victim. But this is the proper weight to put on a deadly weapon. "If you keep your samaya, you cannot make a mistake." The gun was an absolute demand on me to trust my samaya, and an absolute invitation to disaster if I broke it. The actual republic under whose laws I live guarantees me the right to own guns and to use them in self-defense, and that fact illustrates both the best and worst aspects of our national character. It says yes, you really are the ruler of yourself, you are not born to be a ward of the state; all your options are open. The power of self-defense is part of what it means to be a free and responsible agent, and you cannot be alienated from that freedom by law until you prove yourself a threat to the public peace. On the other hand, the same freedom allows any mob on the street to shoot up the town for fun and profit.

We honor our freedom and responsibility, too, primarily in the power to blow each other away. Yet the powers to explore our consciousness with psychedelic drugs, to die by choice, and to assist others who wish to die, are not honored; in these departments we are still wards of the state.

If we persist in it, all of our illusions about the Buddhist path, like bubbles, sooner or later encounter some reality that breaks them. Gurus are not a superior species, they are made out of the same stuff as anyone else, and we trust them at our own risk. Buddhist meditators can and do play competitive games, cause harm, get jealous, and act needlessly, neurotically, gratuitously insulting, even at the highest levels. You could do all the practices of the three yanas and get nothing out of them. "Nothing happens." Buddhism is not an answer to anything, it is a mirror, always turning us back on ourselves.

I was content to remain just another person, with no ambition to be enlightened. Ironically, I found this stage described in Zen Buddhist literature as the fruition of dharma: "In the beginning, mountains are mountains and clouds are clouds; in the middle, mountains are not mountains, and clouds are not clouds; in the end, mountains are again mountains, and clouds are again clouds." But whether any ego had been examined, transcended, or dissolved, or ever existed in the first place, was impossible for me to say. Accepting and being simply who I am is a continuous delight, and I have dharma to thank for that. It may be no big deal, but it is no small gift either.

I continued saying the mantras I had been taught, because they were comforting and relieved stress. They worked especially well for plane rides. If I had to die in the fireball of an exploded jet, the last thing I would want on my lips is the mantra that I learned from Khyentse. The test of whether you are really a Buddhist might be what you trust under the shadow of death, and by that test, I am still a Buddhist.

One fact strongly in favor of the Vajrayana is that I felt no hang-over from it. It did not make me sick, or three feet thick. A mere cult leaves you disgusted and disillusioned, wondering how you could have been such a fool. I did not feel that charlatans had hood-winked me into giving up my powers to enhance theirs. On the contrary, mine were unveiled.

I had the sensation of being "completely without problems," but it gave me no security. There were rugs under me that could still be pulled, and ultimately would be: vigor, stable health, comfort, life. I was left more or less where I was when I began—interested in everything, believing nothing. I felt grateful for what I had learned of Buddhist tantra. It waited for my renewed interest, like a fine Harley in the garage.

20

LOTUS TAKING ROOT

IN THE ASIAN countries where it originated, Buddhism is on the decline. The Muslims inflicted a death-blow on the Vajrayana society of north India during the thirteenth century. The current Communist repression of Tibetan Buddhists is one of the tragedies of our own era. Buddhism is a principal target of the massacres and persecutions that have swept through Southeast Asia. In Japan, the Zen tradition has barely survived the pressures of the modern industrial age.

The place where Buddhist dharma has taken hold most recently with something like the energy of its original freshness is the North American continent. Ironically, here, in the center of materialism, Buddhism is slowly but steadily putting down roots. For the time being, it appears to be limited primarily to small groups of college-educated, middle-class white people; and the only large-scale Buddhist communities in America are composed of Asian immigrants. The non-Christian segment of the Black population leans toward Islam, and the religious interests of Latins largely favor charismatic Christianity, Santeria, or the Roman Catholic Church. Still, the climate of opinion in America is hospitable to Buddhist dharma—it amplifies deep, health-giving tendencies in our culture.

Since the Columbian "discovery," America has always held the promise of a fresh start. That promise is tainted by a history of invasion and slavery, but it is nonetheless real. In this land, Europeans and other immigrants have had the opportunity to confront what they are as human beings, without the shell of rigid class lines and centuries of accumulated baggage. Many came here for the explicit purpose of realizing what they understood as an enlightened way of life. The English in Massachusetts, for example, wanted to found the New Jerusalem in the wilderness, a Puritan version of the dream of Shambhala. Although to us their inspiration appears warped by their Calvinist doctrinal preconceptions, this vision outlasted the doctrine. It was a strong current in the New England utopian transcendentalism of the nineteenth century, long after the Calvinist culture had lost its cohesion and gone into decline.

The Buddhist Way establishes a psychological ground for accomplishing the same end: confronting what we are as human beings, and making a society that will translate the vision of enlightenment into practice. There is no theology in Buddhism that would exclude or repress. Its doctrines can solidify into a nontheistic version of orthodoxy, and in certain places have already done so. But the emphasis within the meditative traditions on practice, on genuine experience, helps to keep the vision fresh and alive. Buddhist nontheism is like an open continent—the continent of the mind, newly discovered, free from rigid class lines and preconceptual baggage. Each time the teachings are searched, weighed, questioned, and put into practice, the tradition is made new.

As early as the age of Emerson and Thoreau, hardly a generation after the first proto-Buddhist teachings from the literature of Sanskrit were made available in English translation, the compatibility between Buddhist dharma and American culture was already perceived. Emerson consciously put aside theist doctrines and attempted to draw his religious inspiration from the immediacy of the moment. Thoreau lived for a time much like a Zen monk; his verbal meditations on how the world drinks from Walden Pond could have been written by contemporary Vietnamese master Thich Nhat Hanh, and many of his sentences are suitable for arrangement as haiku poetry. Whitman's description of being made love to by the universal cosmic tongue sounds like a vision of Krishna and the milkmaids, the erotic devotional lyrics of the Hindu *bhakti* Mirabai, or the unity of guru and disciple in the Vajrayana.

The influence of Buddhism on American cultural life broadened in the late nineteenth and early twentieth centuries. Although he attacked Chinese Buddhism during his fascist period, Ezra Pound was inspired by the imagistic concreteness of Chinese characters; and Henry Miller proclaimed himself a Buddhist. Jack Kerouac wrote from the Buddhist premise of seeking Ordinary Mind in ordinary experience, and the Beat poets of the 1950s studied dharma and revered the aging, smiling, enigmatic figure of D. T. Suzuki, the Zen apostle from Japan who also cast his gentle bolts of lightning at Thomas Merton. Our best poets and musicians have spontaneously assumed proto-Buddhist attitudes toward living and composing, even when they knew nothing about Buddhist philosophy. Native American reality systems have resonated to the living spirit of the land for centuries, and the land itself still holds the memory of their consciousness. The discovery that trees, lakes, rivers, mountains, and clouds are alive is nothing new to them.

If Buddhism has a home anywhere in the world today, it is in America. No country needs it more, or has better resources, energy, and the cultural ground needed to make wholesome bread from its recipe. We need the dharma to retrieve the freshness of the American hope, to save ourselves from the cynicism towards ourselves that has followed the corruption and pollution of our environment and our political system. We need to decondition the American mind, open the stingy hand, reexperience the goodness of the perceptions, pacify the defensive terror that causes us to shoot the stranger at the door, put aside the drugs, the commodities, the endless television fantasies, clean up our trash, and take delight in our next breath. We need to heal the blindness that causes us to poison our sacred garden. We need to appreciate the freedom from control by religious or political dictatorship that our ancestors secured for us; but even more, we need to use that freedom to become kings and queens of ourselves, which we have scarcely begun to do. Use it or lose it.

The dharma can be discovered through the Buddhist tradition, but Buddhism is by no means the only source of dharma. I would define dharma as anything that awakens bodhicitta and brings on the direct experience of egolessness. The teachings of Christ are perfumed with dharma. There is dharma in jazz, in beautiful gardens, in literature, in Sufi dance, in Quaker silence, in shaman healing, in projects to care for the homeless and clean up the inner cities, in Catholic ritual, in meaningful and competent work. There is dharma in anything that causes us to respect the innate softness and intelligence of ourselves and others. When the Buddhist system is applied properly, it does not turn us inward toward our own organizations, practices, and ideas, but outward toward the whole vast world of universal dharma. The system has succeeded when the Buddhist can recognize the true dharma at the core of all other religions and disciplines that are based on respect for the human image, and has no need to reject them.

The spirit of mutual tolerance is a powerful current in American civilization: it comes down through Roger Williams, John Woolman, Thomas Jefferson, Benjamin Franklin, Sojourner Truth, and Frederick Douglass, and has found expression in our own time in the movements for human and animal rights, the beat poets and thinkers, the libertarian trends in the counterculture of the 1960s, and the networks that have sprung up to protect writers and artists from political repression. The Buddhist outlook can help identify the dharma of this spirit, and broaden it from an attitude to a whole way of life.

Buddhism itself, however, promises nothing; like all other human enterprises, it is a coemergent phenomenon. It can be an invitation to open the mind or an opportunity to close it up in a shell inscribed with sutras and slogans. What we do with it depends ultimately, not on the teacher, but on ourselves—just like everything else. To anyone who is thinking about entering the Buddhist transformational system, I would give my wholehearted encouragement, but also this warning: cherish your fundamental doubt at every stage. Doubt is what allows you to experience the system and drop it at the same time.

Ernest Hemingway advised young writers to examine their work with a built-in shit detector. In spiritual journeying, the shit detector is an absolutely essential piece of equipment. Without it, you could end up a number in the body count of a cult massacre. A large part of the path consists of nothing else but keeping this detector in good repair. If it is directed equally at yourself and the reasons for your resistance, there is no cause to fear that it will mislead you into throwing away your lottery ticket. Skepticism is not just ego; it is the very inherent sanity that the path is supposed to unfold.

Buddhism is a good system, but it must be sifted thoroughly with questions. When this is done, it does not remain static, but changes to fit experience, like a living language. Buddhist dharma has a grammar that we cannot invent and must first learn; but it is the learner, not the teacher, who applies it. Otherwise it would have no life.

A myth prevails in some places, especially in the three-yana curriculum, that you must obey and defer to the master until enlightenment is achieved, or at least until the master gives you complete dharma transmission and recognizes you as a roshi, rinpoche, regent, tulku, or five-star general. I believe we are better off declaring ourselves enlightened at the beginning, and then deciding moment to moment what we will do with the teachings. Masters acquire a vested interest in being masters, and tend to remain in whatever system conferred their status. Obey and defer, as long as you can feel dharma in that choice; but do it to enjoy the humorous beauty of deference, to respect your human image in the teacher, and to dance with your own splendid pride, which does not need either to be excused or excised.

There is no such thing as master and student. This is why the relationship works.

GLOSSARY OF DHARMA TERMS

Abhidharma
An early Buddhist psychological text which explains the components of ego and ego-conditioned experience.

Abhiseka
"Sprinkling," "pouring." In the Vajrayana, the initiation of the student into sadhana practice. Abhiseka includes rituals of blessings, empowerments, and instruction by the guru.

Anatman
"No self." The Buddhist doctrine that there is no enduring entity of a self, or ego, which can be preserved from impermanence, or harmed by it.

Bardo [or pardo]
"Intermediate state." In Tibetan Buddhist teaching, there are six intermediate states of consciousness: the moment of death, the state following death, the state of becoming, the state between death and birth, the state of dreaming, and the state of meditation.

Bhavachakra
"Wheel of life." A Buddhist symbol, or schematic diagram, of the ego and its functioning. The structure of the wheel includes, at the center, the basic illusions of ego (kleshas); branching from these like radii, the six realms of suffering; around the rim, the twelve links (nidanas) in the chain of ego-driven causation (karma). The image of the wheel emphasizes that the entire structure is in constant cyclic motion.

Bodhi
"Awake" or "wakefulness."

Bodhicitta
"Awakened heart" or "awakened mind." The "soft spot," or seed of enlightenment, which is latent in all sentient beings. When bodhicitta is aroused, we become capable of unconditional compassion for others.

Bodhisattva
A buddha in training, active in the world; a person in whom bodhicitta has been aroused. The bodhisattva is dedicated to the welfare of others, and takes a vow not to enter nirvana until all other sentient beings have been enlightened.

Buddha
"Awakened one." A buddha has completely dispelled all the illusions of samsara and is fully awake. The founder of Buddhist teaching, Sakyamuni Buddha, or "The Buddha," is only one of a possible unlimited number of buddhas.

Buddha
One of the five buddha families of buddha, vajra, karma, ratna, and padma. Buddha energy is ignorance transformed into all-accommodating spaciousness.

Buddha-dharma
The dharma taught by the Buddha, or Buddhist tradition.

Buddha family
In Vajrayana Buddhism, one of five types of enlightened energy which exist in every situation and every sentient being. In samsara, these families appear to us as obstacles, or kleshas: ignorance, envy, passion, aggression, and pride. Liberated from the illusion of ego, the kleshas manifest their true nature as forms of enlightenment.

Buddha-mind
The capacity for enlightenment which resides in all sentient beings; enlightened mind.

Cakra [chakra]

"Wheel." See "Dharmacakra" and "Bhavachakra."

Daka

"Courageous one." In Vajrayana Buddhism, a male deity embodying buddha-mind who protects the meditator's dharma practice.

Dakini

In Vajrayana Buddhism, a female deity embodying buddha-mind who manifests the creative and playful energies of mind and protects the meditator's dharma practice.

Dharma

"Law," "way," "truth." This word is used as a common noun in Buddhist philosophy to denote simply a process, or event. Spelled with a capital "D," it usually means the teachings of the Buddha.

Dharmacakra

"The wheel of the law"—that is, Buddhist teaching.

Dharmakaya

"Body of truth." One of the three bodies of a buddha, the dharmakaya is formless, unmanifested, encompasses and pervades everything in samsara and nirvana, is beyond all characteristics, and has no beginning, end, or location.

Ego

"I," or self. In Buddhist teaching, ego consists of five heaps (skandhas) of impulses and impressions that create the illusion of an enduring entity. Once afflicted by this illusion, we solidify and defend it with actions motivated by the kleshas. These actions create karma.

Gelugpa

One of the major lineages of dharma transmission in Tibetan Buddhism, the Gelugpas have been established since the fourteenth century. The Dalai Lama is currently the senior master of this lineage.

Hinayana
"Lesser" or "narrow" vehicle. In Tibetan Buddhism, this term refers to the fundamental Buddhist teachings that are essential as a ground for entering the Mahayana and Vajrayana paths. The fundamental teachings include the four noble truths, the three marks of existence, and the practice of shamatha/vipashyana. Theravada Buddhists reject the term "Hinayana" as a description of their own teachings, because of a perceived implication that "Hinayana" is inferior to "Mahayana." The term itself, however, implies nothing pejorative, but simply characterizes the place of a certain group of teachings within the overall Tibetan three-yana curriculum.

Kagyu
One of the major lineages of dharma transmission in Tibetan Buddhism. Senior masters of the Kagyu lineage in modern times have included the Karmapas and Kalu Rinpoche.

Karma
Work, causation, result. As an aspect of suffering, karma refers to the harmful or illusory chain of consequences generated by ego-driven behavior and thought. These consequences help to perpetuate suffering by solidifying the notion of ego.

Karma
One of the five buddha families. A form of enlightened energy which accomplishes work. In the world of samsara, this buddha family appears to us as envy, jealousy, and the compulsion to achieve order.

Karmapa
"One who does the work of Buddha." The Karmapas are a lineage of great Buddhist teachers, established in Tibet since the twelfth century. According to Tibetan Buddhist tradition, each Karmapa has the power to work miracles, and at the time of his death, leaves a letter of instruction with his senior disciples describing where and when he will be reborn.

Karuna

"Loving kindness," compassion, warmth. One of the qualities developed by the awakening of bodhicitta.

Klesha

"Stain," "obscuration," "disturbing conception." The kleshas (ignorance, aggression, passion, envy, and pride) both result from ego and help to maintain it. The true nature of the kleshas is enlightenment, but we are unable to recognize this until freed from the illusion of ego.

Lineage

A line of oral transmission of dharma from guru to disciple. A lineage holder is a disciple who has been given complete transmission and is empowered to choose a successor to the lineage.

Maha Ati

The highest dharma teaching within the Tibetan Buddhist tradition.

Mahayana

The "great vehicle"—a school of Buddhist dharma originating in northern India, perhaps a few centuries after the Buddha's death, although Mahayanists have claimed that the teachings of this vehicle were given by the Buddha himself. The Mahayana developed the ideal of the bodhisattva, the buddha in training who works in the world for the benefit of others. The foundational teaching of Mahayana is the doctrine of sunyata, or emptiness, proclaimed in the *Heart Sutra* as the basis of true compassion. Mahayana Buddhism spread to Tibet, where it was integrated with the Vajrayana, and to China and Japan, where it developed into Ch'an and Zen, among many other sects and traditions.

Maitri

Unconditional friendliness and kindness toward all sentient beings, an aspect of bodhicitta.

Mala
A string of beads used in Tibetan Buddhist practice to keep track of prayer, mantra, and practice repetitions.

Mandala
An integrated system of teachings, teachers, disciples, deities, and/or events, usually depicted in Tibetan art as a circle with a complex inner structure. This structure includes a system of walls, gates, gatekeepers, and presiding deities representing enlightened aspects of mind. In its largest sense, mandala is the whole universe, seen as inherently pure and sacred, filled with buddhas, bodhisattvas, dakas, dakinis, dharmapalas, and protectors.

Mantra
A sacred syllable or incantation; in its largest sense, all sound, experienced as a sacred emanation of buddha-mind.

Ngondro
One of a series of practices in Vajrayana Buddhism that prepare the disciple for abhiseka. Ngondros include prostration, mantra recitation, mandala practice, and Guru Yoga, accompanied by repetitions of the refuge and bodhisattva vows.

Nirmanakaya
"Emanation body," the world of material form. As one of the bodies of Buddha, the nirmanakaya manifests in all realms of existence through various forms to work for the welfare of sentient beings according to their aptitudes.

Nirvana
"Extinction"; in Buddhist teaching, the condition of removal, or extinction, of the illusion of ego and all its karmic effects, including the kleshas and the six realms of suffering.

Nyingma
The "old ones"; the oldest living lineage of Buddhist dharma transmission in Tibet, traceable to Guru Padmasambhava, who lived and taught perhaps during the seventh century.

Ordinary Mind
The experience of mind without ego, see Thamal gye shepa.

Padma
"Lotus"; one of the five buddha families and the enlightened form of passion.

Paramita
"Crossing to the other shore"; one of the six transcendent virtues of a bodhisattva. These are meditation, generosity, discipline, patience, exertion, and egoless wisdom.

Ratna
"Jewel"; one of the five buddha families, ratna is an enlightened form of pride.

Sadhaka
A Vajrayana student who has finished ngondro, taken abhiseka, and been empowered to practice the higher yogas of Buddhist tantra.

Sadhana
A post-abhiseka practice ritual in Vajrayana Buddhism, also referred to as a tantra.

Sambhogakaya
"Perfect enjoyment body"; refers to the experiences and realms of sense and thought.

Samsara
The wheel of suffering created by the illusions of ego. Samsara is the world that results from klesha and karma.

Sangha
The community of Buddhist practitioners. The sangha is the "third jewel" of the triple Buddhist refuge. In becoming a Buddhist, one takes the refuge vow, a repetition of the formula, "I take refuge in the Buddha, I take refuge in the Dharma, I take refuge in the Sangha." Many Buddhist chants and practices repeat this formula.

The ordained sangha are those who have taken monastic vows; the lay sangha are those who have taken the refuge vow and participate in Buddhist study and practice.

Shamatha
"Abiding in peace"; the practice of sitting meditation without object or goal.

Shambhala
A mythic kingdom in Buddhist legend whose members are enlightened; an enlightened society. In the sangha of Chogyam Trungpa, a cumulative system of Buddhist-inspired teachings and practices aimed toward realizing enlightened society without the help of a religious outlook.

Sunyata
"Emptiness"; the Mahayana Buddhist doctrine that all things neither exist nor nonexist, and that human concepts, including the concepts of existence and nonexistence, do not accurately model anything outside themselves.

Sutra
"That which is stitched together"; a teaching proclaimed by or ascribed to the Buddha, that has been handed down through Buddhist tradition in both written and oral form. Sutras are sometimes chanted as part of a particular liturgy.

Tantra
"Continuity"; a practice and teaching of Vajrayana Buddhism that aims toward realizing enlightened mind in the realms of samsara.

Thamal gye shepa
A Tibetan term, and teaching, commonly translated into English by Vajrayana Buddhists as "ordinary mind," or mind without ego. This state can be induced by Buddhist practice, by abhiseka, or by the presence of a great teacher.

Theravada

The Buddhist tradition found in Sri Lanka and other areas of Southeast Asia, that claims to derive from the original teachings of Sakyamuni Buddha as he gave them. Buddhist teachings important in Theravada include the Four Noble Truths, the Eight-fold Path, the *Abhidharma*, and the *Vinaya*.

Vajra

"Indestructible," "Adamantine," "Diamond-like." This term may refer to the original nature of mind and universe, or the tantric vehicle for attaining swift realization of this nature. A vajra (Tibetan, *dorje*) is an object used in Vajrayana practices that depicts and embodies buddha-mind.

Vajra

One of the five buddha families, vajra energy is aggression transmuted into mirrorlike wisdom.

Vajradhatu

A Vajrayana Buddhist organization founded by Chogyam Trungpa Rinpoche, with branches in several countries.

Vajrayana

A vehicle of Buddhist teaching based on the tantras that reached a high level of development in northern India before the Muslim invasions. Vajrayana was brought into Tibet on separate occasions by various teachers, among them Padmasambhava and Marpa the Translator.

Vinaya

A compendium of rules regulating the conduct of Buddhist monastics, and tracing its origins to Sakyamuni Buddha.

Vipashyana

The panoramic awareness, or "wide-angle" perception, developed by shamatha.

Windhorse

The sense of energy, sacredness, cheerfulness, and respect for one's world developed by Shambhala training and induced by certain Shambhala meditation practices.

Yidam

A deity visualized in Vajrayana practice, commonly embodying the energy of one of the five buddha families, and thought to be a form of the guru. Yidams are evoked in tantras as a swift means for the realization of buddha-mind.

Zazen

Sitting meditation practice as taught in the Zen Buddhist tradition. Zazen is essentially the same as Shamatha.

INDEX

Abhidharma: 22, 205
abhiseka: 7, 129, 143, 181, 192
Aeneid, The: 230
Amway: 12
anjali: 145, 208
Anuttara yoga: 193
Apuleius, *The Golden Ass:* 24–25
ashe: 97
Avalokitesvara: 13, 62, 209

Bardo Thodol: see *Tibetan Book of the Dead*
basic goodness: 107, 138
behaviorism: 53–54, 205–6
bhavachakra: 17, **18**
Big Mind: 79, 158, 189, 209, 224, 230
Blake, William: 162
Bly, Robert: 124
bodhicitta: 75, 91, 108, 113, 114, 237
bodhisattva: 76, 85, 86, 87, 104, 144
   and crime, 232
Bohr, Niels: 209
buddha families: 206–08
buddha-mind: 161
Butler, Katy: 6

Cameron, Ewen, Dr.: 201–2
Campbell, Joseph: 123, 124
Capra, Fritjof: 209
Castaneda, Carlos: 28, 129
coemergence: 178, 193–5, 217, 222

dakas: 144, 168, 178
dakinis: 144, 168, 176, 178–9

Dalai Lama: 125, 197, 231
Dante Alighieri: 170, 181, 214–15
Democritus: 21–22
devotion: 136–39, 143, 153, 165, 191–2
dharmakaya: 122, 158, 178, 191
dharmapalas: 144, 168, 179
Donne, John: 16
Dorje, Lodro: 130
Dowman, Keith: 8–9

Eckhart, Meister: 180
ego: 21–23, 80, 105, 138, 143, 193–4
   structure of, 205–6
egolessness: 21–23, 105ff, 193–4, 196
Eight-fold Path: 75
Ekajati: 119, 123, 124, 212
Eliot, T. S.: 124
Emerson, Ralph Waldo: 242
Eros: 19, 20, 146
Evans-Wentz, W. Y. 34

Flight of the Garuda, The: see Shabkar, Lama

Gampo Abbey: 227
Gelugpa: 32
Gelugpa Lama: 171–5
Ginsberg, Allen: 215, 221
Gray, Spalding: 57
Great Eastern Sun: 96, 99
Gurdjieff, G. I.: 27, 28
guru yoga: 135, 155, 177–83, 195

Hayward, Jeremy: 125, 205–6, 209

Hawking, Stephen: 209
Heart Sutra: 13, 22, 62, 209, 217
Hemingway, Ernest: 56, 245
Hilton, James, *Lost Horizon:*
    35-37
Hinayana: 31, 33, 47, 74-75, 105,
    107, 113, 130, 132, 139, 140, 206
Homer: 182, 224
Hum: 157-8
Hume, David: 21

idiot compassion: 85

John, Gospel of: 24, 138
Journey Without Goal: See
    Trungpa, Chogyam
Jung, Carl: 34, 37, 123, 179
    and synchronicity, 151

Kagyu: 32, 34, 119, 135, 136, 144,
    150, 192
Kalachakra Mandala: **198**
Kalachakra Tantra: 62, 196-8
Kalapa Court: 71, 90
Kalu Rinpoche: 7, 91, 136, 185, 196,
    197
    Gem Ornament of Manifold
        Oral Instruction, 155, 158, 179
Kant, Immanuel: 19
karma: 17, 218
Karmapa, Seventeenth, The: 7
Karmapa, Sixteenth, The: 8, 136,
    149, 192
Karmapas: 7-9, 27, 136, 149
Karme-Choling: 83, 152, 190-92
karuna: 106
Keats, John: 3, 217, 221, 222
Kerouac, Jack: 243
Kevorkian, Dr.: 62

Khyentse, Dilgo, Rinpoche: 7, 136,
    149, 152, 153, 179, 189-91, 231
kleshas: 17, 107, 109, 137
    broken up by Vajrasattva
        mantra, 156
    and buddha families, 206ff
Kongtrul, Jamgon Rinpoche: 7-9,
    109, 192-3, 196
Kübler-Ross, Elisabeth: 60-61

Lao Tsu: 24, 27
lhasang: 144

Maha Ati: 32, 34, 211
Mahakala: 120
Mahasukha: 163
Mahayana: 22, 31, 33, 47, 75-82, 84,
    85, 91, 106, 108, 113, 115, 130,
    132, 139, 140, 164, 209
maitri: 106, 112
Maitri program: 207
mala: 135
mandala: 84, 87, 91, 96, 111, 129,
    135, 145, 179, 181, 183, 208, 237
    as ngondro, 135, 167-76
maras: 121
Marks, John: 201-03
Marpa: 27, 134
Maugham, W. Somerset, *The*
    Razor's Edge: 37
meditation: 45ff, 104
    behavioral effects, 53-54, 205
    and death, 60-66
    and healing, 67-71
    and political action, 73ff
Merwin, W. S.: 215
Merton, Thomas: 37-38, 243
Meru, Mt: 71, 160, 167, 170, 174
Milarepa: 27, 38, 134, 185

Milton, John: 223
Mirabai: 243

Naropa: 134
Naropa Institute: 207, 215
Needleman, Jacob: 19, 237
ngondro: 133–36, 146, 155, 195, 203
  erosion of resistance to teacher, 183
  loss of benefits, 201
  recovery of polluted ground, 182
nidanas: 17
nirmanakaya: 122, 158, 178
nirvana: 76, 193, 194, 195
Nyingma: 32, 34, 135, 136, 144

one taste: 193, 194
Ordinary Magic: 221
Ordinary Mind: 3, 150, 180, 223–4
  achieved by Vajrasattva mantra, 155–63
oryoki: 52, 91–92
Oxonian dialect: 94
Orwell, George: 96

paramitas: 78–9, 106, 108–09, 164
Pirsig, Robert M.: 211
Plato: allegory of the cave, 17, 19–20, 210
  mandala and *Republic*, 235–38
Plotinus: 24
Pound, Ezra: 243
prostrations: 135, 143–53
protectors: 119–28, 145, 234

quantum mechanics: 209

refuge: 33, 145
Republic: see Plato

Rich, Thomas: see Tendzin, Osel
Rigden fathers: 93, 98, 100
romantic love and dharma: 104–11, 113–16, 229
Rudra: 131, 137, 139

sadhaka: 129, 201
sadhana: 182, 193, 209
samaya: 130, 137, 163–4, 216, 238
sambhogakaya: 122, 127, 158, 178
samsara: 16–19, 32, 56, 69, 74, 104, 105, 108, 147, 156, 193
samskara: 156, 195
sangha: 33, 87, 111, 112, 115, 145, 149, 150, 208
satori: 157
Sawang, The: 192
Search for the Manchurian Candidate, The: see Marks, John
Seminary: 89–92, 94, 113–14, 129, 131, 165
setting sun: 96, 99
Shabkar, Lama: 204
Shakespeare, William: 17, 222
Shamarpa Rinpoche: 8
shamatha: 45–47, 50–51, 55, 59, 61, 103, 107, 127, 132, 145, 155, 171, 194, 195
shambhala: 36–37, 71, 93–102, 219, 220, 221, 242
Shifting Worlds, Changing Minds: See Hayward, Jeremy
Simmer-Brown, Judith: 104
skandhas: 22, 204–06, 209, 211
spiritual materialism: 39, 43, 127, 132, 194
sunyata: 62, 158
  as escape clause, 209

Sutra of the Noble Three Jewels: 20
Suzuki, D. T.: 38, 243
Suzuki, Shunryu: 26, 117

Tai Situ Rinpoche: 8
tantra: 104–05, 126, 159, 194–99,
    209–12, 239
Tendzin, Osel: 11, 77, 87, 88, 114,
    137, 141, 189, 192, 221, 237
  and AIDS, 3–6, 110, 183–7
  encounters with, 3–6, 83–84,
    89–90. 163–64
  on samaya, 163–64
Thamal gye shepa: see Ordinary
    Mind
thangkas: 213–14
Theravadin: 47, 79
Thich Nhat Hanh: 242
Thinley, Ugyen: 8–9
Thoreau, Henry David: 229, 242
Tibetan Book of the Dead: 34–35,
    62, 381
tonglen: 79–80, 103, 106, 113, 144,
    155, 156, 171, 195
transmission: 131–33, 139–41
Tricycle: 8–9, 57
Trungpa, Chogyam: 3, 10, 11, 20,
    26, 27, 28, 34, 76, 87–92, 111,
    162–63, 172–73, 205
  as Dorje Dradul, 93, 100
  as Lord Mukpo, 93
  as Vidyadhara, 131
  cremation, 2, 151–2
  and chaos, 215
  *Cutting Through Spiritual
    Materialism,* 39
  first encounter with, 38–43
  instructions to Tendzin, 183–5
  intangible presence, 178–9

Journey Without Goal, 193, 206
  and nontheistic energy, 137
  obstacles to rebirth, 189
  on art, 216
  on doubt, 29
  on elocution, 94
  on loneliness, 165
  On Mahayana and the
    bodhisattva vow, 85–86
  on meditation, 15, 48, 49, 61
  on ngondro, 147, 150, 201
  on Ordinary Mind, 162–3
  and passion, 107ff
  picture as protection, 231
  poetry, 219–21
  politics, 77–78, 93ff
  and prostrations: 147, 148, 150–51
  protectors' chants, 120–21, 126–7
  *Shambhala: The Sacred Path of
    the Warrior,* 93
  teaching of Vajrayana, 193
  and transmission, 129–41

vajra: **156,** 157, 209
Vajradhara: 119, 123, 144, 148, 150
Vajradhatu: 8–9, 76–77, 86, 91, 99,
    101, 111, 114, 119, 123, 133, 135,
    192
Vajra hell: 130–33, 164, 208
Vajrakilaya: 189, 212, 235
Vajrasadhu: 120
Vajrasattva mantra: 135, 155–62,
    157
Vajrayana: 6–7, 10, 11, 31, 32–33,
    79, 101, 106, 109–10, 126–7,
    129–41, 143, 159, 163–64, 204,
    206
  as betrayal, 140
  and crime, 235

cultural relativity of, 227–8
and mind control, 202–03,
  209–12
no hangover, 239
reality system, 185
Vajrayogini: 123, **196**
sadhana, 193ff
Varela, Francisco: 125
Vetali: 120
vipashyana: 55–57, 59, 216
vipassana: 47

Watts, Alan: 38
Welwood, John: 107, 221
Whitman, Walt: 242
windhorse: 101–02
Wordsworth, William: 230

Yeats, William Butler: 110, 222
yidam: 144, 145, 168, 179, 189, 193,
  195, 197, 200, 235

Zen: 27, 47, 61, 232, 241, 243

Stephen T. Butterfield is an English professor at Castleton State College in Castleton, Vermont, holds an M.A. from Tufts and a Ph.D. from the University of Massachusetts, learned Tibetan Buddhist teachings and practices from Chogyam Trungpa Rinpoche, Osel Tendzin, Kalu Rinpoche, Khyentse Rinpoche, and Jamgon Kongtrul Rinpoche, has published fiction, poetry, and essays in numerous periodicals including *Beloit Poetry Journal, Nimrod, The Sun,* and *Tricycle,* has written two previous books, *Black Autobiography in America* (University of Massachusetts Press, 1974) and *Amway: The Cult of Free Enterprise* (South End Press, 1985), is a recent and eager student of classical languages, and plays traditional Celtic music with friends.